MW01518199

Leadership and Diversity in Psychology

Leadership and Diversity in Psychology explores the topic of leadership and diversity from a range of different perspectives. The authors draw from professional experience and research to support their reflections on leadership with diverse populations, leadership in organizations and developing leadership style.

Incorporating current theory and up-to-date research concerning current trends towards more relational and integrative work, the book emphasises practitioners' reflections of their own experience. It reflects the contemporary focus towards more pluralistic/integrative practice, which has moved away from traditional orientations involving specific ways of working.

Leadership and Diversity in Psychology will be of great interest to academics and researchers in the fields of clinical and counselling psychology and organizational psychology as well as professional practitioners.

Maureen McIntosh is a Chartered Senior Counselling Psychologist with the British Psychological Society (BPS) and registered with the Health and Care Professions Council (HCPC). She has worked in the NHS since 2002 with older adults and adults. She is an Associate Fellow of the BPS and she was the BPS Chair of the Division of Counselling Psychology (2016–2018).

Helen Nicholas is a counselling psychologist, registered with the Health and Care Professions Council (HCPC), a chartered psychologist with the British Psychological Society (BPS), an EMDR accredited practitioner and a registered coaching psychologist. She teaches on the BSc counselling psychology and clinical psychology and is the course lead for the MSc Counselling at the University of Worcester.

Afreen Husain Huq is a Clinical Psychologist retired from the NHS, having worked in the NHS between 1985 and 2015 with older adults and been involved in diversity work in clinical practice as well as the BPS (formerly the Faculty for Race and Culture, and the FPOP).

Routledge Studies in Leadership, Work
and Organizational Psychology

Foucault on Leadership
The Leader as Subject
Nathan W. Harter

Leadership and Diversity in Psychology
Moving Beyond the Limits
Maureen McIntosh, Helen Nicholas, and Afreen Husain Huq

Leadership and Diversity in Psychology

Moving Beyond the Limits

Edited by
Maureen McIntosh, Helen Nicholas and
Afreen Husain Huq

Routledge
Taylor & Francis Group

LONDON AND NEW YORK

First published 2019
by Routledge
2 Park Square, Milton Park, Abingdon, Oxon OX14 4RN

and by Routledge
52 Vanderbilt Avenue, New York, NY 10017

Routledge is an imprint of the Taylor & Francis Group, an informa business

British Library Cataloguing in Publication Data
A catalogue record for this book is available from the British Library

Library of Congress Cataloging in Publication Data
Names: McIntosh, Maureen, editor. | Nicholas, Helen (Psychologist),
editor. | Huq, Afreen Husain, editor.
Title: Leadership and diversity in psychology : moving beyond the limits /
edited by Dr. Maureen McIntosh, Dr. Helen Nicholas, and Dr. Afreen
Husain Huq.
Description: Abingdon, Oxon ; New York, NY : Routledge, 2019.
Identifiers: LCCN 2018049125 (print) | LCCN 2018050726 (ebook) |
Subjects: LCSH: Psychology—Vocational guidance. | Psychology—Practice.
| Leadership. | Multiculturalism.
Classification: LCC BF76 (ebook) | LCC BF76 .L43 2019 (print) | DDC
150.23—dc23
LC record available at https://lccn.loc.gov/2018049125

ISBN: 978-1-138-36163-8 (hbk)
ISBN: 978-0-429-43260-6 (ebk)

Typeset in Bembo
by Cenveo® Publisher Services

Contents

Contributors

Editors

Afreen Husain Huq is a clinical psychologist retired from the NHS, having worked in the NHS from 1985 to 2015 with older adults and involved in diversity work in clinical practice as well as the with the BPS (formerly the Faculty for Race and Culture, and the FPOP).

Maureen McIntosh is a chartered senior counselling psychologist and is HCPC registered who has worked in the NHS since 2002 with older adults and adults. She is an Associate Fellow of the BPS and she was the BPS Chair of the Division of Counselling Psychology (2016–2018). Maureen has trained as a Mindfulness [level 1] Teacher and she has published and co-authored several publications.

Helen Nicholas is a counselling psychologist, registered with the Health and Care Professions Council (HCPC), a chartered psychologist with the British Psychological Society (BPS), an EMDR accredited practitioner and a registered coaching psychologist. She teaches on the BSc counselling psychology and clinical psychology and is the course lead for the MSc Counselling at the University of Worcester. Her qualifications include a Doctorate in psychotherapeutic and counselling psychology (PsychD) from the University of Surrey, a foundation in systemic family therapy and EMDR accreditation. In addition to her academic role, she runs a private practice in Somerset where she specialises in working across the lifespan with adolescents, adults and older adults. Helen has a particular interest in depression, anxiety, trauma and neurodegenerative diseases. Her volunteer roles within the BPS began in 2010 and include past roles as chair of the British Psychological Society (BPS), Division of Counselling Psychology and the BPS South West Branch. Helen's current roles include being an active member of the BPS training committee for counselling psychology, the BPS ethics committee and a BPS trustee. Helen also sits on the Health and Care Professions Council, fitness to practice panel. Her research interests and publications are in the areas of counselling psychology, work-life balance, supervision, personality traits, neurodegenerative diseases, and ethical and professional issues in psychology.

Authors

Sharon Akinkunmi is a chartered counselling psychologist and Associate Fellow of the BPS (British Psychological Society). The title of AFBPsS is awarded in recognition of several years' experience and contribution to the field of psychology. Her experience in mental health spans 20 years, with children, young people, adults and older adults from diverse backgrounds in various contexts. These include inpatient, low secure, community and educational settings and over ten years' managerial experience working as a team leader of a youth counselling service, managing and supervising others as a psychologist in the private sector. Sharon now works in the NHS as a Specialist Practitioner Psychologist. She has worked with those with moderate to severe mental health, learning difficulties, ASC (Autistic Spectrum Conditions), including older adults with dementia and their carers. Sharon is also the Deputy Chair of the BME (Black & Minority Ethnic) Network in her NHS Trust. This role led to becoming a participant on the WRES (Workforce Race & Equality Standard) Expert Programme, NHS England, raising awareness on issues relating to race equality. She has a passion to impact the lives of others positively and values fairness, openness and honesty. Self-development is also important to her.

Sharon is an effective communicator, open to new ideas and lifelong learning. She is also married with three children. Her hobbies include singing and hairdressing. She also enjoys running and cycling. In her spare time, she also hosts a woman's forum where she holds seminars and conferences addressing women's issues.

Ben Amponsah is an accredited member of the British Association of Counselling and Psychotherapy (MBACP Accred) and a member of the British Psychology Society (MBPsS). He qualified as a counsellor in 2004, having worked in therapy since 2002. Ben attained his first degree in psychology at the University of Bristol in 1991. He then completed his diploma in Counselling Studies at the University of Manchester in 2004 and has subsequently practiced at the LGBT Foundation in Manchester, where he is now a Senior Counsellor. Ben has also worked for many years in the Employee Assistance Programme (EAP) Industry and in the field of Solution-Focussed Brief Therapy (SFBT) and most recently Eye Movement Desensitisation and Reprocessing (EMDR). Ben uses Integrative Counselling as his main model for counselling. Ben has been running a successful private counselling and consultancy practice since August 2013. Ben is also a Psychologist and, having partly completed the

Independent BPS course for the Qualification in Counselling Psychology (QCoP), is soon to commence a professional doctorate in Counselling Psychology at Glasgow Caledonian University (September 2018). Ben has successfully completed an internal training course at Freedom from Torture and is engaged in continued professional development on psychological therapy with torture survivors. Ben has been working as a volunteer counsellor, on a part-time basis, at Freedom from Torture since October 2010. Ben considers himself an amateur creative writer and is active on many fan fiction gaming forums, but has not, as yet, published there.

Daisy Best is currently a principal lecturer on the doctorate in counselling psychology at Teesside University. She has some responsibility for supporting staff within the School of Social Sciences, Humanities and Law, to meet the Enterprise and Business Engagement Agenda. Between 2014 and 2017, Daisy was the Programme Director for the Doctorate in Counselling Psychology at Teesside University. Daisy is a school governor for a primary school in Middlesbrough and she is the Director of North Yorkshire Psychological Therapies, a private psychology service. Daisy was previously employed within the NHS, where she undertook the role of Acting Deputy Head of a Psychology department. Daisy has completed the BPS Leadership and Development Programme and a Teesside University Academic Leadership Programme. She has presented at various conferences and has undertaken a range of research, mostly in the area of domestic violence. Daisy has directed films that promote Counselling Psychology; https://www.youtube.com/watch?v=JcDKz5J-90s. Daisy contentedly lives within the North Yorkshire Moors National Park with her wife.

Neha Cattra (née Malhotra) is a chartered counselling psychologist who qualified in 2015 and has worked in large multi-disciplinary teams within adult mental health settings since qualification. She currently works in a busy AMHT in the city of Oxford. She has an interest in mentoring and supporting others, and as such also works as an external research supervisor at the Metanoia institute. Neha has a special interest in difference and diversity, as well as training and teaching in creative ways. An active volunteer throughout her life and career, she is currently a member of the conference committee for the Division of Counselling Psychology, British Psychological Society. As part of the BPS Leadership Development Programme, Neha successfully completed in 2015/2016. She established 'The DCoP Research Hub' and led an audit of the BPS, which was subsequently published as 'A report on the social justice, equality, diversity and inclusion audit of the British Psychological Society'. Recently married to a pottery-mad doctor, she splits her time between Oxford, London and North Wales. Neha is often found expressing her creativity in the kitchen, having travel adventures and whiling away afternoons people-watching in quirky coffee shops.

Roxane L. Gervais is a chartered psychologist and a registered occupational psychologist. She has a diverse skill set inclusive of applied research, data analytic processes, managing projects, as well as mentoring and developing technical staff. Roxane researches and promotes solutions to work-related issues. This research covers stress and well-being at work and has led to her facilitating training on work-related stress and well-being as well as undertaking stress audits within organisations and developing workshops. Her research focuses also on assessing women over the life-course, especially with respect to their work patterns and practices; she explores organisational practices, such as work-life balance, engagement, resilience, and organisational change processes that allow a more holistic view of today's workforce. Due to the changing work environment that includes globalisation and a stronger focus on diversity, her research includes generational differences and other diversity issues. She has presented her research at international conferences and contributes to her profession by editing papers for four journals and two international conference committees. Roxane has edited two books, one exploring those resources available to women who work and another on the global aspects of outsourcing. Roxane volunteers with one of her professional bodies, the British Psychological Society, to assist in ensuring that both the science and practice of occupational psychology is maintained and reinforced. She gained her PhD at the University of Hull. Roxane has worked in diverse organisations and at present is a senior psychologist at the Health & Safety Executive in the United Kingdom.

Lorraine Gordon a consultant counselling psychologist since 2009, trained at UCL and City University. She began her career providing psychological therapy in primary care over 20 years ago. Lorraine has since gone on to develop a speciality in working with complex and severe presentations in adult mental health, predominantly with the South London and Maudsley NHS Foundation Trust. For ten years she specialised in working with psychosis in various settings in Lambeth and Bromley, becoming the psychology lead for a borough-wide Early Intervention in Psychosis Service in Newham. Lorraine has demonstrated a keen interest in culture and diversity, coordinating a module on cultural issues for a counselling psychology course. She has also been a counselling psychology course tutor as well as lecturer on a number of counselling and clinical psychology and other post-graduate programmes including recently at the IOPPN part of KCL. Lorraine co-produced a course on 'psychological therapies' with a service user and provides teaching at the Recovery College affiliated with her present trust. With further practitioner level post-graduate training and accreditation, Lorraine mainly uses schema-focused therapy and CBT to inform her practice; she is also an EMDR-trained therapist. For a number of years Lorraine has been Head of Service as well as psychology lead at a borough–wide integrated psychological therapies team based at the Maudsley Hospital. A clinician first and foremost, in 2010 Lorraine published an article with Jerome Carson on 'Recovery and wellbeing: the new paradigms for mental health services'.

Misha Jechand is a business psychologist with a strong interest in people and organisations, currently specialising in assessment and selection at British Airways. She is responsible for advisory on assessment and selection tools and methodology across the organisation, as well as upskilling new assessors and promoting best practice initiatives. She has previously worked as a Learning and Development Specialist within Professional Development and Training for Network Rail, where she designed a series of training courses for aspiring bridge examiners. Following this she worked as a consultant for TMP Worldwide, where she worked on a number of assessment and selection projects across a variety of organisations and industries. Her commercial experience is built upon an excellent academic background from Aston Business School, with an MSc in Work Psychology and Business. In addition, she is working towards becoming a chartered occupational psychologist and is enrolled on the Stage 2 Doctorate Qualification in Occupational Psychology. Outside of work, she enjoys travelling and experiencing new cultures. Her travels over the last year have included Dubai, Singapore and South Africa. In addition, she enjoys writing and has authored a series of blogs called 'Reflections'. This is her first published piece of writing and her passion for diversity and inclusion influenced her to write this.

Ute Liersch is a counselling psychologist in training at Regent's University. Psychology is her third career. She worked in international hotel management for many years before returning home to Germany. There she created an educational company, which she successfully sold 12 years later. Witnessing the developmental trajectory of her pupils inspired her to a late career change. She moved into psychology. Since then she worked in a hospice, with the bereaved and dying, with chronic pain clients and survivors of torture and with people who have long enduring mental health problems. Ute is trained in third-wave behaviourism, existential-phenomenological thinking and is on the teacher trainer pathway for mindfulness, Bangor University. She hosts stress–resilience workshops for organisations inside and outside the UK and is a visiting lecturer for the 2018–2019 academic year at Birkbeck, University of London. As a child, she was deemed unsuitable for higher education. Her dyslexia, dyspraxia and dyscalculia were only diagnosed in 2011. Trying to hide her difficulties for many years, this article is her coming out, sharing experiences and strategies. Ute says: 'I have clawed my way into academia'. She has been published in the Journal of Psychotherapy and Counselling Psychology Reflection. She presented at the Counselling

Psychology Conference 2017 and the BPS Developmental Conference in 2012. She has written handbooks and weekly columns for the Helen Doron Educational Institute and e-learning tools for Croydon Health Service NHS Trust. As a child, she did her parent's head in with countless short stories and poems.

Tasim Martin-Berg is Deputy Programme Leader and Lecturer in Counselling Psychology, Glasgow Caledonian University and Consultant Counselling Psychologist, First Psychology Scotland. An active volunteer throughout her career, she is currently Training Lead for the Division of Counselling Psychology and Division of Counselling Psychology Scotland, British Psychological Society. As part of the BPS Leadership Development Programme, Tasim successfully completed in 2015/2016, she investigated 'How training programmes and DCoP can best support leadership development for its members and trainees' and published 'A report on the social justice, equality, diversity and inclusion audit of the British Psychological Society'. Tasim is deeply passionate and enthusiastic about the counselling psychology training process and is privileged to be able to work with students in this context. Having worked in a diverse range of settings, she currently runs a busy independent practice providing psychological therapy, supervision and consultation to individuals, teams and organisations. Her areas of interest in teaching, research and practice are: social justice and counselling psychology; partnership with third sector organisations; developing anti-discriminatory and anti-oppressive practice; feminist psychology and psychology of women; working with survivors of childhood sexual abuse and gender-based violence; acceptance-based cognitive behavioural therapies, including dialectical behaviour therapy; working with individuals with the sorts of difficulties associated with a diagnosis of borderline personality disorder; and LGBTQ+ issues and families. Tasim is mummy and co-parent to her two children and lives with them in a pink cottage near the sea in rural South East Scotland.

Nicola Massie is a consultant counselling psychologist in clinical practice with adults with an intellectual disability and with adults in a mental health service. Since qualifying by the Qualification in Counselling Psychology in 2007 Nicola has worked clinically and developed her leadership skills as a senior psychologist in multi-disciplinary teams and has led and contributed to initiatives to develop services in learning disability teams across South Wales. She also presents and provides training to counselling psychology trainees to support and develop an understanding of and confidence to work with people with an intellectual disability.

Nicola has also focused on developing her leadership skills to promote the contribution of counselling psychologists in Wales through clinical practice, mentorship and formal networking opportunities including with

Welsh Government, through the Welsh Branch of the British Psychological Society, and sitting on applied psychology groups working in the health service. Nicola has contributed to the Welsh Branch of BPS Policy Advisory Group, led and co-led consultations, contributed to events in Welsh Assembly Government and represented Wales in the group that revised the Professional Practice Guidelines (2017).

Nicola was the Chair of the Division of Counselling Psychology from 2013 until 2018 and during this time she was successful in leading the division to raise the profile and contribution of counselling psychology and significantly develop training opportunities in Wales.

Maureen McIntosh is one of the editors of this book and the author of the Chapter 1, 'The legacy of black oppression: Growth and resilient leadership'.

Lyndsey Moon is a Chartered Psychologist, Chair of the MOU Coalition and Associate Fellow at Warwick University.

Zenobia Nadirshaw is a consultant clinical psychologist, having worked for 42 years in the National Health Service, and Professor at the School of Health Studies, University of West London. Through her clinical practice and academic work lecturing, publishing and chairing several committees of the British Psychological Society and its Division of Clinical Psychology, she has raised the profile of double discrimination for people with learning disabilities as well as mental health problems as well as mental health problems from Ethnic Minority Groups. She is a recipient of several national and international awards and is now an honorary member of the British Psychological Society.

Sarah Supple qualified with a doctorate in psychotherapeutic and counselling psychology from the University of Surrey in 2003. Following that she worked in Northampton in both an outpatient psychology department and a community mental health team. During that time, she had articles published in the DCP and DCoP publications. Seeing is believing: Adapting cognitive therapy for visual impairment. *Counselling Psychology Review*, 19 (3). She also wrote a chapter for a book entitled, *New Ways of Working in Mental Health, the role that counselling psychology plays in the evolution of working in mental health services*. She then moved to Suffolk to work in an outpatient psychology department before having her first child. On returning from maternity leave, Sarah worked in the adult acute services, covering two inpatient acute wards and two crisis resolution and home treatment teams. During that time, she also undertook training as a CAT practitioner. In February 2016, she took up a post working with children and young people's services in Lowestoft, providing psychological training and consultation as well as some direct clinical work with teams, including social care (child in need and child protection teams), early help teams, the children in care teams, the leaving care teams and other linked services.

Simon Toms is a chartered psychologist and associate fellow of the British Psychological Society. He is also a chartered scientist with the Science Council, principal practitioner with the Association for Business Psychology, published author, and PhD graduate. Simon is a graduate of the Division of Occupational Psychology's Leadership Development Programme. One of Simon's fields of interest lies in non-traditional working arrangements, most notably the employment of temporary agency workers—an area in which Simon has completed a PhD, published a book, conducted further research, and presented findings at national and international conferences.

Rachel Tribe works at the School of Psychology, University of East London. She is a trustee of two international mental health charities: the Centre for Research and Evaluation—International Federation (Careif) and the UK: Sri Lanka Trauma Group. In 2014 she was awarded the British Psychological Society Award for Challenging Social Inequalities in Psychology. She is active in national and international consultancy, training and research. She has experience working in the private, public, charity and academic sectors. She has worked clinically with a range of diverse communities. She was a member of the the World Psychiatric Association's Task Force on Migration and Mental Health, the Royal College of Psychiatrists' expert panel on Improving Services for Refugees and Asylum-Seekers and the British Psychological Society (BPS) Presidential Task Force on Refugees and Asylum Seekers. She co-wrote the BPS guidelines with Dr Kate Thompson on Working with Interpreters in Health Settings, in 2017. Professor Tribe also co-edited a book on Working with Interpreters in Mental Health with Dr Hitesh Raval, re-issued in 2014. Her latest book is Lane, P. & Tribe, R. (eds) (2017), Anti-discriminatory practice in mental health for older people. She is currently working on the 3rd edition of Tribe, R & Morrissey, J. (eds), *The Handbook of Professional, Ethical and Research Practice*. She has published over 85 journal articles and book chapters She recently established with colleagues, a mental health and well-being webportal for refugees, internally displaced people and those working with them: https://www.uel.ac.uk/Schools/Psychology/Research/Refugee-Mental-Health-and-Wellbeing-Portal

Tony Wainwright is a clinical psychologist who has worked in leadership positions in the NHS, first as professional head of the psychology department at King's College in London and then in Cornwall Partnership NHS Trust, where he was professional head of service and director of quality. He currently teaches on policy, leadership, ethics, human rights and public health in the psychology department at the University of Exeter, where he is a senior lecturer.

He is a member of the British Psychological Society's (BPS) Ethics Committee and its immediate past chair. He currently represents the BPS on the European Federation of Psychologists' Associations Board of Ethics, Board of Human Rights and Psychology and is co-convenor of their Board of Promotion and Prevention. He is a member of the editorial group for Division of Clinical Psychology, Clinical Psychology Forum, where he is the lead for ethics and is also the reviews editor. He is a member of an international multidisciplinary network considering the role of psychology in euthanasia across Europe. He is currently co-editing a special issue of the European Psychologist on human rights and psychology and co-editing a textbook on human rights education for psychologists.

Tony Ward is an associate professor of Health and Counselling Psychology at the University of the West of England (UWE), Bristol. He also teaches on the Masters in Clinical Psychology at the Université Paris VIII in France. His main professional interest is in working therapeutically with clients that are experiencing neurological conditions, such as myalgic encephalitis, multiple sclerosis, head injury, stroke and various types of dementia. He was a co-author of the *Test of Everyday Attention* published in the 1990s, which remains a bestselling test battery for the neuropsychological assessment of attention. He is also interested in psychotherapeutic approaches to common mental health conditions, including depression, anxiety and trauma. Dr Ward is a keen proponent of the therapeutic advantages to be gained from a deeply integrative approach to client work. He has worked with various colleagues including Mick Cooper and John Mcleod on the development of a pluralistic approach to depression. He has recently written articles on how neuroscience can provide a level of unifying theory across different therapeutic schools. Dr Ward teaches on the professional doctorate in counselling psychology at UWE, and recently has been responsible for developing teaching on leadership. During the pilot phase of this work, it became obvious that the issue of diversity in relationship to leadership is a neglected topic.

Laura Anne Winter is an HCPC Registered Counselling Psychologist, Chartered Psychologist with the BPS and lecturer in Education and Counselling Psychology at the University of Manchester. She is also a Fellow of the Higher Education Academy. Her work involves teaching and supervising students on the doctorate in counselling psychology at Manchester and conducting and disseminating various research projects. She has also been involved in a number of leadership roles in relation to the doctorate programme, for example, working as Interim Programme Director and Placement Co-ordinator. Her therapeutic practice has been predominantly focused in NHS and third-sector settings, most recently working with working age adults who have been labelled with 'severe and enduring mental health problems'. Laura has published widely in the fields of counselling psychology and education. Her research explores the interrelationships between inequality and social and political issues, emotional wellbeing and educational experience. She has a particular interest in social justice in psychological and counselling professions and education and has conducted work exploring the presence of social justice ideas and practices within both counselling and educational psychology. She has a particular interest in ideas of 'relational equality': a subject which she recently wrote about in an article in the *Oxford Review of Education* entitled 'Relational equality: what, how and why?' Recently she has been involved in editing the fourth edition of the flagship textbook 'The Sage Handbook of Counselling and Psychotherapy' (with Colin Feltham and Terry Hanley).

Chapter summaries

Part I Leadership with diverse populations

Chapter I The legacy of black oppression: Growth and resilient leadership

This chapter will explore aspects of the legacy of slavery, black oppression and the cultural and political landscape that set this oppression in motion. There is an examination of the systemic negative ideologies that strive to keep power within the dominant culture, whether that be intentionally or unintentionally. Issues such as slavery, racism, prejudice, cultural oppression, internalized racism, microaggressions, identity and intersectionality, unconscious bias, growth, resilience, leadership and inequalities will be explored. Consideration will be given to why sophisticated barriers exist within society and organizations which prevent many more people of colour from progressing in life and being in leadership roles.

Chapter 2 The role of leadership for gay black practitioners: How do we craft authority from micro-aggressions and multiple identities? A personal story

Trait leadership behaviours and models as posited and researched by many social scientists such as Zaccaro (2004), Blake and Mouton (1964) and Hersey and Blanchard (1970) are topics that have long had an intrinsic appeal to me for a myriad of reasons. The main ones being that of a young black gay boy and then man trying to forge his way in a predominantly white culture. And to do so in a way that I could effectively not only push back against the many micro-aggressions (Sue, 2010) that I experienced, but also turn those slights and prejudices into something lasting and positive. I did this at first as a pupil at a predominantly white independent school, vowing to be one of its stars, and then by joining the army as an officer—one of the first commissioned into a whole Army Corps. Finally, by forging ahead in my future careers in both the Employee Assistance Programme (EAP) industry and then in the world of LGBT rights and finally in counselling per se. Throughout it all, the twin struggles between my gay and black self were to the fore, at certain times one and then the other in the ascendant, but it is only most recently that I am learning to feel at peace with both. That has allowed me to essay some elements of leadership within my chosen field, counselling psychology, and consider, at the same time, how this intersectionality (Crenshaw, 1989) really works for me. That is what has motivated me to write this chapter— that taking up the mantle of leadership whilst representing the intersections of diversity can hopefully shine as an example to many others who come after me.

Chapter 3 The different aspects of equality in the leadership agenda in the BPS

The chapter explores in some detail about how the British Psychological Society (BPS) and psychologists can equip themselves with the tools and attitudes to be leaders of change. The author displays her wealth of knowledge and experience regarding equality and diversity issues. This change in relation to diversity and equality means that institutions and services must engage with Black and Minority Ethnic (BME) individuals in ways that embody equality. The author speaks plainly about what is needed from psychologists to create a fairer system to engage with BME communities to prevent discrimination. In the latter part of her chapter she speaks robustly to the BPS Senior Management team and Trust Board about being more representative of the needs of diverse groups by changing policies and practices rather than just writing guidelines on diversity.

Chapter 4 Young black males' attitudes towards therapy

This exploration focuses on young black males and their attitudes to psychological therapy. Young black African Caribbean males are overrepresented in the mental health and criminal justice systems and seemingly underachieving in education in the UK. However, African Caribbean males are also part of our future generation, the potential leaders who can also contribute positively to society, as many of them are. However, it can be argued that the media may not always help to portray black men in a positive light. I am a black female-chartered counselling psychologist who has worked with young people from diverse backgrounds in various settings. My research findings showed that young black males felt they should 'sort things out for themselves' when dealing with their emotional difficulties. There were cultural issues that they felt would affect the therapy process. Therapy was viewed by them as a waste of time, feminine and a sign of weakness. Family upbringing was a factor which was perceived to strongly influence young black men's behaviour regarding seeking help. These young men felt they should 'protect' themselves from 'the system', meaning mental health services, the police, social services, etc., or other institutions set up to 'help and support', of which psychological therapy was seen to be a part. The young men seem to develop their own coping strategies and would only engage in psychological therapy as a last resort. These areas will be discussed in addition to how we as psychologists, therapists and other mental health practitioners can improve our approach by taking these areas into account.

Chapter 5 Social justice, leadership and diversity

This chapter will discuss what is meant by social justice in relation to counselling psychology specifically and psychology generally within the UK, as well as briefly considering social justice in the wider context. It will discuss if there is a role for counselling psychologists and psychology in promoting social justice through challenging social inequalities and exclusion and promoting anti-discriminatory practice. It will review the role of counselling psychology in potentially foregrounding inclusive best practices which celebrates diversity and provides leadership on this issue. *Diversity in this context will refer to a multiplicity of perspectives and experiences, many of which will be encompassed by the protected characteristics as defined by the* Equality Act *(2010)*. It will discuss how counselling psychology might provide some leadership on this issue using the framework of social justice. *Leadership in this context will be defined as an individual, group or professional group or organisation who may show or promote leadership in others to facilitate change*. It will then discuss the possible skills and theories psychologists have at their disposal to undertake work which promotes social justice and equality and takes into consideration human rights. It will provide a range of examples of where psychologists have undertaken social justice work using their training and skills and provided leadership in a range of contexts outside the consulting room. The chapter will argue that taking an active leadership role to encourage the promotion of social justice is at the centre of our work as a profession, a division and as individual counselling psychologists.

Chapter 6 Ethics and social justice

This chapter examines the ethical challenges faced by psychologists concerning issues of social justice that go beyond individual one-to-one work. The British Psychological Society (BPS) has published the Declaration on Equality, Diversity and Inclusion that sets out clearly the importance of addressing these wider social and political problems. At the same time the BPS Ethics Committee has widened the scope of its Code of Ethics and Conduct to include some reference to these contextual areas and has plans to develop its work more actively in the field of human rights. We include some discussion comparing the Universal Declaration of Ethical Principles for Psychologists, and the Universal Declaration Of Human Rights. Psychologists must pay attention to the enormous impact on the wellbeing of individuals, families and communities of social injustice. The chapter discusses these impacts where inclusion and exclusion are played out and how in research we need to carefully consider the way multiple characteristics that may lead to exclusion or discrimination can carefully be considered to ensure we only use non-oppressive approaches. The chapter also addresses the way we as psychologists are organised. Is the BPS itself living up to its own standards? An account of an audit undertaken of the Society's work by the Social Justice, Equality, Diversity and Inclusion Task Force is reported and from this some pointers are set out for how the BPS might use the opportunity provided by the current restructuring to recalibrate and reset its culture so that it more actively takes account of social justice and human rights.

Part II Developing your leadership style

Chapter 7 Power and privilege in psychology: Can we have egalitarian leadership?

This chapter considers the question 'Can we have egalitarian leadership?' whilst aiming to reflect upon and stimulate thinking about 'diversity' and to present a social justice perspective in relation to this. Such a view suggests that diversity is about power imbalances, privilege and oppression (Allen, Balfour, Bell & Marmot, 2014; Cutts, 2013; Smail, 1995; Winter, Guo, Wilk & Hanley, 2016). I suggest that diversity fundamentally relates to *equality*. Drawing on my recent work in education, I reflect on the idea of relating to each other as moral equals and the need to think about equality not only as about tangible differences in resources, but also as about our relationships (Mangan & Winter, 2017; Winter, 2017). Following this, I discuss what we might mean by 'leadership' and, using case examples, I try to provoke and stimulate thinking about power and privilege issues with leadership in psychology. Specifically, I suggest that leaders, by virtue simply of their role, have a greater degree of a particular type of power than those they are 'leading', and that this perhaps raises concerns from a diversity perspective. I then reflect upon the various ways we might mitigate this power imbalance in leadership relationships (as we do in our therapeutic work). This might for example involve engaging in explicit meta-communication and dialogue in these interpersonal relationships, to communicate our respect for the other as our equal human being. I do not aim to provide answers, and I also do not expect that all readers will agree with my ideas on things that might be problematic in relation to leadership. Nevertheless, I hope to stimulate deeper thinking about some commonly held ideas and assumptions held in psychology (and society), and to encourage critical thinking about what we mean by 'social justice'.

Chapter 8 Disability and identity: Reflections on my journey as a disabled woman, student and counselling psychologist

This chapter reflects on the journey of a registered blind psychologist thinking about the experience of being disabled within the psychological community. It looks back at how training as a psychologist and later as a CAT therapist informed the thinking and values that went on to facilitate the development of a disabled identity. This was in part through reflecting on the negative constructions of disability, initially within psychology and then more broadly within our society. This helped the author to reflect on how to think differently about disability and reflect on how to make it a positive part of one's identity and about how taking a leadership role was integral to this. This process was started by exploring the research within the field of psychology at the time the author undertook her Doctorate. The author considered the social construction of disability within psychological research and within the psychological community itself. This chapter will discuss how CAT ideas enabled further reflections about what reciprocal roles and procedures may have been played out in relation to the issue of being disabled. For example, striving to be viewed as 'amazing' to avoid being seen as tragic. The chapter reflects on how CAT as a discipline relates to disability and what reciprocal roles get played out within therapeutic relationships. The chapter examines how to create more helpful reciprocal roles and procedures regarding the author's and others relationship with and the construction of disability. The chapter includes how the author felt her leadership role was taken on reluctantly, but out of necessity, meaning that to survive being disabled in a non-disabled world she had to learn how to notice, name and address exclusion, marginalisation and discrimination. The author of this chapter took on a leadership role to address such issues, as she felt not doing this risked being blocked by barriers of discrimination and restrictive presumption.

Chapter 9 Dyslexia: Shackles far beyond the written word

Why is it so difficult for a person with dyslexia, dyspraxia and dyscalculia to enter higher education—even to work in academia? Is it because Dyslexia Support is not sufficient? Is it because we are not intelligent or motivated enough? Ute Liersch critically considers these questions by investigating the genesis of dyslexia, by exploring the helpfulness and hindrances of a diagnosis of dyslexia and by challenging the non-dyslexic reader's assumptions. She invites us into her life as a dyslexic and how she clawed her way into academia, always carefully sharing what she learned along the way. This chapter offers a genuine eye-opener to those for whom correct spelling seems like second nature, who cannot understand the phenomenon of dyslexia.

Chapter 10 Managing self, managing others: What does owning one's perspective add to leadership when you are a black woman in the NHS?

A keen knowledge of ourselves, our self-concept and identity and how we manage interactions with others undoubtedly is advantageous in the complex process of negotiating and taking up authority. Counselling psychologists have a leadership vantage point providing a platform from which vision and values can be seen and heard. Diversity at all levels in an organisation such as the NHS is of paramount importance. The chapter invites readers to open themselves to the possibility that black women can lead effectively and describes how emotional intelligence is an essential component of effective leadership.

Part III Leadership in organizations

Chapter 11 The challenges of authenticity: Leadership as a lesbian

This chapter synthesises Daisy's personal experience as a lesbian with leadership experience in addition to the literature and research that has explored the issues of lesbians as leaders. Daisy explores the conscious choices that lesbians make about how much they hide or share their sexual orientation within the workplace and beyond, and the implications for those who are in a leadership position, in whatever capacity this leadership role may exist. This is framed within the context of living in a heteronormative world where prejudice is both implicit and explicit. The influences of personal support on career success, the impact of discrimination and prejudice and the transformation approach to leadership are discussed. Gaps in the evidence base for lesbians in leadership are highlighted and suggestions for how lesbians can support themselves and be supported by others to develop as leaders are explored. This chapter promotes the impact of discrimination towards lesbians within the workplace and highlights the uniqueness of lesbians as leaders in the hope that more lesbians will feel empowered to work towards leadership. It also highlights the paucity of research that exists within this area, with the intention of encouraging further discussions and positive action.

Chapter 12 Social justice, leadership, and multi-cultural competency amongst applied psychology trainees

This chapter considers how psychologists that have responsibility for training in the various applied areas of the discipline can raise awareness of issues around diversity in trainees. It is suggested that this is an important topic when considering leadership. Many psychology trainees will aspire to reach the higher echelons of the profession, and in doing this, they will inevitably have to consider taking on leadership roles. The topic of diversity is, however, rather neglected in mainstream texts on leadership, which is rather incongruent with the strong emphasis on social justice which is now put forward as a core value for the profession. The chapter argues the point that awareness of diversity and cultural competency are essential in applied psychology, not only in terms of practice with clients, but also in terms of values and drivers which inform perspectives in terms of leadership. It is argued that in encouraging students to see themselves as future leaders, they should appreciate the need to reflect upon their professional values when in such roles, through, for example, championing social diversity. The chapter focuses on ethnic diversity as one key strand, as an example of the kinds of issues which trainers need to consider. Suggestions in the literature are highlighted in terms of how trainers can raise awareness of diversity issues in this area. There is a summary of the various suggestions at the end of the article. It is also suggested that courses should articulate a clear statement of values, so that trainees are in no doubt at the outset as to the expectations that they will be asked to fulfil. The chapter will be of interest to trainers across the fields of applied psychology.

Chapter 13 Reflective leadership in a multi-disciplinary team

This chapter is a reflection on ideas about and the experience of facilitating reflective leadership. The context for this exploration is the clinical work that is undertaken within multi-disciplinary teams which offer support for individuals with an intellectual disability. Teams supporting individuals with an intellectual disability work to empower their service users and challenge the difficulties presented to these individuals that are often a consequence of the environment and communities in which they live, work and make relationships. Intellectual disability teams typically focus on inclusion by understanding the effect of the environment. Psychologists working in intellectual disability teams are often trained and skilled in working with systemic models that engage with difference and diversity. In this chapter, ideas about diversity are, however, in relation to thinking differently about leadership. Working in teams to support people and systems that are related to intellectual disability is often challenging and can be highly stressful and emotional. Multi-disciplinary teams are configured with the expectation that they work as a team and may share goals, plans and hoped for outcomes. The stressful nature of the work can lead teams both to split and project the stress that is experienced by the team members. In the case of the example given, the stress was a consequence of team members striving to give the best support possible for a service user with whom they had become emotionally connected. Facilitating leadership that does not include support for team members to reflect on, engage with and be supported with their own thoughts and emotional responses to their work may lead to team members finding it difficult to work together and even become overly stressed themselves. This chapter explores ways in which to mitigate against this.

Chapter 14 Women in senior management: Exploring the dynamics of diversity in attaining senior leadership positions

Leadership is a core component of the work environment. Good leadership can enhance employees' performance and engagement levels, drive productivity and support employees' overall well-being. It is especially relevant as organisations become more diverse, which requires leadership that is purposeful, strong, proactive and facilitative, to explore and promote all the benefits that a diverse workforce brings. While the importance of leadership is not in doubt, those who lead still tend to be drawn from a limited homogenous group, with women and women from black and other minority ethnic (BME) groups less likely to fill senior leadership positions. This chapter provides context to the paucity of women—and especially those women who identify as from BME backgrounds—in such positions. It outlines the conscious and unconscious biases that continue to exist within the workplace that drive how women, and particularly BME women, are perceived and treated in terms of leadership opportunities. These perceptions endure despite equality legislation to eliminate unfair work practices that are in place in Western countries generally and that are developing globally. The persistence of unfair work practices indicates that there are inherent biases that need to be challenged consistently if the leadership competencies of BME women are to be accepted and used. This chapter outlines the benefits that using a diverse pool in senior leadership positions would bring to organisations, and how organisations could promote and put in place more fair practices to ensure this occurs.

Chapter 15 Diversity from an organisational perspective: Past, present and future directions

Diversity and inclusion are becoming an increasingly important topic on the agenda for organisations. Organisations who understand the value of having a diverse workforce are more likely to benefit (Stockdale & Crosby, 2004; Noe et al., 2003). Benefits include a stronger employer brand, increased employee engagement and performance, a variety of talent and experience in the workforce, innovative thinking, a culture of openness and an increased talent pool. The aim of this chapter is to inform individuals about the activity which is present today in organisations to promote diversity and inclusion, especially at senior leadership levels. This chapter captures the personal reflections of the author on how diversity and inclusion were viewed whilst she was growing up, how her working experiences have transformed her perception and how she envisions the topic to develop in the future. The author explains her personal experience that being female and coming from an ethnic minority group, there have been many times where she has been discouraged from pursuing her passions due to the perceptions of others. However, within the roles she has undertaken over the last few years she has seen the promotion of diversity and inclusion within organisations and worked on several initiatives herself. Having a diverse representation across the leadership board will still take time; however, if young people grasp opportunities now and develop the skills required, there is no reason why this cannot happen in the future.

Introduction

*Maureen McIntosh, Helen Nicholas and
Afreen Husain Huq*

> Courage is what it takes to stand up and speak. Courage is also what it
> takes to sit and listen.
>
> Winston Churchill

There is significant awareness in psychology of the impact on leaders and leadership as society becomes increasingly diverse. For many years the emphasis
has been on increasing the number of leaders with specific attributes, such as
women or those from ethnic minorities, to reflect a truer representation of
society. The book taps into the current surge of interest in how to develop
our leadership skills.

The inspiration for this book on leadership and diversity arose out of the
personal experience of the first editor, in her leadership role as Chair of the
Division of Counselling Psychology *(2016–2018)*. The second editor, born
and raised in South Africa, was inspired to bring the voices of psychologists
from different backgrounds together in a collection of chapters that allows for
their experiences and stories to be told. She has also held several leadership
positions and is involved in the BPS leadership and development programme.
The third editor was enthused by colleagues' inspiration to undertake this
formidable challenge of compiling relevant material for a book on leadership
and diversity, having worked in the NHS for over 30 years and having survived the challenges of being the token Black/Asian clinical psychologist in
the system.

There are very few people of colour within leadership positions, and the
varied reflections from the contributors highlight that diversity is about
a multitude of important areas such as race, ethnicity, sexuality, gender,
power, social justice, equality, disability, identity, the intersection of these
areas and so much more. This book has a contemporary 'edge' which is
achieved through a focus on practitioners' reflections of their own experience. It incorporates current theory, up to date research and references
concerning current trends towards more relational and integrative work.
The book reflects the progression in the direction of a more pluralistic/

integrative practice, moving away from traditional orientations involving specific ways of working.

There are 15 chapters that argue a variety of points of view to demonstrate to the reader how the practice of leadership can be used to widen knowledge, empower people and change systems by connecting to rich ideas.

The authors are from different backgrounds, and they write about their area of interest and what has inspired them to contribute to this very relevant, exciting and thought-provoking topic. Many of the authors are themselves from a minority group and they discuss their experiences about many issues, for example, disability, dyslexia, BME, intersectionality, gender, lesbian, gay and social justice. Talking about being from a diverse group does not assume all minority groups are disadvantaged, rather it demonstrates the complexity of experience and how easily it is presumed that fairness and equality within systems exist for all.

The focus of the book is about 'moving beyond the limits' when obstacles prevent individuals and organizations from leading on equality, social justice and diversity matters. The chapters fall broadly into three parts. The first part is a collection of accounts of leadership with diverse populations, including an historical perspective from the first editor, in addition to the voices of other authors on gender, sexuality, power, privilege, equality and social justice. The second part draws on how psychologists and mental health professionals can develop their leadership style, often in challenging and difficult situations. This part takes the reader on a personal journey through the stories of the authors and how they overcame some of the difficulties they have faced because of their own diversity. The third part pays attention to leadership in organizations and how the authors have challenged organizational structures. The authors also write about leadership within the context of diversity from the perspective of psychologists that have personal and professional experience about the topics in which they speak.

As editors, we hope the varied perspectives on diversity and leadership will inspire further discussion, reflection and learning in leadership, clinical and research practice. Overall, this book explores leadership with diverse populations, leadership styles and leadership in organizations, with emphasis on power issues in relation to others and managing self and others. In addition, taking advantage of opportunities as they arise in the work place whilst utilising setbacks as a learning experience. It is important for practitioners to be aware that alternative positions can be adopted, and hopefully this book will help to open the minds of practitioners to new ways of working including reflecting on their own practice. We encourage the reader to share their own knowledge, generate debates and reflect with colleagues to change, and act where they see inequality and discrimination.

In conclusion, we hope the reader will engage with a critical exploration of the meaning of diversity and leadership in their clinical and leadership practice to develop an understanding of its complexities whether conscious or unconscious.

Reference

BrainyQuote. Winston Churchill Quotes. Retrieved from: http://www.brainyquote.com/quotes/winston_churchill_161628.

Part I

Leadership with diverse populations

Chapter 1

The legacy of black oppression: Growth and resilient leadership

Maureen McIntosh

Introduction

> My Great Grandmother's Great Grandmother was a slave.
>
> (McIntosh, 2015, Scene 9)

As I sat watching this thought-provoking play called *Dominoes* I was struck by this powerful and heartfelt statement about the conflict that arises within a person's sense of who they are, and how this is often deeply rooted in one's history. The lead character in the play is a mixed-race woman who goes way back into the past of her ancestors to explore some of the hidden aspects within her family's story. What is revealed is a complex narrative that surrounds the history of the racial group she is a part of; this opens the door to a new way of embracing all facets of her sense of self.

Oppression is described as "the exercise of authority or power in a burdensome, cruel, or unjust manner" (dictionary.com). The history of enslaving people from Africa is beyond the scope of this chapter; however, it cannot be overlooked because this was a defining, traumatic turning point in black people's history of oppression, and fight for recognition, freedom, and equality. It is well documented that African people were forcibly taken into slavery because they were viewed as an inexpensive way to gain inexhaustible manpower (History.com). The behaviour of the British in slavery (Sherwood, 2007) is "morally wrong or evil" (Cambridge online dictionary). These owners mistreated their slaves whilst putting in place systems of sexual and physical violence and psychological abuse, in addition to recompensing submission (History.com). This abuse of power maintained a system that set slaves apart from one another, leaving them helpless to fight against their captors (History.com). The aim behind such levels of cruelty was to make slaves into unresisting individuals so their masters could have complete authority over them by not treating them as human beings

(Feblowitz, 2010). However, instead of breaking black people's spirit with the "lash, cane, raised hand" or through hangings as described in "slave narratives", the captors failed (Feblowitz, 2010, p. 1) due to slaves' unwillingness to give in and their desire to be the master of their own life choices (Feblowitz, 2010).

In 1863 Lincoln delivered an "emancipation proclamation", which meant that some areas within America, slaves were legally free; however, slavery was not "abolished" until the 18 December 1865 (History.com). Before the British relinquished their laws supporting slavery, there was an uprising by slaves fighting for their freedom in the Caribbean. In the UK they eventually passed the "emancipation act in 1833" (The National Archives). The government paid £20,000,000" (National Archives) to recompense slave owners for earnings they lost due to the passing of this law. Freedom was delayed by five years until 1838, and during that time in the British Caribbean "masters continued to ill-treat and exploit" black people (National Archives). Figures from the *Guardian* available online (Smith, 2006) suggest that "28 million" black people were "sold into slavery" [1450–19th century] and the UK profited greatly by delivering annually more than "300,000" black people to slave owners (Smith, 2006).

It took many more years for an American President to apologise for America's part in slavery. It is reported that President Clinton (CNN, 1997) did not feel that his country should "compensate" African Americans for the harm that was caused, because it was such a long time ago when slavery occurred. However, he did address in an interview that something needed to happen to confront the consequences of slavery. He expressed in rather striking terms that the matter is incomplete and still resonates to this present day. Clinton explained, *"I think it has to be dealt with…there's still some unfinished business out there among black and white Americans"* (CNN, 1997). Bennet (1998) wrote in an online article for the *New York Times* that whilst visiting Africa, President Clinton presented a carefully constructed apology, where his statement accepts that there is something erroneous about profiting from slavery:

> Going back to the time before we were even a nation, European Americans received the fruits of the slave trade and we were wrong in that.

Tony Blair on behalf of the UK government expressed *"…we are sorry…"* whilst emphasising that it should not be forgotten that slavery is "unacceptable" (BBC News, 2007). It can be argued that it is a significant undertaking when governments across the world denounce inhumane acts such as one group of people believing that they have the right to own another human being. Nevertheless, these speeches hardly make a difference when some of the systems that society and institutions are built on embody racist ideals that inevitably prolong the legacy of black oppression. This can make it difficult to move forward with full confidence of real change.

As the first black person to be the Chair [July 2016–6 July 2018] of the British Psychological Society, Division of Counselling Psychology (DCoP), I felt that the DCoP truly embraced the importance of diversity, and I was proud to serve for the benefit of the membership, moreover for all those who never thought there would ever be a black chair. Trying to highlight the inequalities that beset many people of colour can be tricky to explain when to some it may appear that black people do not face the same challenges as our forefathers who experienced slavery, fought for black civil rights in the 50s and 60s or against apartheid (1948–1994). On closer inspection and with an unbiased eye one can clearly see that *"the masters tools will never dismantle the masters house"* (Lorde, 2007, p. 110) and those who have power are often unwilling to change the structures that keep the power within the dominant group. A fellow counselling psychologist introduced me to this book written by the black feminist Audre Lorde. Her book gave me strength during a time when my role as a leader within a large well-known institution within my professional and voluntary roles was being challenged in unhelpful ways. I felt that it seemed hard for some individuals to respect and hear my voice. Lorde (2007, p. 110) postulates that *"black people have historically been stripped of their language and forms of expression and forced to communicate in the language of the oppressor"*.

An examination of the research, commentary, and negative stereotyping of black people in the media, the black person's lived experience, and institutional racism within the police force, organisations and in psychiatry demonstrate very clearly the struggle black people often experience. Moreover, the incidents where black people are killed in communities show where power remains and that racial inequality is very much present today in all areas of society.

Cultural Oppression, prejudice and racism

> This inequality is generally the result of a history of colonialism, genocide and oppression in which the material, intellectual, spiritual and emotional resources of one people are put in service of another through force, deception and disrespect for their ways.
>
> (Bivens, 1995, p. 1)

Schiele (2005, p. 803) sees "cultural imperialism as cultural oppression", which is defined by Young (1990, p. 59) as a widespread distribution of "the dominant group's experience and culture as [being] the norm" (cited in Schiele, 2005, p. 803). When the voice of the dominant group is valued more than other cultures, the consequence is that the voice of minority ethnic groups goes unrecognised (Schiele, 2005). Bivens describes (1995, p. 1) "racism as a system of oppression based on race…" and this comes about because of the "privilege" held by the dominant culture who have a disproportionate amount "…of systemic power…" (Bivens, 1995, p. 1). Carbone (2010, p. 1) suggests that there is a link between "poverty and race" that creates a divide because it places the "power" and entitlement in the hands of the racial group which has the most influence whilst treating others as insignificant based on their "race and class". The media highlighted the exposition which demonstrated that there is "racial inequality in the UK" between "ethnic minorities and white people". It is argued that it is important that those who are from the dominant culture consider that "being white" places them in the category of being superior to "the detriment" of those from minority groups (NASP, 2016, p. 1), if they choose not to use their power in ways that helps others.

It can be an important step in the right direction if individuals in seeing this failure to be tolerant and understanding, try instead to "break down the barriers of cultural ignorance and value judgements" (McIntosh, 2017, p. 19). The difficulty lies at the heart of institutions and societal and political systems that are meant to protect the rights of all equally regardless of their racial background. Sadly, it often takes the tragic loss of yet another black person to uncover the depths of racism, prejudicial attitudes and bias that exist. For example, in the case of the public enquiry into the death of Stephen Laurence it highlighted the level of "institutional racism" within the Metropolitan Police (The Guardian, 1998), when it is meant to be a trustworthy organisation.

There are many incidences where stories of racism are depicted, and conversations are taking place, whether it be through movements like Black Lives Matter (blacklivesmatter.com), in communities, in politics, films, plays, on the internet, and within music. People are fighting for social justice, equality, and a fairer, safe society for all, where people are not judged on the colour of their skin or ethnic group. Black Lives Matter (Thrasher, 2015) has affected the way many black people have come together stronger in the face of adversity through converging and proving that black people are valuable members of society that deserve respect.

Unfortunately, the Equalities Act (Legislation.gov.uk, 2010) has not prevented "discrimination" and prejudice (Mcleod, 2013, p. 1). I remember one day trying to cross a busy road and as I stood there waiting for the light to change a car drove past and the person shouted the 'N' word quite loudly at me. As I crossed the road I did not realise that this was a "micro-assault" (Sue et al., 2007, p. 278). I felt quite shocked that someone would go to all that trouble to offend someone they do not know. Looking back, I also recollect that a Caucasian colleague I worked with many years ago spoke honestly about his experience of meeting black people when he was a child. He explained that his parents instructed him to cross the street if he saw a black person walking down the road. It was over 20 years ago when those two events happened, but I recall it so clearly and it makes me think about how people can hold onto so much prejudice and ignorance about a racial group.

Watching the powerful and disturbing video by Childish Gambino (2018) entitled *"This is America"* is educative in its delivery of modern day America and its legitimised brutality and gun violence. The video makes uneasy watching, as Gambino moves scene by scene demonstrating the lethality of gun violence on the innocent. This is a reality that is seen every day through the media, on the internet, and within communities. In the video Gambino pauses, and the silence is palpable, then the music begins again, and it ends with Gambino, his eyes filled with fear as he runs for his life.

In the UK currently, there is an increase in knife crime that is taking the lives of young black people, which is devastating for families, communities, and future generations. And yet the fight goes on for tolerance and justice within society where one can observe multicultural groups coming together to highlight the fight against racism and gun and knife crime as they advocate for peace. There are no easy answers about how to eradicate racism or what will help young black people believe that there are alternative ways of taking control of their destiny in life. The National Association of School Psychologists (2016, p. 1) argues that society must have these "tough conversations", and psychologists who work in schools have the competencies that can create "systems-level change" by taking a lead and encouraging discourse about this issue to "produce positive outcomes" for all concerned (p. 1).

Internalized Racism

> [Is]the acceptance of negative attitudes, beliefs, ideologies, and stereotypes perpetuated by the White dominant society as being true about one's racial group.
>
> Molina & James, 2016, p. 3

When reflecting on the definition of internalized racism it is important to consider what the impact upon the individual and racial group is when individuals, organisations, the broader society, and the political landscape keep in place frameworks that have little or no respect for the multicultural communities that reside within it. For some, this lack of respect communicates an unhelpful belief that black minority ethnic groups are not worthwhile human beings and inferior when compared to others. Many black ethnic minorities resist oppressive systems by striving to work harder than their peers from the dominant culture to demonstrate their knowledge, skills, and competencies through "achievement, perfectionism, and assimilation", (Banks & Stephens, 2018, p. 95) to challenge the label of "inferiority" which is at the core of "internalised oppression" (Banks & Stephens, 2018, p. 95).

There is a powerful argument to move away from attributing this problem to the black person with remarks like, they have a *chip on their shoulder* and instead take the view that "internalized racism...is structural" (Bivens, 1995, p. 1) and deeply embedded within all areas of society. The consequence of such negative infrastructures of oppression endeavours to keep the "power" in the hands of the dominant culture, whilst eroding the "power" of black minority ethnic groups by trying to instil "fear [of] our own power and difference" (Biven, 1995, p. 1). This can be seen within organisations, institutions, and society where black minority ethnic groups are fighting to be heard and to be allowed into positions of power where they can demonstrate leadership and have influence at all levels of society, including politically.

Many influential writers and activists—Nelson Mandela, Martin Luther King, Frantz Fanon, James Baldwin, and many more—have spoken about the black man and how the oppression of our identity is something black people are continually fighting against. Last year, I attended The Guild of Psychotherapists' film screening and group discussion of James Baldwin's *"I am not your Negro"*. Hoffman (2016) evaluates this film (Peck, Baldwin & Jackson, 2016) which explains through Baldwin's words and through film footage a powerful, uneasy truth about the oppression of black people. I sat with many others both black and white watching this film, which included images of brutality and dehumanising acts upon black people over decades, including modern times. I watched and listened to the commentary trying to make sense of why. I was struck by something James Baldwin observed as the problem and that is the *fear* and *ignorance* within the dominant culture to truly see black people as equal.

Baldwin (1962) wrote to his nephew something that I believe still resonates today in the minds of many and in the systems that maintain racial inequality:

> You were born where you were born and faced the future that you faced because you were black and for no other reason. The limits to your ambition were thus expected to be settled. You were born into a society which spelled out with brutal clarity and in as many ways as possible that you were a worthless human being. You were not expected to aspire to excellence. You were expected to make peace with mediocrity. Please try to remember that what they believe, as well as what they do and cause you to endure, does not testify to your inferiority, but to their inhumanity and fear.

Baldwin (1962) states an uncomfortable truth that has been observed since slavery and that is of the low expectations that are built into the infrastructure and sadly, in the minds of some individuals. He encourages his nephew not to view this racist behaviour as a sign that black people are inferior, instead that those who choose to hold such perceptions are in fact showing how afraid they are of equality and of sharing power. This is what black people and those from the dominant culture who do not ascribe to such ideologies are fighting for: A recognition that truly acknowledges that fundamental changes need to take place.

Micro-aggressions

> Micro-aggressions [are] brief and commonplace daily verbal, behavioural, and environmental indignities, whether intentional or unintentional, that communicate hostile, derogatory or negative racial slights and insults to the target person or group
>
> Sue et al., 2007, p. 271

Schiele (2005) suggests that when negative meanings about black people are conveyed it becomes a barrier to the black minority ethnic group progressing and creates a feeling of "ethnic self-depreciation" (p. 806).

Sue et al. (2007, p. 278) elaborate on three types of micro-aggressions:

1 Microinsult (Often Unconscious) Behavioural/verbal remarks or comments that convey rudeness, insensitivity and demean a person's racial heritage or identity.
2 Micro-assault (Often Conscious) Explicit racial derogations characterized primarily by a violent verbal or nonverbal attack meant to hurt the intended victim through name-calling, avoidant behaviour or purposeful discriminatory actions.
3 Microinvalidation (Often Unconscious) Verbal comments or behaviours that exclude, negate, or nullify the psychological thoughts, feelings, or experiential reality of a person of colour.

The person who experiences these micro-aggressions routinely finds ways to protect themselves by ignoring these behaviours to survive in their environment. Often the "perpetrator" accuses the individual of being "overly sensitive" (Sue et al., 2007, p. 278), and the person experiencing the micro-aggression is persuaded not to pursue the matter further (Sue et al., 2007). "Intersectionality" can disentangle "the complexities of inequality" (Petrova, 2016, p. 6) that exist when one's identity falls into several different areas such as race, gender, and class. Petrova (2016, p. 5) suggests that the term "intersectional discrimination" has more utility because it refers to the "multiple discrimination" that some individuals face. I am aware that

I have identities that are within these intersections and although I have a Doctorate degree that may afford me a certain level of status, my racial background often means that I will be viewed less favourably by some because of the colour of my skin.

I recollect attending a meeting in a well-known organisation where I was advocating as a counselling psychologist for a publication on culture and diversity. After that professional meeting I reflected on how bruised I felt from my experience during the debate. The majority in the room were Caucasian and I felt like a lone voice defending this publication, except for one person who spoke out to reflect on the power disparities within the room regarding my ethnic position. Deep down in my heart I did not want to agree to what was being asked of me because it went against my professional identity as a counselling psychologist. However, in that moment I conceded and put my own feelings to one side and stayed silent. We had a battle to get the articles published but with the support of black colleagues and others who generally believed in the publication, we were able to have the document published (Ade-Serrano, Nkansa-Dwamena, & McIntosh, 2017) through sheer perseverance.

On another occasion I had to attend a scheduled meeting where I was representing the interests of counselling psychologists. Again, I was the only black person in the room and ten minutes before the meeting began I was left with an uneasy feeling when I was asked by one of the people leading the meeting if I was in *the wrong meeting*. I felt quite embarrassed when this person came over and quietly said that to me. I knew I was in the right place, but I gave the person the benefit of the doubt and I informed them of my job title and who I was there to represent. This person went on to say that I could choose not to stay if I have other things to do because others in the meeting from my professional modality could be the representatives (even though they were there in another capacity), moreover these individuals were also from the dominant culture. I went over and spoke to my colleagues about what had been suggested to me and they appeared genuinely puzzled by this person's behaviour. My two colleagues who have always been kind and supportive encouraged me to stay in the meeting. Unfortunately, the micro-aggression was deeply felt, and I left the meeting making the excuse that I could be doing other things. In truth, I was left feeling uncomfortable, embarrassed, and excluded. Sue et al. (2007, p. 279) explain that black people face micro-aggressions routinely in their daily lives which has a "cumulative" impact that can affect individuals' "well-being". As I reflected on my experience and discussed it with others, I did not allow it to prevent me from finding my voice within that forum. Often it can feel like a battle; you have some success, but it is always a battle. The repetition of negative encounters to silence the black person's voice, whether intentional or unintentional, is commonly experienced by black people.

Implicit/explicit bias

Bias is the negative evaluation of one group and its members relative to another.

Blair, Steiner & Havranek, 2011, p. 71

When looking more closely at the issue of bias, research shows that there are differences in how implicit and explicit bias are understood (Blair et al., 2011, p. 71). "Explicit bias" is stated clearly and the person is cognizant of their view and is driven to do something about it (Blair et al., 2011). Whereas "implicit bias" consists of a different "process" that is "unintentional and unconscious" and this can be triggered by "situational cues" for example "a person's skin colour or accent" (Blair et al., 2011, p. 71). There are computerised tests known as "Implicit Association Tests" (Greenwald et al., 2009; Lane et al., 2007, cited in Blair et al., 2011, p. 72) that can identify whether a person has this type of bias. Implicit bias has been shown to exist in many types of situations, including in "healthcare", creating substandard ways of communicating with those from ethic groups (Fazio et al., 1995; Greenwald et al., 2009; Dovidio et al., 2002, cited in Blair et al., 2011, p. 72). "Stereotype threat" is also an issue that can impact on "patient–clinician communication" when the client may experience "stress" because they suspect that an unfair opinion will be formed about them based on "negative stereotypes" (Steele, Spencer & Aronson, 2002, cited in Blair et al., 2011, p. 75). Studies have shown some positive outcomes when examining how to diminish implicit bias within people. One such research showed "admired African Americans" to people and the results were that "implicit bias" had lessened (Dasgupta & Greenwald, 2001, cited in Blair et al., 2011, p. 75). Studies suggest that when the person faced with such biases "affirm [their] self-integrity" it decreases "racial" disparities in level of achievement within academic environments (Cohen et al., 2006; Cohen et al., 2009; Miyake et al., 2010, cited in Blair et al., 2011, p. 75).

Arguably, it is part of the landscape and no matter how much you try not to racialise every encounter one is usually faced with some form of bias. Therefore, it is the responsibility of everyone to bring awareness to how they are communicating to develop new ways of engagement with others that is built on honest acceptance of the person so that real change happens.

Identity, growth and resilient leadership

...Black people throughout the Diaspora develop affirmative identities, even in the face of racial oppression.

Neville, Viard & Turner, 2015, p. 248

Masten (2001, p. 2) describes that "resilience" embodies "good outcomes" despite "serious threats to adaptation or development". Ledesma (2014, p. 1) posits that "resilience" in connection to "leadership development" is about "thriving and hardiness". Throughout history it is often said that black people demonstrate qualities such as "hardiness" because of their ability to "endure difficult conditions [with] courage" and they can "thrive" notwithstanding the many inequalities that exist to prevent them from flourishing in life (dictionary.com).

In many ways I have lived my life more courageously in the eyes of those who have supported me than I have felt myself at times. I have had to grow into my skin and embrace all aspects of who I am in the face of many challenges. My resilient-self developed growing up and seeing my mother's strength and listening to stories about my grandmother. My sense of self as a black person was strong then and now. On reflecting on my leadership style, I would categorize it as someone who is "democratic" and wants to contribute to the "growth and well-being" of others by "sharing power", in addition to demonstrating "transformational leadership" by "inspiring" others (lfhe.ac.uk).

It is disconcerting that there are still fewer black people in senior roles. Randhawa (2018) argues that there is a preponderance of "diversity" in "London's workforce" but unsurprisingly there is a lack of "diversity" within "leadership". I have reflected on the lack of black people in senior positions in a previous communication to the members of DCoP when I talked (McIntosh, 2018) about Randhawa's (2018) online article where she states that "closing the gap on BME representation in NHS leadership [is] not rocket science". It is a huge issue considering that currently there is so much written about race, inequality, and diversity. In the National Health System [NHS] "43%" of its employees are from a "black minority ethnic" group [BME] and only "14%" hold a "board-level" role (Randhawa, 2018). I have experienced what I felt to be discrimination when as the only black psychologist in a CMHT at Band 8a, my post was deleted.

Arguably, the NHS statistics present a bleak reality which suggests that black oppression is still here. BME individuals who work in the NHS are experiencing "discrimination" (Chand, 2018); and are "more likely" to experience "bullying than white colleagues" (Mundasad, 2016). In the report on bullying (Mundasad, 2016) there is an argument that the NHS *"…must not be defensive or complacent, but must change our cultures, biases, attitudes and behaviours as well as improve our processes and policies"* (Danny Mortimer, chief executive of NHS Employers). Strong words; however, I am curious about why there is so much resistance to sharing power and treating black people with respect.

In the early days of my role in a large organisation I consulted with other senior psychologists who had knowledge and experience of the systemic processes in this institution I had taken a leadership role within. I trusted them to honestly answer my question about whether I was being treated differently because of my cultural background. Very sincerely, the message I received was not to give up. Another colleague told me that maybe they, meaning the people in this organisation, needed time to get used to me. When trying to make sense of my experiences and talking to other black people and black psychologists one can often be the only black person in a meeting or in a leadership role in the room. I believe there is a negative assumption that black people cannot progress and hold leadership positions.

If one is from the dominant culture it is the norm to only have people that look like you in the room making decisions. I have often walked into a room or joined a meeting and there is a look of surprise which is palpable when a white person is expected to be *Dr Maureen McIntosh*. After getting over that racist hurdle, there is always another and another when my credentials are questioned through prejudiced, patronising, disingenuous smiles. I believe this is referred to as a "micro-insult" (Sue et al., 2007, p. 278). In conversation with a senior psychologist within the NHS I was informed that due to my high standards of work and efficiency, I was labelled as an engine because of how much work I could take on. I honestly believe that this person felt I was being given a compliment. It took a little while and my rejection of this label for this individual to realise that I was offended by it and in my eyes, it was just another "micro-insult" (Sue et al., 2007, p. 278). If I am thought of as an engine by others, then as an organisation they can treat me without compassion.

Over time, I have learnt not to buy into negativity, as this is not part of my self-identity, and the historical experience of slavery, racism, and discrimination has given black people through the generations a strength of spirit that is at the core of who we are. I have chosen not to *"look at [my]self through the eyes of others, [or] measure [my] soul by… a world that looks on in amused contempt and pity"* (Du Bois, 1989[1903]:3, cited in Pyke, 2010, p. 551). I have chosen to continually stand up and do my very best, showing leadership and strength by remaining open to learning whilst developing kind communication with those I interact with, to show that all human beings deserve to be valued and treated fairly and with respect.

Finding the courage to assert myself in the face of adversity is something I do to maintain my integrity as a human being, black woman, mother, sister, daughter, friend, counselling psychologist and doctor. I always like to think of myself as a person that tries to *move beyond the limits* of the many obstacles that are put before me and I encourage others to find their strength too.

I have discovered that poetry is a form of expression that allows me to go a little deeper to connect with my resilient self. Lorde (2007) illustrates this beautifully through her writing as it reflects the capacity within poetry to begin as a budding seed and develop towards *"…those ideas which are until the poem—nameless and formless, about to be birthed, but already felt… [and] we learn more and more to cherish our feelings and to respect those hidden sources of our power from where true knowledge and, therefore, lasting action comes"* (pp. 36–37).

I am inspired by Lorde's poetic words to end my chapter with my own poetry.

My Journey

Beautiful part of my journey of self-discovery
Is to be open.
My past life already lived,
I can rise above and see with a different lens the meta-characteristics
that illuminate my strengths and values.
That take me in new directions.
At every juncture I can challenge myself,
I take the perspective that I am arriving,
fully here, present in my own life and ready to live it.

McIntosh, 2015

References

Ade-Serrano, Y., Nkansa-Dwamena, O. & McIntosh, M. (2017). Race, Culture and diversity. A collection of articles. British Psychological Society, Division of Counselling Psychology.

Banks, K. H. & Stephens, J. (2018). Reframing Internalized Racial Oppression and Charting a way Forward. *Social Issues and Policy Review, 12*(1), 91–111. Retrieved from https://doi.org/10.1111/sipr.12041

Baldwin, J. (1962). A Letter to My Nephew. *The Progressive.* Retrieved: 05/08/2018 from https://progressive.org/magazine/letter-nephew/

BBC News Channel. (2007, March 14). Blair 'sorry' for UK slavery role. Retrieved: 10/06/2018 from http://news.bbc.co.uk/1/hi/uk_politics/6451793.stm

Bennet, J. (1998, March 25). Clinton In Africa: The Overview; In Uganda, Clinton expresses regret on Slavery in U.S. Retrieved: 07/05/2018 from https://www.nytimes.com/1998/03/25/world/clinton-africa-overview-uganda-clinton-expresses-regret-slavery-us.html

Bivens, D. (1995). Internalized Racism: a definition. Women's Theological Center. Retrieved: 10/06/2018 from http://racialequitytools.org/resourcefiles/bivens.pdf

Black Lives Matter. Retrieved from https://blacklivesmatter.com/about/

Blair, I. V., Steiner, J. F. & Havranek, E. P. (2011). Unconscious (Implicit) Bias and Health Disparities: Where Do We Go from Here? *The Permanente Journal, 15*(2), 71–78.

Cambridge Online Dictionary. Retrieved from https://dictionary.cambridge.org

Carbone, S. A. (2010). Race, Class, and Oppression: Solutions for Active Learning and Literacy in the Classroom. *Inquiries Journal/Student Pulse, 2*(01), 1–4. Retrieved from http://www.inquiriesjournal.com/

Chand, K. (2018, July 9). The NHS relies on its BME staff – so why do they still face discrimination? Retrieved: 5/8/18 from https://www.theguardian.com/society/2018/jul/09/nhs-bme-staff-discrimination

Childish Gambino (2018, May 5). This is America. Retrieved from http://smarturl.it/TcIgA

CNN Politics (1997, June 17). Clinton Opposes Slavery Reparations. Retrieved: 07/05/2018 from http://edition.cnn.com/ALLPOLITICS/1997/06/17/clinton.race/

Cohen, G.L., Garcia, J., Apfel, N. & Master, A. (2006). Reducing the racial achievement gap: a social-psychological intervention. *Science*, *313*(5791), 1307–1310 (cited in Blair et al, (2011), p. 75, op cit).

Cohen, G., Garcia, J., Purdie-Vaughns, V., Apfel, N. & Brzustoski, P. (2009). Recursive processes in self-affirmation: intervening to close the minority achievement gap. *Science*. *324*(5925), 400–403 (cited in Blair et al., (2011), p. 75, op cit).

Dasgupta, N. & Greenwald, A.G. (2001). On the malleability of automatic attitudes: combating automatic prejudice with images of admired and disliked individuals. *Journal of Personality Social Psychology*, *81*(5), 800–814 (cited in Blair et al., (2011), p. 75, op cit).

Dictionary.com. Retrieved from https://www.dictionary.com/

Dovidio, J.F., Kawakami, K. & Gaertner, S.L. (2002). Implicit and explicit prejudice and interracial interaction. *Journal of Personality Social Psychology*, *82*(1), 62–68 (cited in Blair et al., (2011), p. 72, op cit).

Du Bois, W. E. B. 1989[1903]. *The Souls of Black Folk*. New York: Grove Press (cited in Pyke (2010), p. 551, op cit).

Feblowitz, J. C. (2010). Breaking the Cycle: Violence, Control and Resistance in American Slave Narratives. *Inquiries Journal/Student Pulse*, *2*(01), 1–5. Retrieved from http://www.inquiriesjournal.com/a?id=126

Fazio, R.H., Jackson, J.R., Dunton, B.C. & Williams, C.J. (1995). Variability in automatic activation as an unobtrusive measure of racial attitudes: A bona fide pipeline? *Journal of Personality Social Psychology*, *69*(6), 1013–27, (cited in Blair et al., (2011), p. 72, op cit).

Greenwald, A.G., Poehlman T.A., Uhlmann, E. & Banaji, M.R. (2009). Understanding and using the Implicit Association Test: III. Meta-analysis of predictive validity. *Journal of Personality Social Psychology*, *97*(1), 17–41 (cited in Blair et al., (2011), p. 72, op cit).

History.com Staff. (2009). Slavery in America. Retrieved: 06/05/2018 from https://www.history.com/topics/black-history/slavery

Hoffman, J. (2016). *I Am Not Your Negro review – James Baldwin's words weave film of immense power*. Retrieved: 05/08/2018 from https://www.theguardian.com/film/2016/

Jamaican Patwah definition. Retrieved: 10/06/2018 from http://jamaicanpatwah.com/term/Tallawah/

Lane, K.A., Banaji, M.R., Nosek, B.A. & Greenwald, A.G. (2007). Understanding and using the Implicit Association Test: IV: What we know (so far) about the method. In: Wittenbrink, B., Schwarz, N., editors. *Implicit measures of attitudes*. New York: Guilford Press; 2007. pp. 59–102 (cited in Blair et al., (2011), p. 72, op cit).

Leadership Foundation for Higher Education. 10 x Leadership Styles. Retrieved: 06/05/2018 from https://www.lfhe.ac.uk/en/general/lf10/ten-times-tables/10-leadership-styles.cfm

Ledesma, J. (2014). Conceptual Frameworks and Research Models on Resilience in Leadership. *SAGE Open*, 1–8, DOI: 10.1177/2158244014545464.

Legislation.gov.uk. (2010). *Equality Act 2010*. [online] Available at: http://www.legislation.gov.uk/ukpga/2010/15/contents

Lorde, A. (2007). *Sister Outsider: essays and speeches*. Trumansburg, NY: Crossing Press.

Masten, A. S. (2001). Ordinary Magic Resilience Processes in Development. *American Psychologist, 56*(3), 227–238 DOI: 10.1037//0003-066X.56.3.227

Mcleod, M. (2013, October 15). Theresa May's immigration bill is a valuable tool for racist landlords. *The Guardian*, pp. 1–3. Retrieved: 05/08/2018 from https://www.theguardian.com

McIntosh, M. (2017). Making sense of idioms of distress and cultural expression in psycho-therapeutic practice. In Ade-Serrano, Y., Nkansa-Dwamena, O. & McIntosh, M. (2017). *Race, Culture and diversity. A collection of articles.* (pp. 17–28). British Psychological Society, Division of Counselling Psychology.

McIntosh, M. (2015). Poem: *The Journey.* Unpublished.

McIntosh, M. (2018). Letter from the Chair. *DCoP Announcements,* (April). British Psychological Society, Division of Counselling Psychology.

McIntosh, P. (2015). *Dominoes.* Unpublished. Scene 9.

Miyake, A., Kost-Smith, L.E., Finkelstein, N.D., Pollock, S.J., Cohen, G.L. & Ito, T.A. (2010). Reducing the gender achievement gap in college science: a classroom study of values affirmation. *Science, 330*(6008), 1234–1237 (cited in Blair et al., (2011), p. 75, op cit).

Molina, K. M. & James, D. (2016). Discrimination, internalized racism, and depression: A comparative study of African American and Afro-Caribbean adults in the US. *Group Process Intergroup Relations, 19*(4), 439–461. doi:10.1177/1368430216641304.

Mundasad, S. (2016). NHS: BME staff 'more likely to be bullied than white colleagues'. *BBC News.* Retrieved: 05/08/2018 from https://www.bbc.co.uk/news/health-36427577

National Association of School Psychologists. (2016). *Understanding Race and Privilege* [handout]. Bethesda, MD: Author.

Neville, H.A., Viard, B. & Turner, L. (2015). Race and Recognition: Pathways to an Affirmative Black Identity. *Journal of Black Psychology, 41*(3), 247–271.

Peck, R., Baldwin, J. & Jackson, S. L. (2016). *I Am Not Your Negro.* United States. Magnolia Home Entertainment.

Petrova, D. (2016). Equal Rights Review Special Focus: Intersectionality. Vol.16. Retrieved on: 05/08/2018. www.equalrightstrust.org/.../Equal

Pyke, K. D. (2010). What is internalized racial oppression and why don't we study it? Acknowledging racism's hidden injuries. *Sociological Perspectives, 53*(4), 551–572. Retrieved from http://www.ucpressjournals.com

Randhawa, M. (2018). Closing the gap on BME representation in NHS leadership: not rocket science". Retrieved 15/04/2018 from https://www.kingsfund.org.uk/blog/2018/03/bme-representation-nhs-leadershipretrieved

Smith, D. (2006). Blair: Britain's 'sorrow' for shame of slave trade. Retrieved: 05/08/2018 from https://www.theguardian.com/politics/2006/nov/26/race.immigrationpolicy

The Guardian (1998, February 24). The Macpherson report: summary. Retrieved from https://www.theguardian.com/uk/1999/feb/24/lawrence.ukcrime12

Thrasher, S. W. (2015, August 9). Black Lives Matter has showed us: the oppression of black people is borderless. *The Guardian,* pp. 1–3. Retrieved: 05/08/2018 from https://www.theguardian.com

Schiele, H. J. (2005). Cultural Oppression and the high-risk status of African Americans. *Journal of Black Studies, 35*(6), 802–826.

Sherwood, M. (2007). Britain, slavery and the trade in enslaved Africans. *Institute of Historical Research.* Issue 12. Retrieved from https://www.history.ac.uk/ihr/Focus/Slavery/articles/sherwood.html

Steele, C., Spencer, S. & Aronson, J. (2002). Contending with group image: The psychology of stereotype and social identity threat. In: Zanna M. *Advances in experimental social psychology*. New York: Academic Press, pp. 379–440 (cited in Blair et al, (2011), p. 75, op cit).

Sue, D. W., Capodilupo, C. M., Torino, G. C., Bucceri, J. M., Holder, A. M. B., Nadal, K. L. & Esquilin, M. (2007). Racial Microaggressions in Everyday Life Implications for Clinical Practice. *American Psychologist*. *62*(4), 271–286. DOI: 10.1037/0003-066X.62.4.271

_____ The National Archives. Emancipation. Retrieved: 18/08/2018 from http://www.nationalarchives.gov.uk/pathways/blackhistory/rights/emancipation.htm

Young, I. M. (1990). *Justice and the politics of difference*. Princeton, NJ: Princeton University Press (cited in Schiele, H.J.(2005), p. 803, op cit).

The role of leadership for gay black practitioners: How do we craft authority from micro-aggressions and multiple identities? A personal story

Ben Amponsah

Introduction

Leadership is defined in a myriad of ways by many different professional bodies, academic institutions and organisations, and varies depending on the culture from which it is seen. Theorists debate whether it is primarily dependant on traits, such as is posited by seminal research on trait leadership, (2004); behaviours as in Blake and Mouton's behavioural theory of leadership model, (1964); or situations as defined by Hersey and Blanchard's influential Situational Leadership Model of the 1970s. For the purposes of this essay, however, I will use a definition that speaks to me from my own personal, Western perspective and one that I cite from M. Chemers (1997) as: 'a process of social influence in which a person can enlist the aid and support of others in the accomplishment of a common task.' The key element here is how leaders can pull in others to aid them in those goals.

Authority and leadership are terms often used interchangeably, such as in the military or in business, but they are not the same. In my view whilst authority can be seen as the positions that leaders take up (CEO, Colonel etc) it can also be seen as the end-product of that leadership. Certainly, in the context of what I am going to write about, I will distil leadership down to that product towards which we should aim, which arises from our lived experiences of race and sexuality, that then facilitates our ability to influence others. Here I do not want to enter into wider debates on the corrupting effects of authority, such as Milgram researched in his famous 1963 experiments, later discussed at length in his 1974 book *Obedience to Authority*. This is because I want to primarily cleave to how we can use positive leadership to create a sound authority, forged by our experiences, as those who stand on the great junctions of intersectionality, to bring a clearer focus to our efforts at social justice.

Micro-aggressions, the casual degradation of any marginalised group, are the stock in trade of those of us who exist as minorities in a majority world. The term, first coined in 1970 by psychiatrist Chester M. Pierce to describe the experience of black Americans at the hands of their non-black counterparts, has now been stretched to encompass race, gender, sexuality and a host of other identities. Derald Wing Sue has written authoritatively on the subject in his 2010 book, *Microaggressions in Everyday Life*. There has been some 'pushback' against the term by some in the world of psychology who accuse its proponents of perpetrating a 'pseudoscience' on the world (Nagai, 2017), but as a black gay man, the term really resonates with me and I have been engaged for the last fifteen years, at least, in a struggle to work out how to turn these subtle slights from a sense of victimhood and blaming into something positive and lasting.

This chapter is the exposition of what I have discovered so far.

My story

My tussles with the idea of what it means to be a leader started when I was twelve: I remember it very well—it was 1981 and I was a somewhat socially awkward adolescent, acutely aware of my rarefied status as one of only three black boys in a preparatory school of 400. One of the others was my twin brother, but he was a star of sports, a rakehell and a maverick and therefore completely unsuited to the authority positions of School and House Monitor that were eagerly sought after by the fledgling Fifth Formers. I failed dismally to secure either prestigious appointment and as I tearfully digested the one position I did attain (Head of the Boarding House Library), I made a vow to never again be found wanting. 'I will be not only School Prefect but also House Captain in the senior school', I swore solemnly and not only did I achieve those positions, but I was also Club Captain and a major sports figure, just like my twin brother had been at Prep School.

As I contemplated just how far I had come, what I did not really have a clear idea about was what fire had driven me to become *someone* from my experiences of being *no one* five years before—here what I mean is that the experience of being just another boy was deeply inimical to me from that early age: people were observing and scrutinising me for all sorts of reasons—I would give them something to marvel at. I think that my twin brother was exercised by a similar dynamic, but he opted for the rebel path. For me it was about my sense of status and belonging and the ability, from there, to exercise leadership in a world that felt overwhelmingly white. That was the cultural conflict with which I was wrestling at that time. Sexuality had not properly emerged as a factor for me, by then, though I was aware I was attracted to people of the same sex. My fervent hope was that it was just a teen phase that would pass. It is interesting to me that this aspect of my personality, which has always reached for positions of authority where I can exercise leadership, started at an early age. Looking back on that time now, I can feel some of that sense of powerlessness that so many people of colour experience, where they do not reckon they *can* do anything about it. At that stage in my young life I *could* do something and, through sheer force of personality, made the stuffy private school establishment sit up and notice me. This was through a process of demonstrating responsibility and leadership in my peer group, by being someone the schoolmasters could 'rely' on and someone who was also popular across a range of the usual school factions (athletes, geeks, academics, outcasts even).

Before university, flushed from success at school, I commenced the process of becoming an army officer—a career that my family and friends counselled was utter madness, since the military in the late 80s/early 90s was renowned for being racist. I ignored those concerns, for to become a paragon of authority—against all the odds—would be my biggest triumph yet and what purer example of an authority figure, exercising life and death leadership, could there be?

First, however, it was at university that the simmering issue that I had hoped would go away, my sexuality, emerged. It was, as realisation dawned, whilst frequenting gay clubs in my final year and enjoying (almost) guilt-free gay sex, that I realised that this was a part of me that was not about to go quietly into the night. It was not until many years later that I even heard the term intersectionality, but this was what I was experiencing, and I did not like it at all—it made my already uneasy sense of personal identity suddenly much more complicated. There I was overcoming the racial challenge by fronting up and seizing positions that I did not instinctively feel were mine to have, and suddenly here came a new aspect of myself that would also require struggle and a fight for which I did not feel at all equipped. There is ample evidence for how people from ethnic minorities are seemingly disadvantaged by the colour of their skin—the recently published research by the 'Inequality Project' supported by *The Guardian* (Duncan, September, 2017) found that "Black, Asian, and minority ethnic" BAME people were represented in only 3% of the top jobs in all sectors despite making up 13% of the population.

In the end my task was made easier by the fact that homosexuality was then outlawed in the army and so, conveniently, I was 'compelled' to return to the closet from which my nascent university experiences had me emerging. That was the deal with the devil that I was prepared to make to realise my dream but one which seemingly put me in conflict with my emerging sexual identity. Interestingly, I still frequented gay clubs on army leave (even when at the Royal Military Academy, Sandhurst, at the start of my career) and had a couple of boyfriends, but all well away from the prurient gaze of the military. My identity as a person in a leadership position was seemingly complete and I revelled in my ability to disrupt expectations of what a British army officer should be. What were those expectations? From my experiences as a Territorial Army (TA) officer at university and then a commissioned regular, it soon became clear that I should be white and generally upper middle class. I encountered no other black officers until I had joined and remember being deeply insulted by one of our DS (Directing Staff), a Captain, at our final exercise at the Royal Military Academy, Sandhurst (RMAS). He delighted in telling me how they used to have the odd black man in their regiment who was then nicknamed 'darkie' or similar. To put into context my previous thoughts about acquiring positions of authority that I did not feel were mine to have, here is a stark fact: when I joined the army, I was the first and only black officer ever commissioned into all fifteen (at the time) Royal Tank and Cavalry Regiments. That was a corps of some 10,000 soldiers with around 1,000 officers. By the time I left, six years later, I was still the only black officer, and during all my time in the army I only ever encountered Black officer in the army as a whole, in an artillery regiment that we took over UN peacekeeping duties in Cyprus.

My sense of being apart and something of an interloper was compounded, often, by the attitude of some of the soldiers. It was always a bit of a game to see whether sentries at barracks would check my identity card, which clearly showed that I was an officer, and salute me. Many did not salute, and they were reprimanded in no uncertain terms for it, me telling them that it was the Queen's authority they were failing to salute not me—a rather convenient excuse for their disrespect but, by the letter of military custom, correct. I remember clearly being told on one such occasion by a more senior officer and mentor, not long after I had just joined my regiment: 'you have to be better than your white brother officers', something that I never stopped hearing at Sandhurst. This proved to be a lesson I would never forget and one which placed a burden of striving for perennial over-achievement on me. It was he who made sure I never let the sentries get away with not affording me the proper respect at the gates and who had taken up that position of white ally that is often sadly necessary for BAME people to achieve their potential. When I look back now I am saddened that it needed to be so, but at the time I was eternally grateful for his wise words and support and suspect that there are many, like me, who feel similarly.

So, there I found myself, in the early 1990s, with sexuality firmly in the background, cultural/racial identity to the fore but doing what I had always wanted to do: exercising a huge amount of authority by dint of my position and ability. It felt satisfying and empowering and, like before at school (and at university to an extent), I felt most comfortable in my skin in this sort of scenario: plucky and bold black kid challenges the cultural tropes and reaches for positions hitherto unknown for people of my cultural heritage. I had already been the first black House Captain at a major public school and now here I was being told by generals that I could, soon enough, be the first black commanding officer (Lieutenant Colonel) of a British Army regiment. Of course such an idyllic state of affairs was never going to last forever; not least because, though I could confront and challenge the subtle and not so subtle racism that I encountered almost daily—a trooper using the 'N' word to describe my rugby playing skills; a brother officer declaring that I wasn't like other black people—I was 'one of' them apparently because of how I spoke and my public school sensibilities, far from the 'chippy' attitudes that they had experienced, they said. The same was not true of my sexuality, for to challenge the daily homophobia was to expose myself and if I did that I would be administratively discharged (it was only whilst at Sandhurst that it ceased to be a criminal offence, punishable by six months in the Military Corrective Centre, Colchester, and then discharged dishonourably). Four years into my army career, with every lie that I told about who I was dating or grinning through gritted teeth at the constant homophobia, I knew that covering up my sexuality was doing me more harm than good and was not sustainable, so I engineered a posting back to the UK from Germany and then determined to resign my commission. It gave me the opportunity to experience the club scene and acceptance of my sexuality from my new friends in Sheffield (somewhere I had become acquainted with because an officer friend of mine was stationed there with the UK diving team). I loved it. Suddenly new possibilities were in sight: a chance to embrace the full panoply of my own intersectionality—a brave new world.

In the end leaving the military, upon which so much of my identity as a young black man with status and meaning rested, was relatively easy and painless, not least because the imperative to break free from what, to me, were the stifling bonds of military life with all its prejudices writ large, had become urgent. It was upon leaving that I was finally able to come out properly to all my friends and family, not just a select few and those in Sheffield. It was a time of wonder and of discovery but also a dark time, in many ways, as I stumbled into inappropriate relationships and yearned to be loved. I, like many gay men who have been released by the truth of coming out, over-indulged in the 'scene', in sex and drugs and in the rock and roll lifestyle of unadulterated gay hedonism. It was, at once, a release and a millstone around my neck, for I was now having to confront, in a psychosexual context, the many attachment issues that posing as a straight man and joining the army had papered over. It was not long after leaving the army that I moved from Sheffield to Manchester to be more closely immersed in gay life and not long after that I first experienced therapy.

I had, by this stage, started a new career as an Employee Assistance Programme (EAP) professional and so was now familiar with counselling and what it could offer. The first bout I had was as part of my own EAP support and was provided by a counselling psychologist. It was, of course, after yet another seemingly promising relationship had broken down prematurely and agonisingly and I wanted to know what it was that I was contributing. My therapist took an integrative, highly person-centred approach. Although the therapy got me thinking about how my mother's imprisonment on multiple occasions throughout my young life and the suppression of my sexuality had seriously affected my capacity and ability to form solid intimate same-sex connections, it didn't really equip me with the tools to do anything about it. It was only after I decided that I would like to do as my therapist did and enrolled in a postgraduate counselling course that, with the help of the personal development groups and the personal therapy we were obliged to have, I was able to finally come to terms with several aspects of myself that I simply had not before. Close friends and family remarked, around the time that I was completing my course, how at peace I was with myself—not something that could have been said in my turbulent 20s when, even though I was engaged in a career that provided me with some of the things I craved, it had not been a formula for ongoing growth.

In the mid-2000s, while working as both an EAP professional and therapist, I joined the thriving LGBT northwest charity, the Lesbian and Gay Foundation (LGF), now the LGBT Foundation, and became an LGBT activist. Their directors admitted that there was very little BAME representation in their literature or indeed on the scene itself, so I started by doing some promotional work for them. I was eager to get involved not least because here, at last, was a way to bring these two competing strands of my identity together: the cultural and racial. It was the latter which was now, again, striving for recognition after having to take a back seat, for a while, to that of my sexual identity. There I did what I have done throughout my life and sought a leadership role, first getting myself on the Board of Trustees and then, in 2004, being appointed Chair after a short stint as Deputy Chair. This was to ensure that I was now in a position, much like I had been in the army, to directly influence policy from my place as strategic leader of the charity, using my own unique leadership style that focused mainly on building effective partnerships and taking firm, decisive action, where needed. That said, I will acknowledge that it has necessarily moved from a more authoritarian leadership style when in the army to a more democratic one now, which is part of the journey I have taken from officer to therapist. It was a satisfying place to be, not least because I was now also settling into my new skin as a qualified therapist and aspiring counselling psychologist-to-be.

Leadership in the profession

I have necessarily condensed my life story for reasons of expedience, but I hope the preceding chapter has provided a taste of the sort of drivers and influences there were on my identity and on where and how, post-army, I could once more craft a leadership role that might embrace these two powerful aspects of my sense of self. In addition, there was a nascent realisation that I might also derive authority both from my interest in researching some of these elements of intersectionality and from my role and contribution to the Division to which I belong: the British Psychological Society's (BPS) Division for Counselling Psychology (DCoP).

As I came to complete the research proposal for my Counselling Studies Diploma, a question came to me again and again: 'what is the impact of being both black *and* gay for the therapist'? Here I was not concerned, as other bits of research have been, with the impact on the white client of being counselled by a black counsellor but what the effects are on a black counsellor of being a minority within a minority, of being invisible, of the many instances of both subtle racism and covert homophobia directed at us from clients, the settings in which we work and the people we work with. Researching the literature, or lack of it at the time, excited me greatly, as here I could see another opportunity to forge for myself a role of leadership within my new profession: no one seemed to be researching this in any great depth! Yet here I was living that experience in my professional life every day. Eventually I honed and refined the question into what was going to be my research for the Qualification for Counselling Psychology (QCoP), but I did not stay the course and the research was never formalised. I still aim to pick it up when I finally take up the place I have won at Glasgow Caledonian University (GCU) next September 2019. I appreciate that the literature and indeed even the research is likely to have shifted in the last seven years since I crafted the QCoP research proposal, but I am very much looking forward to getting back into this vital field as my ultimate hope is to provide some insight for those of us who stand on the intersections of race and sexual identity as therapists—insight that will help us to practice better and feel more at one with those alternate aspects of ourselves as we do.

Research, however, is just one of the ways that I was discovering that I could re-craft that sense of authority and leadership in my new life as a counselling psychologist. Another was to directly join, participate and influence some of the groups within the Division itself. I joined the DCoP Northwest Branch very early on in its inception, and very soon found myself as its Honorary Secretary, responsible primarily for communications and, through monthly newsletters and control of our distribution list, I became someone well known amongst the NW Counselling Psychologists. Moving into roles of influence is something that I have repeated recently by joining the Conference Committee, a post that I have really loved but that is also influential: the DCoP Conferences are a fantastic vehicle for knowledge gathering and networking, both of which are vital for transitioning to positions of authority where real leadership can be exercised.

I am also a member of the Division's Black and Asian Counselling Psychology Group (BACPG), but I have only been a passive member to date. I have asked myself why I have not been more involved—my excuse has always been it is too London-centric, but I do wonder whether there are other influences. The only answer that I have elicited thus far is that participation of that group might, for me, be overtly of the cultural/racial stance and I do not want to be pigeonholed as a black counselling psychologist—not when the last fifteen years seem to have been all about how I can be seen as both black *and* gay and what I can effect from that intersectional classification. That is what I was when Chair of the LGF; that is what I was proposing in my research; that is front and centre for me when moving for positions of leadership within the Division, and maybe the BACPG speaks to me of something that is too one dimensional. I am still reflecting on it.

Social justice is also a vital component of this new leadership identity for me and I am part of the Division's Social Justice Network (SJN). Again, I have not really been an active participant, but I have attended some of their events and I passionately believe that an integral element of challenging and overcoming the twin ills of racism and homophobia is striving with all our might to live, work and breathe social justice and all its facets in how we counsel, what we do, the politics we pursue (controversially for some) and how vocal we are being as counselling psychologists. The current Chair of the Division, Dr Christina Richards, said in the (September, 2017) *Counselling Psychology Review*, 'But where it is we who must act as professionals—to make decisions about counselling psychology as a profession; to decide on behalf of clients who cannot; and, vitally, to effect social change in the wider world – listening is simply not enough'. As a black gay man who has been oppressed and marginalised it is something to be able to speak out for social justice from a place where people take note, and this is something that has become a real driving force for me in both the counselling that I provide but also in the roles that I have undertaken. And who knows? Today the Conference Committee, tomorrow maybe the Executive Committee and beyond.

Intersectionality

But why is being both black and gay so important in the context that I write this chapter? What does it say about leadership, example and authority and the ability to craft it? I have often witnessed jokes about people spanning this divide along the lines of 'you've got it *really* bad—you're both black and gay!' Or 'you drew the short straw'. I have even heard it said in a way that a certain positivity is implied and have been guilty of using the same tropes myself as a way of ingratiating myself or endearing myself to a majority group (the army to name but one). But regardless of whether this can be seen in a light-hearted or more sinister way, it has always seemed to me that there is power in being someone who spans the lines of identity and it is this that I have tried to hone and craft in my post-army years. That power seems to derive from the ability to speak about lived experiences for these marginalised groups in ways that make people sit up and listen. This has been true in my life: I have found that people are less inclined to dismiss what I say because they recognise that I have first-hand experience of intersectionality and my boldness and confidence mean that I am not afraid to speak out about them in the cause of furthering equality and social justice. These searching reflections of self would not be possible, of course, without an in-depth look at what these identities mean and which only really started for me when I proposed my Counselling Diploma and QCoP research. The problem with just researching aspects of identity such as sexuality, are highlighted by Colin Hicks and Martin Milton in *The Handbook of Counselling Psychology* 3rd Edition (2010), who make the very apposite point that elements like sexuality cannot be studied without due reference to other sociological factors such as race (Eliason, 1996).

Intersectionality was first defined by human rights lawyer Kimberlé Crenshaw, in 1989, as the interconnection of multiple, overlapping social identities which can then open the way to multiple routes of oppression or discrimination (Crenshaw, 1989). To understand this is to understand how injustice and social inequality occur on a multidimensional basis, she argues, and this is certainly the thrust of current interest in this vital field: to understand social injustice and inequality is to then be able to take effective steps to combat it. Admittedly there is much more that can be done, and the UN has recently released a set of goals to transform our world, with reducing inequality as goal 10 (January, 2016). That comprises economic, environmental and social equality with the last taking pride of place amongst the better-known areas of the environment and economy. This is something that has increasingly been a central theme in our profession and I have been heartened to see that it has risen to the fore of what we, as counselling psychologists, stand and fight for. It took me a while to realise that the growing discourse on this subject put me in a position of prominence and influence. Now I have a vehicle and a term with which to shape my own narrative, one that has taken me from public schoolboy to therapist and LGBT activist via the army: a strange and circuitous journey by anyone's reckoning. For me this represents a new way to campaign that finally melds these identities and how I see them in a way that I can use.

So, on the one hand, I intend to craft authority through the research that I propose and on the other through example and position, in order that I can link these elements into the passion that I have for social justice. Intersectionality is important because it is all about shining a light on the multiple levels of identity that can lead to multiple levels of discrimination. At its rawest level my desire to become a therapist and counselling psychologist is about helping people back onto their feet in a way that brings them into equality with their peers, with society and themselves—to bring an equalising balance.

Ultimately it is in this fight against injustice and a deeper understanding of what it means, for me, to be both black and gay, that will, I hope, enable me to better deal with and overcome the micro-aggressions that all of us in minorities endure on a regular basis. The increased insight into who I am— all parts of me—what I am doing now and what I intend to still do will stand as a rebuke to these taunts and taints and will allow me to pursue these aims without being weighed down by the anchor of my own struggles.

Conclusion

When I was asked to contribute to this book my first response was 'why me?' I did not think that, as someone who has not even yet qualified, I had anything to offer such an august publication. It has only been in writing that I realise this is not the case and my story, spanning, as it does, my initial struggle to fit into the rarefied and privileged environments of preparatory and public school, the army, business and then my current identity and profession as a therapist and soon to be qualified counselling psychologist, is very relevant. Across these have been a fight to be recognised, to be someone who can make a difference both to my clients in their quest for social and mental health justice but also to the wider world of psychology, through the research that I am proposing into how intersectionality impacts us as therapists. Add to this the positions that I intend to take within my Division and within the British Psychological Society and I again ask myself: today the DCoP Conference Committee, tomorrow the world? I feel that my experiences of intersectionality, the constant push back against injustice, have compelled me to seek out ways in which I can be recognised—to put my head above the parapet—to use military terminology. Only in those rarefied places have I been able to effect change and get people to challenge their own sense of prejudice. Maybe that is why I have done it in settings where I am always in a small minority? It has been effective for me so far and I intend for it to be more effective still. Finally, it has been tremendously empowering for me to see our previous Chair, an authoritative black woman, as leader, for it sets for me an example of what might be. It feels like the Division has been moving towards a platform of delivering social justice over the years I have been involved and I see an imperative for those of us who seek a leadership role in that story to be completely immersed in issues of intersectionality and identity. My contributing to this publication feels, for me, an important part in that ongoing journey.

References

Blake, R. and Mouton, J. (1964). *The Managerial Grid: the Key to Leadership Excellence.* Houston: Gulf Publishing Co.

Chemers, M. (1997). *An integrative theory of leadership.* Lawrence Erlbaum Associates, Publishers.

Crenshaw, K. (1989). Demarginalizing the Intersection of Race and Sex: A Black Feminist Critique of Antidiscrimination Doctrine, Feminist Theory and Antiracist Politics. *University of Chicago Legal Forum, 140:* pp. 139–167.

Eliason, M. J. (1996) Identity formation for lesbian, bisexual and gay persons: beyond a minoritising view. *Journal of Homosexuality, 30,* 31–58.

Herd, M. (2017). The Inequality Project: the Guardian's in-depth look at our unequal world. The Guardian, 25 April [Online] www.theguardian.com/inequality/2017/apr/25/inequality-project-guardian-in-depth-look-unequal-world-equality

Hersey, P. and Blanchard, K. (1969). Life cycle theory of leadership. *Training and Development Journal, 23*(5), 26–34.

Hicks, C. and Milton, M. (2010). Sexual Identities: Meanings for Counselling Psychology Practice. In S. Strawbridge & R. Woolfe. (Eds.). *Handbook of Counselling Psychology (p. 269).* 3rd ed. London: Sage.

Milgram, S. (1974). *Obedience to Authority; An Experimental View*. New York: Harpercollins.

Nagai, A. (2017). The Pseudo-Science of Microaggressions. *National Association of Scholars*. Retrieved from https://www.nas.org/articles/the_pseudo_science_of_microaggressions

Richards, C. (2017). Editorial: *Counselling Psychology Review, British Psychological Society, 32*, 3.

Sue, D. W. (2010). *Microaggressions in Everyday Life: Race, Gender, and Sexual Orientation*. Hoboken, New Jersey: John Wiley & Sons.

United Nations. (2016). *Sustainable Development Goals: 17 Goals to transform our World Report 2016*. Available at: http://www.un.org/sustainabledevelopment/sustainable-development-goals/

Zaccaro, S.J., Kemp, C. and Bader, P. (2004). Leader Traits and Attributes. *The nature of Leadership*. Thousand Oaks, CA, US: Sage Publications Inc.

Chapter 3

The different aspects of equality in the leadership agenda in the BPS

Zenobia Nadirshaw

The ethnic minority population in England and Wales is 14%; this figure is expected to increase up to 30% of the UK population by 2050. Psychologists are now fundamental to the organisations of health service, education services and social care services. They are now in positions to influence the public at large as well as key decision makers and to discharge power through the process of setting up and co-ordinating, planning and 'programming' these institutions. Psychologists with their other colleagues including academics can determine the ethos and ideological framework of the institutions, design policies, procedures and practices, delegate duties and responsibilities, determine content and allocation of resources and define criteria for need and prioritisation (Nadirshaw, 1999). The common definition of psychology—the scientific study of behaviour and experience—appears to refer to the behaviour and experiences of a select group of people with training values, knowledge and 'technology' still rooted in western psychological science and minimally informed by the different and diverse groups that currently exist in British society. Eurocentric and ethnocentric perspectives still persist within the profession, and middle-class values still dominate most of these perspectives—including in the applied practice of psychology, the teaching courses and academic debates and discourses.

Having worked in the field of psychology for the past 40 years, the author believes that psychology needs to develop services based on diversity as a basic principle that recognises the following:

- **D – Different**
- **I – Individuals**
- **V – Valuing**
- **E – Each other**
- **R – Regardless of**
- **S – Skin**
- **I – Intellect**
- **T – Talent**
- **Y – Years**

Psychologists need to ensure that services are offered in non-stigmatising, non-institutional settings in the community with and by the voluntary sector and that diversity and difference are positively valued. Psychologists need to develop cultural competencies in knowledge, skills and attitudes that question the stereotyped views and beliefs that they hold about racially and culturally different clients and question the use of traditional mainstream psychological practices against racist and prejudiced beliefs and xenophobic conditioning.

Psychologists, as part of their helping and caring role, need to help Black and Minority Ethnic (BME) people with emotional and mental difficulties to find their way back to meaningful existence, relationships and restored identities and to assist BME people in working through the damaging experiences of racism, discrimination and disadvantage.

Role and responsibility of psychologists: Academic and applied practitioners

Psychologists need to show a genuine willingness and desire to learn about other cultures and their diverse variants relating to perceptions of psychological care, mental health and mental well-being. They need to take a holistic view within a person-centred approach, which includes taking a person's religious, cultural and spiritual beliefs about a person's mental health and mental well-being. As part of ensuring that psychologists' work and clinical practice contribute to the benefit of BME service users, psychologists need to undertake race equality impact assessments and see how policies and procedures employed by their services directly impact BME service users (for example, use of the Mental Health Act with compulsory sections which transfers people directly into the mental health in-patient or forensic services rather than allow them to be treated by primary care services). All this needs to be done at the academic level as well as owning this issue at the individual practitioner level.

Psychologists need to move away from the status quo wherein culture, 'race' and ethnicity become the **problem**. The Knowledge and Skills Framework (KSF) identifies diversity as one of the six core dimensions that NHS staff have to develop in terms of their core skills and competencies. As part of that, it would be expected that all practising psychologists should develop a productive working relationship with culturally and linguistically diverse groups of people by:

- Avoiding different types of biases, for example, cultural bias and unconscious bias and finding new ways (verbally and non-verbally) to build rapport and respect.
- Using and working with trained interpreters in assessment, formulation and intervention work as well as research work.

- Pre-assessing and pre-incorporating ethnic identity (including its fine gradations, region, class and generation) which can have impact on process and outcome on psychological work.
- Acknowledging their own ethnocentricity and hostility to people who are 'different' and being white in the helping profession (Ryde, 2009). Psychologists need to acknowledge that people can change—irrespective of their differences and psychological distress.
- Re-looking at current models of mental health which traditionally reflect Western constructions and incorporate other world views of psychological well-being into their practice (Milton, 2018).

The British Psychological Society's (BPS) *Generic Professional Practice* (2008) defines good psychological practice for all applied psychologists, and the BPS *Code of Ethics and Conduct* (2006) identifies four key ethical values:

- **Respect** for individuals, cultural and role differences including client and the public
- **Competence** in the continuing development of high standards in professional work
- **Responsibility** to clients, to the public and to the profession and science of psychology
- **Integrity**, honesty, accuracy, clarity and fairness in their interactions with all persons

It is expected that all applied psychologists and academicians will be guided by and follow the above four ethical values and will have the necessary skills and abilities to work with **all** sections of the British community, including the black and minority ethnic (BME) groups and refugee communities and other discriminated groups based on age, sex, sexual preference, class, religious and cultural beliefs.

Psychologists need to recognise that multi-ethnic groups are not homogenous groups and there are wide regional and local differences amongst these groups split by language, dialect and regional variations. Each ethnic community has a distinct identity, and the religious focus may also vary. The recently published practice guidelines (BPS, 2017) highlight the work that psychologists should be doing with reference to other populations (people with intellectual disabilities, working with people of faith, religion and spirituality, working with sexual and gender minorities and with people who are socially excluded, including people with cultural difference).

Psychologists must fully understand the concepts of 'race', culture and ethnicity and not to use them interchangeably. Race is a biologically meaningless concept to apply to people, and even the artificial divisions between the so-called racial groups are nebulous and unstable, biologically, socially and physically (Owusu & Howitt, 2000; Fernando, 2014). All psychologists and academic departments have responsibilities to incorporate learning out-comes and continuing professional development (CPD) activities in terms of training requirements to work with people from **all** sections of British society.

For psychologists to understand the double/triple discrimination suffered by people from diverse and ethnic religious backgrounds, they should be aware of the following concepts:

- The interchangeable use of the terms 'race', culture and ethnicity leading to either the perception of black and minority culture, 'race' and ethnic-ity as unitary or an assumption that knowing about these cultures solves the problem of equality, fairness and availability of services.
- The maintenance of the colour-blind approach in service where 'one size fits all' resulting in a lack of formal recognition of the varied diverse needs as well as of these needs being ignored, unacknowledged or assumed to be the same.
- The lack of appropriate, culturally relevant psychological therapy not available to certain BME communities.
- Being discriminated on grounds of 'special' needs which puts them in the 'cultural pathology' section instead of acknowledging that they have different needs.

Psychologists must acknowledge the vital part and role played by carers and their access to carer's assessments, rights to receive appropriate support and finances.

Working with difference

In the light of the author's long-standing NHS experience and having worked in NHS and Social Services settings for over 40 years, these are the helpful recommendations for the practising applied psychologists:

- Psychologists should ensure better and fuller compliance with a range of policies and strategies and legislation that promotes equality for all people.
- Psychologists should develop and implement ethical practice through continuing professional development activity which reinforces personal and professional standards as well as ethical practice (Nadirshaw, Gray & Golding, 2006).
- Psychologists need to be part of the solution of redressing inequalities because of issues of racism and cultural insensitivity. We need to accept ideas of spirituality, religion and the different values of the diverse eth-nic communities against the values of the dominant sections of British society. For example, where there are services which are not mind-ful of a person's distress, a holistic assessment in all settings of applied practice needs to be done. Psychologists need to acknowledge different

cultural values, spiritual and religious beliefs as well as different beliefs about physical health and mental health well-being. The late psychologist Pittu Laungani (2007) commented on similarity and differences between Eastern cultures and Western cultures in terms of the value systems adopted by the Western (English) perspective versus Eastern values. The identified four core values that distinguish British approaches from Indian approaches. They are:

- Individualism/Communalism (Collectivism)
- Cognitivism/Emotionalism
- Free will/Determinism
- Materialism/Spiritualism

Practising psychologists should be aware of such differences when working with people from diverse backgrounds.

- It is incumbent on all psychologists to acknowledge the contribution of nine inherited characteristics to develop better outcome for their clients, staff and students. Psychologists need to address the different life situations and life circumstances experienced by users who wish to use mental health services. We need to hear their voices based on their personal experiences and respond accordingly in a human and beneficent way.
- Psychologists need to understand the different concepts of health and illness within different established ethnic groups like the Indian, Pakistani, Bangladeshi and Afro-Caribbean groups as well as the newly arrived communities from Europe and the refugee communities from Syria, Turkey, Somalia, etc.
- Psychologists need to understand the history of racism and the early development of Western psychology and culturally biased testing in favour of white middle-class children (Fernando, 2010).
- Psychologists need to be aware of the stereotyped beliefs and assumptions which manifest in thinking about culture and ethnic groups and working within health, education and social services systems that produce such assumptions and biases. The one-size-fits all imperialistic tendency must be eradicated and modified to incorporate and reflect the current changes in society, as British society is now a multi-ethnic and multi-cultural country.
- Psychologists need to be working within the community and with voluntary organisations to address issues within society which contribute to prejudice and racism, inequality and negative perceptions of minority ethnic groups by the media. Issues such as poor housing, lack of education and appropriate job opportunities, as well as the social standing of ethnic minority groups within contemporary British society needs to be addressed.
- Psychologists need to be aware of the impact of culture, ethnicity and religion in the assessment, formulation and intervention processes in therapeutic work and the use of norm-referenced tests which do not

include minority ethnic groups as part of their standardisation (for example, intelligence tests).

- For Psychology, psychotherapy and academic departments to embark on the exercise of ethnic monitoring and to assess its impact on practice by setting standards in the following areas:

  - Publicity about psychology as a future career for BME students at the undergraduate level; training at the post-graduate level on working with difference and understanding the concept of double discrimination as a result of visible difference arising from gender, sexual preference, ethnicity, religious beliefs, 'race', culture and ethnicity. For an old female who has a learning disability, the impact of triple discrimination is overwhelming for that person.
  - Psychology/psychotherapy departments to make their workforces representative of the communities they serve and to increase the availability of psychological therapies for BME people.
  - In order to offer an appropriate, culturally sensitive psychological service, the following needs to be looked at:

    - Psychologists/therapists to adapt therapy and therapeutic practice to different cultural groups and people of different backgrounds.
    - Psychologists to understand and respect the different concepts of mental and physical health and mental illness that exist within the Indian, Chinese and African traditions (for example, mental illness being caused by spirit possession in India and by talking to spirits of dead forefathers in Africa).
    - Psychologists/academicians/researchers to examine their own beliefs, their stereotyped, prejudiced attitudes and feelings towards the 'other'. They need to work on their own personal attitudes and cultural history when working with people who have been subject to oppression, discrimination and devaluation. Working through their personal belief systems about the 'other' and recognising and valuing people who do not ascribe to Westernised norms of behaviour, patterns of living and child rearing practices are some of the ways that psychologists can move away from the intellectual and emotional colonialism that still abounds within the profession.
    - Psychologists to take a critical view of psychology by posing questions relating to psychology and psychiatry being neutral sciences and the range of Westernised assumptions and beliefs of diagnosis, labelling and working in mental health systems, educational, forensic, child and family services (Kinderman, 2014).
    - Psychologists to develop skills and work to advance the development of inclusive and meaningful knowledge and practice with and for diverse communities (BPS 2015). Experts by experience

need to be asked about the relevance and appropriateness of the psychological work done with them rather than to them.

- Psychologists to work via a twin track approach—at the individual level and at the team level—and to be trained and speaking respectively with people whose first language is not English and who do not understand the Western mental health care system. Other barriers that could be experienced by BME and refugee communities are not trusting the mental health services, being fearful that their children will be placed into care and the perception that people have 'special' rather than different needs.

- Psychologists to work with the ethnic voluntary sector and be guided by community psychology section principles and aims and objectives. They need to move away from an individualised view of mental health. Psychologists to work with the Black Voluntary sector to offer a 'whole'/combined community care service involving clinical care as well as teaching, training and education about the differing needs of multi-ethnic populations as well as training, advocacy, commissioner's communication and job descriptions and help and support provided to this group of people.

- Psychologists working within academia and training courses must establish diversity strategy groups with links to the ethnic voluntary sector and users of psychology/psychotherapy services.

- In keeping with the Equality Act (2010) and equality of opportunity within the BPS and all its sections and divisions, psychologists should increase the number of applicants and trainees to Psychology programmes from different ethnic and culturally diverse groups. Training course organisers should publicise psychology at school and undergraduate levels, to expand the nature of work experience outside the normal route of assistant psychologists working within NHS and Social Services settings. Similarly, graduates from other, less-known university psychology courses need to be given similar opportunities for interviews, and strategies need to be developed to increase the number of male psychologists and ethnic minority psychologists within the profession.

Leadership styles

Haslam, Reicher and Platow (2011) talk of identity leadership, inclusive leadership and leader style. Identity leadership is when the leader's primary function is to 'represent', manage and promote the sense of shared social identity that underpins a group's existence and purpose. Inclusive leadership is where the leader/leaders build positive relationships with their followers and ensure that all group members are encouraged to participate in group activities that bear upon the leadership process (strategy development, governance, goal setting). A leader's style is about 'the means by which a leader influences the followers to contribute to group goals' by using different styles of leadership which could focus on relationship between group members or focus on the task using autocratic, democratic or laissez faire styles.

Leadership is about the process of influencing others in a manner that enhances their contribution to the realisation of the group goals of the organisation. The BPS and the new Senate need to set and establish goals that will fulfil the need for the organisation to be seen publicly as implementing diversity and inclusivity within the policies and procedures and staffing structures.

Steven Covey (2002) talks about eight characteristics of principle-centred leaders. These traits not only characterise effective leaders but also serve as signs of progress at the personal level, the interpersonal–trust level, the managerial–empowerment level and the organisational–alignment level.

These leaders are:

1   Constantly learning and being educated by their experiences, developing new skills and expanding their competencies, by being service oriented and being responsible for the overall service that is provided.
2   Radiating positive energy in an energy field that surrounds them, transforming confusion into contemplation and positive energy.
3   Believing in other people and their unseen potential, principle-centred leaders refuse to label, stereotype or categorise people. They visualise peoples' potential and assist in the growth of staff.
4   Leading a balanced life by reading, watching, observing and learning and being simple, direct and non-manipulative in their communication styles. They think in terms of continuum, priorities and hierarchies and are balanced, temperate, moderate and flexible in adapting to changing circumstances.
5   Seeing life as an adventure due to their security. They do not need to categorise and stereotype everything and are welcoming of change rather than safety, protection and maintenance of old habits. They remain flexible and adaptable.
6   Being synergetic, being change catalysts and using the strengths of others to overcome their own weaknesses.

The third edition of the BPS Practice Guidelines (2017) identify the fact that psychologists 'at any stage of their career' are likely to find themselves in a position where they are required to demonstrate or model leadership.' Leadership in the context of leading change is quoted and described as 'accepting responsibility to create conditions that enable others to achieve shared purpose in the face of uncertainty.' Contemporary leadership styles are more aligned to working within a team or a system rather than being directive. It requires a high level of skills in developing, managing and maintaining 'professional relationships'.

The Board of Trustees, the Senate and Senior Management Team need to be knowledgeable about legislation, as it impacts on the working environment and for all staff to be aware of the issues of power and control that can manifest themselves in the inappropriate use of such issues. When these issues arise, it would be important to access Human Resource policies on discrimination and inequality and to ensure that all staff have union representation if the need arises. Relevant health and safety guidelines need to be in place and all staff need to be cognisant of them—including harassment, bullying and whistleblowing policies. Complaints on such issues need to be monitored at a six-month intervals, and visible, formal and corrective action needs to take place (including taking a case to an employment tribunal). There is a need for staff at all levels to fully understand the working of positive managerial and leadership styles and to know that the organisation is truly reflecting a positive approach and action plan within and outside of the organisation with reference to discrimination, equal opportunities, diversity, inclusivity and social and racial justice.

The Division of Clinical Psychology of the BPS produced an Equality & Diversity Policy Statement in 2015 in which they have produced a list of guidelines and legislation. See Table 3.1.

Table 3.1 A paradigm shift needs to be undertaken within the BPS and all its divisions and sections

From	To
An organisation that controls through power and retains the status quo.	Knowing all the subsystems and their influence in moving the agenda of difference and diversity to be an all-inclusive concept with psychologists and staff sharing equal responsibility for this. For staff and psychologists to understand and use the Human Rights Act 1988 and for the BPS to respect and protect human rights for those who have protected characteristics under the act (age, disability, gender reassignment, marriage, civil partners, 'race', religious belief, sex and sexual orientation). Identifying through appropriate Human Resource Policies on direct and indirect discrimination and failure to provide a reasonable adjustment.
I can't, I don't know how	I can, and I know how, for the Chief Executive Officer and his/her Trustee board and Senate to develop a model of leadership that is true to the realities that confront them. Rhetoric must be avoided, and action must become meaningful which corresponds to the social and organisational reality. A person experienced in the concept of inclusivity, social justice and disability needs to be on the Trust Board and Senior Management Team.
Consultation with community groups	The world of action of partnership working and engaging communities at local and national levels.
Treating the protected characteristic groups as a problem	Recognizing issues of fairness and equity and finding ways in order to bring social and political change for these groups via collective action.

The BPS and its senior management, leaders and all staff need to be aware of diversity and equal opportunities. They need to be alert to the differences that exist between these two topics as well as to fully understand the range of social differences which refer to social **GRRAAACCEESS**

- **G**ender
- **R**ace/**R**eligion
- **A**ge/**A**bilities/**A**ppearance
- **C**ulture/**C**lass
- **E**thnicity/**E**mployment
- **S**exuality/**S**pirituality

Diversity and equal opportunities

There is a difference between diversity and equal opportunities (Kandola, personal communication, 1980).

Diversity	Equal Opportunity
Concept that recognizes the benefits to be gained from differences.	Concept that traditionally has been to legislate against discrimination
Business-needs driven	Legally driven
Internally initiated	Externally initiated
Qualitative focus	Quantitative focus (numbers)
Assumes pluralism	Assumes assimilation
Proactive	Reactive
All differences	Race, gender, disability

Diversity is neither about reducing standards nor about removing prejudices. It is about recognising that they exist and then questioning them before one acts. Diversity is not about language and political correctness. It is a standard by which performance is measured. For example, does the workforce, wherever possible, reflect the communities that they serve (particularly in the Leicester area where the Asian population is higher compared to the local white population). Ethnic record keeping of staff is necessary to measure progress in careers and how employment policies and diversity training are working. These should be audited, checked and presented as a standing agenda at both Trust Board and Senior Management levels. There should be managerial accountability and an understanding that managers are equipped with the requisite experience and training to ensure that there is involvement of social GRAAACCEES group members within the Trust Board membership.

An action plan at individual level, group level and organisation/BPS Society level should be under-taken:

Individual level:

- To be aware of the changing nature of society and to be aware of cultural and other diversities that now exist. For example, in the UK alone in the LGBT community, between 2005–2015 there were 140,000 civil partnerships that were entered into. By comparison in the year 2016 there were 60,000 civil partnerships that were entered into (Schraer & D'Urso, 2017). It is anticipated that by 2050 up to 30% of the UK population will consist of people from ethnic minority backgrounds (Coombs, 2014) (Ref: www.rt.com. Article published 6 May 2014 10.24).
- To acknowledge 'difference' and act in ways that supports equality and values diversity and to be sensitive to social exclusion, racism, discrimination and power imbalance. It would be important to accept one's own cultural values and test beliefs about 'the other'.

Group Level: The BPS could set up a diversity subgroup within its existing workforce to ensure a psychologically healthy work place in which staff at all levels of seniority and disposition feel comfortable and productive. One of the Trust Board members could have this as a special responsibility and engage with all the employees of the BPS on a regular basis.

Organisation Level: It is important that the BPS understands and is aware of the social, political and professional issues which underpin current delivery of services in clinical and academic departments. The base of psychology is not neutral and is arguably reflective of the values held in the dominant culture.

The BPS and its workforce and members need to be aware of the professional power which resides in:

- Access to relevant knowledge, experience and expertise—being claimed as only available to members of the professional group—thereby perpetuating a mystique and notion of exclusivity surrounding professional knowledge and expertise.
- The authority to take decisions over lives of other people, for example, vulnerable people with mental health problems and people with learning disabilities who are reliant and dependent on powerful professionals in the Health, Education and Social Services settings for assistance, guidance and help to live their lives in an ordinary, non-discriminatory manner.
- Being able to dispense services or withhold information from experts by experience/service users.

- The ability to structure face-to-face interaction (interviews, meetings, reviews) in ways that are advantageous to the professional person; for example: content of agenda, procedures and time and location of meetings.

The BPS needs to

- Work with other professional organisations like MIND, MENCAP, Race Equality Foundation and The Mental Health Foundation who are committed to acknowledging difference and diversity in a positive manner and set a framework, incorporating its vision, aims, objectives, principles and priorities that underpin this joint work.
- To have a clear definition of social inclusion, social justice, intercultural relations, and positive attitude to racism and inclusivity and to share that with the workforce and BPS membership.
- To focus on developing healthy workplace environments using new policies and procedures to develop satisfaction and confidence in the staff. It is suggested that the recently developed BPS document psychology at work: improving wellbeing and productivity in the workplace, be advertised as widely as possible via a website link or through the production of hard paper copies (BPS, 2017).
- Strategies need to be in place which can address the tensions that might be created in addressing difficult situations. A win–win policy/strategy needs to be in place for managers and staff whereby staff from BME backgrounds or other personal characteristics feel confident of being treated fairly and equitably.

Staff and senior managers need to be clear about inclusivity and inclusive practice. The latter means:

- To expect, respect and work through diversity and difference in a positive way.
- To understand the issues facing diverse client group members, including the BPS staff, and to be able to respond positively to their specific psychological needs.
- To provide accessible and appropriate services within their area of competence in inclusivity and equality practice.

The BPS and its divisions and subsections need to bring about diversity issues within their organisations.

The business case for diversity and inclusivity includes:

- Legislation
- Demography
- Creativity within teams for recruitment and selection

- Talent management
- Retention
- Flexible working hours
- Critical thinkers for lived experience; the role of power in supervisor-supervisee relationships; therapeutic practise and academic teaching; re-appraisal of Westernised models of psychology and their usage in everyday practice and in teaching and incorporating diversity in a positive manner.
- Understanding the value base against which the work of the psychologists can be understood (service users' rights, consent to treatment and research, effects of psychotropic medication, balancing the personal and political).

Conclusion

Legislation in the form of the Equality Act 2010 highlights the need for reducing socio-economic inequalities and to decrease discrimination and harassment relating to the personal characteristics of 'race', culture, ethnicity, class, sexual preference, disability and gender. Practising psychologists, applied practitioners and academicians and the British Psychological Society need to move away from the traditional ways of working, thinking and researching, The author hopes that the solution suggested in this chapter replaces myths and old adages and the time for change within the overall profession comes to fruition very soon and the complex diversity of a plural society incorporating human behaviour and experience in all its socio-cultural and socio-political context moves rapidly ahead towards a better humanity worldwide.

References

British Psychological Society. (2017). *BPS Practice Guidelines* (3rd ed.). Retrieved from: https://www.bps.org.uk/sites/bps.org.uk/files/Policy%20%20Files/BPS%20Practice20 Guidelines%20(Third%20Edition).pdf

British Psychological Society. (2017). *The Psychology at Work: Improving well-being and productivity in the workplace report*. Retrieved from https://www.bps.org.uk/news-and-policy/ psychology-work-improving-wellbeing-and-productivity-workplace

British Psychological Society. (2015). *Inclusivity Strategy 2016–2018*. Retrieved from https:// www1.bps.org.uk/.../Division%20of%20Clinical%20Psychology/.../dcp-inclusi...

British Psychological Society. (2008). *Generic Professional Practice Guidelines*. Retrieved from www.bps.org.uk/sites/default/files/.../generic_professional_practice_guidelines.pdf

British Psychological Society. (2006). *Code of Ethics and Conduct*. Retrieved from https:// www.bps.org.uk/psychologists/standards-and-guidelines

Coombs, K. (2014). Up to 30% of UK population will be from ethnic minorities by 2015 – study. *RT question time*.

Covey, S. (2002). *Principle centred leadership*. London: Simon & Schuster UK Ltd.

Fernando, S. (2010). *Mental Health, 'Race' and Culture 3rd Ed*. Palgrave Macmillan.

Fernando, S. (2014). Globalisation of Psychiatry – A barrier to mental health development. *International Review of Psychiatry*, *26*(5), 551–557.

Haslam, A., Reicher, S., & Platow, M. (2011). *The New Psychology of leadership, Identity influence and power*. East Sussex: Psychology press.

Kandola, personal communication, 1980.

Kindermann, P. (2014). *The New Laws of Psychology*. London: Robinson/Constable and Robinson.

Languani, P. (2007). *Understanding Cross Cultural Psychology*. New Delhi: Sage Publications.

Milton, M. (2018). *The personal is political. Stories of difference and psychotherapy*. London: Palgrave.

Nadirshaw, Z. (1999). Clinical Psychology. *In K. Bhui & D. Olajide (Eds.), Mental Health Service Provision for a multi-cultural Society*. London: Saunders.

Nadirshaw, Z., Gray, I., and Golding, L. (2006). The British Psychological Society and CPD. *In L. Golding and I. Gray (Eds.), Continuing Profession Development for Clinical Psychologists. A Practical Handbook*. Oxford: BPS and Blackwell Publishers.

Owusu, B., and Howitt, D. (2000). *Psychology beyond Western perspective*. Leicester: BPS Publication.

Ryde, J. (2009). *Being White in the helping profession. Developing effective inter-cultural awareness*. London: Jessica Kingsley Publishers.

Schraer, R. & D'Urso, J. (July, 2017). Gay rights 50 years on: 10 ways in which the UK has changed. *BBC*.

Chapter 4

Young black males' attitudes towards therapy

Sharon Akinkunmi

When I reflect upon young people, I see them as our future, the ones who can become our potential leaders. Given the 'right' support, direction and intervention, many of the young people I have worked with and are in my sphere of influence can have the opportunity to progress. They can become the influential leaders and take prominent roles in our society, as some of them will go on to be. However, at times, from a media perspective, I often see the opposite being portrayed about young black males.

I will be reflecting and focusing on my psychological work with young black males and their attitudes to therapy, as well as thinking about how our society views black men and their roles as future leaders (if they are seen in this light) and if not why not? Based on my own research, I will be looking at how black males are viewed in mental health, education as well as other institutions. As they are also part of the next generation. I will be exploring areas and considering what can be done to address this.

In our society today, in relation to psychological well-being and education, as young inspiring leaders, young black males seem to be disadvantaged. There seem to be many obstacles and barriers on the road to becoming a leader and demonstrating these qualities. This can be seen in the education system and other institutions such as criminal justice and mental health. Even though there may be many examples of young black males' achievements, some of the young black males I have encountered and worked with have often felt that they are overshadowed by negative portrayals in both literature and the media. Research in this area with other young black males also supports this, as the media shows them to be good at sports, but not very intelligent (Cushion, Moore & Jewell, REACH 2011).

This research carried out by REACH, has also been confirmed by journalists that these stereotypes also contribute to the underachievement of black males. Hurd, Zimmerman & Reischl (2010) have shown that role models' behaviour may positively or negatively influence young black males' attitudes.

There is also an overwhelming pool of evidence in the US and UK that there is an over-representation of black people in the criminal justice system, mental health hospitals and secure settings (McInnis & Moukam, 2013).

Both from research into black people and mental health and from my experience of working with black people, they are more likely to be offered medication than talking therapy as a treatment option (Fernando, 2010). Black males specifically are also more likely to be diagnosed with schizophrenia (MIND, 2013).

For this exploration, the term black is being used to describe people of African and African Caribbean descent. This over-representation can be considered on reflection to be linked to evidence that suggests that men and black males specifically, are more reluctant to seek help for psychological distress in comparison to women (Liddon, Kingerlee & Barry, 2017).

From speaking with young black males on my own and reading other researchers' work, there are other barriers to accessing psychological therapy for black and ethnic minorities. I will be exploring this in more detail, with reference to overcoming these barriers. This will include finding ways to empower, encourage, support, and further understand young black males. The aim is to help young black males recognise their positive contribution to society and the role they play as contributing to our future generation of leaders.

To gain knowledge and insight into the contributing factors which influenced young black males' attendance (or non-attendance) to therapy, I conducted focus groups with semi-structured questions. In analysing the data, grounded theory was used as it aims to preserve the narratives of the participants (Glaser & Strauss, 1967). Themes were gathered from the interview data and the transcripts.

The results from my investigations revealed some of the attitudes that the young black males interviewed had towards therapy. Themes such as self-reliance and mistrust of the 'system' were quite recurrent. In their opinion, the 'system' referred to mental health services, the police, social services—and any other institutions set up to 'help and support' the public. They felt as if they should 'sort things out themselves.' Therapy was viewed as a 'waste of time' and a 'feminine' approach to the situation —with femininity being equated to 'weakness.' Psychological therapy was, however, considered to have some positive benefits by some participants. I will explore these further—including how we, as psychologists/therapists and other practitioners working with young black males can hopefully improve our practices. This will also include strategies psychologists can implement to empower young black men, shaping them into future leaders and positive contributors to society and how psychologists can learn to listen more carefully to the views and perspectives of young black males to influence those in leadership roles who influence policies and are part of delivering and developing services.

Introduction

Previous research has shown that men are less likely than women to seek help for psychological issues, as mentioned by Liddon et al. (2017). The UK suicide registrations also suggests men are more likely to commit suicide than women,

Suicides in the United Kingdom - Office for National Statistics" (ONS, 2016). Yet according to studies men are still less likely to seek psychological support in comparison to women as mentioned prior (Addis & Mahalik, 2003). An explanation for this disproportionality may be the emotion-based approach that psychological support offers, which is not in line with the solution-based perspective which men seem to operate with (Liddon et al., 2017). That said, reviewing the literature from a psychological perspective, other more complicated issues may also play a role.

Black people and men, in particular, are also less likely to be referred to psychotherapy/psychological therapy. They are more likely to be offered medication than talking therapies as mentioned prior. Also, black males who are from an African Caribbean heritage are more reluctant to engage in these services and are likely to be in a severe state before they do (Mental Health Foundation, 2018). A reluctance in engaging in therapy or any psychological help can also be linked to a fear of treatment and fear of hospitalisation. This fear has been found to be a factor in mental health service users and particularly for black people in this system. This is due to the link with power, control, and discrimination which seems to form a vicious circle (Sweeney, Gillard, Wykes & Rose, 2015). There are also other factors to consider, such as racism and the invisibility struggle that also play a role according to Franklin and Franklin (2000). The invisibility syndrome can be described as the subjective sense of psychological invisibility, which takes the form of a struggle with feelings, including one's beliefs that personal talents, abilities, and character are not acknowledged or valued by others, nor by the larger society, because of racial prejudice. The invisibility syndrome is also related to what is known as racial identity development. Racial identity development is the dimension of one's' own personal identity. The awareness and sensitivity to one's own context and individual life experiences/encounters have a dominant racial worldview. An example of this is if a black male with a dominant racial worldview may be dependent on his context. In other words, the young male is therefore influenced by family, peers, and other social factors, which can also influence the therapeutic encounter. This supports a black/African perspective in comparison to a Euro-centric perspective, which is more individualistic, as discussed earlier. I found this amongst some of the young black males interviewed too.

This is not a new phenomenon Maxime's (1986) work with young black males found this too. When the black men were brought up in environments which were predominately 'white' they tended to form negative opinions of themselves as black people and against other black people too. Images of 'being black' were internalised as negative which they did not identify with and were also repulsed by these images. This confirms the more recent work by Akbar (2001) and Kambon and Bowen-Reid (2010) about black people who develop a self-destructive orientation and continue the cycle of hurting themselves. An example of this can be seen in young black males who don't seem to value themselves or others and are involved in crime, killing one another on the 'street.'

However, it is essential to understand this about young black males in the UK who may be in different stages of their racial identity. Stereotypical images and other such influences could be contributory factors to understanding the violence and rage being demonstrated by some young black males against one another in society today. From the research sighted, it was also identified that it is necessary to have positive role models and images for young black males. These images are being developed via the media, such as the former US president, black professionals, black chancellors and black MPs (McInnis & Moukam, 2013). This is also what some young people have also stated they want to see more of in the media.

Nevertheless, in relation to therapy, psychological input such as talking therapy has been seen to be a 'Eurocentric style' of approach to ethnic minority young males seeking help. From the research I carried out this was also a prominent theme among the young people. Ethnocentric refers to an approach to therapy which places value on individualism (Woolfe, Dryden & Strawbridge, 2003), as compared to community and relationships which black people seem to value. Self-worth is based on external things and knowledge. Also, the acquisition of 'objects' is considered a Eurocentric model. This is in comparison to a more Black/African psychology perspective, which is about understanding one's culture and cultural history and their impacts (Long, 2017). This perspective also places value on self-knowledge, spiritual, symbolic imagery and self-worth being intrinsic.

From experience and from research evidence it has also been noted that a Eurocentric style may or may not work with a black person depending on where a black person is in their concept of self. For example, a culturally 'mis orientated' black person according to the Afrikan Psychology Approach would be considered to have a more alien–self, which is more oriented to a Eurocentric style of relating. Also, as a black psychologist and from my experience of working with the black community, I recognise that not all black people consider themselves to be 'African,' for example, black people from the Caribbean. These black cultures are all very different. However, it can also be argued again that those that may not want to be associated with their 'blackness/Africaness' may have a more 'alien self–concept,' as Kambon and Bowen-Reid (2010) explains. However, 'Afrikan' psychology has also been seen to be a term with limitations, and the question has been asked why it is necessary (Ratele, 2000). The unasked question is, why is there a need to use the adjective Afrikan psychology, instead of merely taking all psychology done on Africans and non-Africans samples as psychology, period. It appears that what some scholars seek to do with the term Afrikan is to distinguish between different ways of thinking about being Afrikan/Black, and psychology (Mkhize, 2004; Nwoye, 2015). This approach has been developed mainly in the US and this approach is also gradually growing in the UK.

There is a need to develop these approaches in the field of psychology across all disciplines in the UK. This relates to counselling psychology due to the core philosophy it has of the discipline that focuses on the high demand of developing self-awareness, which is in line with the core competencies of the profession's BPS guidelines. It appears that there is still a lot of work to be done in the UK in the development of leaders looking at diversity and considering race and culture. There are still areas of difference which we need to try and understand and explore further in the therapeutic encounter.

From my findings and research evidence black adolescents express themselves differently (Lu, Lindsey, Irsheid & Nebbitt, 2017). This can be described as having a blunt effect, which may be viewed as apathetic. They may also express psychological distress through physical health concerns. It has been proposed that it is important to know the unique way that black adolescents express themselves and clinicians need to be more aware of their complaints about interpersonal struggles and physical discomfort, concludes Lu et al. (2017).

Research carried out in the past (Watkins & Francis, 1988) in America has also outlined the difficulty of getting black males into therapy. High 'dropout' rates have also been found amongst those who do take up therapy. Some of the suggested reasons for these ratings are, for example, being stereotyped by the therapist, the inability of the therapist to provide a culturally responsive form of treatment and a lack of training in ethnicity/cultural diversity. Another factor was an overgeneralization in the application of cultural knowledge by therapists. Without taking individual differences into account was another reason contributing to dropout ratings. However, on reflection, high dropout rates cannot be attributed to the therapist's lack of cultural sensitivity alone; other factors play a part in this.

Factors such as mistrust are considered to play a part in dropout rates. Having worked with this client group, I have found as well as from research evidence that at times, if a black person presents as wary or untrusting within therapy, this can be viewed as defensive and paranoid. This is also based on research which offers insight into why a black person may be mistrusting. This has been argued to be based on their experiences in broader society in a predominantly white setting. This could be due to the experience of personal discrimination and societal racism (Eleftheriadou, 2010). However, it has also been emphasised that this 'defensive' persona by a black person can also be thought of as healthy to protect from being hurt and exposing vulnerabilities.

Therapists/professionals working with black youth, for example, they may not be able to tell what is characteristic or a reflection of the client's culture, socioeconomic status or whether it is a combination of the two. This can lead to misdiagnosis and difficulties in assessment/treatment plans in a therapeutic setting in relation to black males (Fernando, 2010). Racial mistrust is the term used to describe this process where black adolescents, males, tend to distrust white dominant society, which can act as a psychological defence mechanism

(Thompson, Neville, Weathers & Poston, 1990). I found this in the young people I interviewed too. This process could be a factor in the therapeutic setting as described earlier and can contribute to early dropout rates. Racial mistrust has also been argued to be a protective factor to help against the negative self-images being formed by black males (Zimmerman, Ramírez-Valles & Maton, 1999). It can also hinder the forming of a therapeutic relationship, which is an essential component in any therapeutic/psychological therapy process (Clarkson, 2003), hence early dropout rates for young black males. It has been proposed that a white therapist who struggles with a black client who seems to be blaming white people for example for their predicament' should aim to look beyond the blame (Watkins & Francis, 1988). This can be done by being ready as a therapist to explore the hurt behind the blame. This would also require the therapist to demonstrate compassion, congruence, and a black empathic approach.

However, this concept of mistrust is not only experienced between a white therapist and a black client in therapy. This can also be experienced by a black therapist and a black client too. I have found this in my experience and when carrying out this research. This could relate to an 'anti-self' orientation concept described earlier. This type of black person has hostility to their own sense of being 'black.' So, they would not trust a black professional either and could, therefore, display this same mistrust toward them.

One could argue that young black males are in greater need of psychological therapy due to these research findings, as they are being considered 'problem youth.' Or is it rather a 'problem context?' For example, the 'problem context' refers to the experiences of black males (Livingston & Nahimana, 2006, p. 206). Williams (2018) and Nazroo (2017) also refer to the consequences of discrimination and racism that ethnic minorities face not only in the US but in the UK. Rather than viewing black males as a 'problem' a more helpful approach especially in the therapeutic context is to look at the wider problematic context and to recognise the black experience as one of strength and resilience against oppression from the past to support growth and build leaders for the future. This perspective focuses on understanding the journey of black people from the ancestry struggle and its impact on future generations.

According to research (Memon, Taylor, Mohebati, Sundin, Cooper, Scanlon & De Visser, 2016) into barriers to accessing mental health services amongst black and ethnic minorities, it has been found that these barriers can be overcome by having a more effective range of balanced support services, which include psychotherapeutic and psychological counselling services as necessary. It was also proposed that these services should be culturally appropriate and have the appropriate training and support to deliver individually tailored and culturally sensitive care.

Barriers can be overcome through training in culturally sensitive issues, engaging with black and ethnic minorities, and raising awareness on mental health in the black and ethnic minority communities. This includes the benefits of appropriate services. Some argue that these services should be led by black professionals such as the Black Association of Black Psychologists, which also promotes research by black psychologists. However, with the appropriate training and identifying of issues that need addressing these barriers can be overcome. Not only black professionals are the best equipped to work with black people. Training can help develop multicultural competence, and this has been seen in various services developing around the country as well as in training courses for therapists. Nasfsiyat is just one of those examples of services in the UK.

The qualitative study I carried out used grounded theory to uncover the 'meanings' which young black males attribute to therapy. This was with the aim to understand the possible barriers to accessing these services for the young black male and the ways forward to what may encourage them to engage in such services. Group interviews were conducted with young black men aged between 16–25 years. Fernando, British Psychiatrist argues that there is a need for leadership both within the government and also within mental health. Black males, in particular, need a voice along with other ethnic minorities. They need not only to be heard but also to have services that address these issues and act upon them, not just tokenism of having a black person in a leadership role and having no influence to change policy and make decisions, especially in the area of mental health.

Reflecting on the experiences of black males in relation to psychological therapy

Three focus groups were held with young black males, which consisted of six individuals in each group. They were held within Educational and Youth Support Settings. The participants were 18 young black males aged between 16–25 years. All participants described themselves as UK Black Caribbean or Black African. Opportunity sampling was the sampling procedure employed to recruit the participants. Ethical approval was obtained, and consent was obtained from all participants in this study.

Analytical approach

Data were then analysed using grounded theory, following the method that was devised by Glaser and Strauss (1967). This form of analysis was used as it offers an approach which is suited to qualitative research, which is of an exploratory nature. This approach aims to describe how the participants see their 'world,' rather than how the 'world' appears to an outside observer. Grounded theory aims to discover how groups of people define their realities on the basis of interpersonal interactions. Grounded theory accepts that there are plural truths and that reality is socially constructed. There are various forms of grounded theory; however, this research is adopting the original grounded theory by the above researchers mentioned prior. This approach emphasises the need to allow the data to naturally emerge. This was done by the initial analytical step to 'open up' the data and breaking it down into meaningful concepts. By applying this method, it helped to discover the thoughts, ideas, and meanings contained in the interviewees' narratives. This process requires the coding to stick closely to the data, as well as constantly comparing and summarising. Questions such as 'what does this data suggest?' and 'what is happening here?' are asked. These summaries are referred to as codes.

Results of the main code/themes: Last resort

Most of the young men felt that they would only turn to counselling/therapy because of desperation. Desperation was described as on the verge of what they considered to be a mental breakdown. Some young men said 'you don't care until something critical happens'; 'you wouldn't think of counselling.'

Disconnecting one's emotions

'Street life' is the term used to describe being 'on road' and engaging in criminality. It was felt that young black males were involved in this type of anti-social behaviour as they had disconnected themselves from their feelings: 'we see another black person, and there's intimidation, so we think take him out sort of thing, there's no love.'

Protecting street 'cred'

This was a way to guard against feeling vulnerable or weak by their peers to protect their 'street credibility.' This is the image of being the 'hard man on road who can deal with any kind of beef' (trouble/fighting etc.): 'Some people they want status but some they ain't got nothing to live for and some because they are bottling things…'; 'I don't think kids on the street think counselling is cool.'

Discussion: Reflections on the themes from the young males' narratives

There was an underlying theme throughout the interviews with the young black males that they should 'sort themselves out,' when it comes to their emotional difficulties. This is another way of saying they need to look out for themselves because therapy was seen to have negative consequences with little benefits. Therapy would only be considered as a last resort, if considered at all. This research supports results from Branney & White's (2008) study with white males who communicated that their emotional difficulties/ psychological problems should be dealt with by themselves too. Autonomy or self-reliance was the term used to describe this (Lindon et al., 2017).

Therapy was viewed as a feminine activity, a sign of weakness and an indication that they cannot cope. The results support research carried out in the UK and the US, with young black males and males over 25 years (Williams, 2017).

Other similarities were the way that young black males perceived therapy/ therapists as being fake, uncaring, and unqualified. This has been depicted in the media with the use of stereotypical images of therapists. Findings were also consistent with research carried out in America by Franklin et al. (2000). More recent research in the UK also suggested this.

Summary and discussions

Therapy was perceived as a 'system' that is against young black males, as something to be feared or to keep away from. This contributed to their mistrust of the counselling 'system.' The 'system' was viewed as labelling and had stereotypical images of young black males which they felt they needed to protect themselves from.

The implication of these findings suggests that there may be a need for psychological therapy services to look at the overall image of the services that are being provided and promoted. This includes ways to raise awareness and encourage cultural diversity, which may help to change the perception of this profession.

This has been identified in the National Framework for Mental Health Delivering Race Equality in Mental Health Care Action Plan (2012). Research carried out by the Department of Health (2012) also stated that there is a need for written plans in services to address issues on improving mental health services for BME groups. There should also be a commitment from the leadership. This needs to be seen from chief executive levels to senior leadership boards and those working directly with these groups such as young black males and other minority groups. Recommendations were made with regard to the Department of Health, NHS Commissioning Boards, Public Health England, Quality Care Commission, and providers of mental health services to be able to make a direct change. This is with the aim to provide greater support for the improvement in service delivery and outcome for black males and other BME groups in general.

The Division of Counselling Psychology within the British Psychological Society (BPS) also set out recommendations in the Division of Counselling Psychology (2015) addressing the issues of Race, Culture, and Diversity in 2015. It was considered that multicultural and multiracial issues need to be taken seriously. A proposal was put forward for all counselling psychology courses in the UK to have a formal module introduced during training to develop multicultural competence. The module would be to 'address race, culture, and ethnicity as well as understanding the complexities' (DCoP, 2015).

It is clear from the findings that black males do seem to believe that therapy can have some benefits too. Although it was considered mainly a more Westernised way of dealing with emotional issues, as discussed, there were values placed on this process to an extent. There were diverse views and comments in terms of therapy being beneficial. However, it was suggested that it would only be embarked on as a 'last resort' (only if these young men were in a desperate situation).

The African psychology perspective as mentioned earlier seeks to look at the assessment and formulation of integrating cultural sensitivity. This has been seen in the development of these approaches in training courses such as clinical psychology. Assessment tools are being developed to include a better understanding and awareness of the needs of black people.

There is a need to educate trainee psychotherapists and psychologists regarding issues of race and culture. This can be applied to any type of ethnic mix, and it is an ongoing process. Multicultural competence is the term used to describe the recognition and the reality of race within the therapeutic hour. It was found that these therapists felt that specific skills needed to be exercised within the therapeutic setting when working with a black client. Some of these skills were being direct but also sensitive to issues that pertained to race and openness/acceptance of the effects of racism.

As counselling psychologists and other professionals working with race, culture, and diversity, it is critical to explore our own biases as recommended by DCoP (2015). This in relation to developing self-awareness and being open and honest about our own 'assumptions, positions of power and privilege,' especially working with black males to be able to explore these areas and their impact on the therapeutic relationship.

It may be necessary to also do further consultation and research in this area with young black males, to be able to set up services that aim to meet their needs. Services need to be representative of the group they want to target. This research could focus on larger sample sizes across various boroughs. It could also investigate the few services that are working with the black community. This includes voluntary organisations, etc., that may be engaging young black males and finding out what is effective. Work with young black men 'on the street' may also be necessary to understand their views. However, it is also important to recognise that some participants may feel despondent to a degree, as they may think that they are not being represented. It is essential to include the voice of black communities when setting up services in their communities.

Concerning counselling psychology/psychotherapy there is a need to emphasise this area. This may mean the possibility of recruiting and training male therapists/psychologists into the mental health field. It is imperative for education and training to take place in black communities, as it will enhance both young people's and adult's understanding of therapy. Information in schools, youth centres, youth offending services, and other agencies would be central to adopting this approach too. This includes educating families and other organisations working with parents, as the young men in this study also acknowledged the significant impact their family environment had on their attitudes and behaviours.

In the light of some of these issues presented, it would seem one would be suggesting that only black male therapists would be able to relate to young black males. However, research has shown that this is not the case. It is crucial that young black men feel able to identify with their therapists, whether black or white (Ward & Besson, 2013). An awareness of issues regarding race and culture is essential for the development of cultural competence in the therapist. There are pockets of what is considered 'good' practice in some organisations. Nafsiyat, a multicultural therapy service, targets clients from BME backgrounds as well as promoting cultural competence within its therapists.

The way forward concerning young black males and therapy has been discussed in terms of employment and training. Increasing public knowledge on the benefits of psychological treatment, from a black perspective, is another approach which can be used to spread information to broader sections of the community. This form of public education is already taking place in America—with the association of Black Psychologists (Akbar, 1999).

The fact the sample size of the study is small (18 participants) and only includes individuals from one borough, it could be argued that the study lacks external validity. However, that would only apply if the study was being analysed in isolation. The findings of this study correlate with previous research, some of which has been conducted in other countries.

In conclusion, with appropriate support and culturally sensitive services addressing their psychological difficulties, young black males could make positive contributions and live productive lives.

References

Addis, M., & Mahalik, J. (2003). Men, masculinity, and the contexts of help seeking. *American Psychologist*, *58*(1), 5–14. doi: 10.1037/0003-066x.58.1.5.

Afrika, L. (2009). *Melanin*. Long Island City, N.Y.: Seaburn Pub. Group.

Akbar, N. (2001). *Visions for black men*. Tallahassee, Fla.: Mind Productions.

Branney, P., & White, A. (2008). Big boys don't cry: depression and men. *Advances in Psychiatric Treatment*, *14*(4), 256–262. doi: 10.1192/apt.bp.106.003467.

Clarkson, P. (2003). *The therapeutic relationship* (2nd ed.). London: Whurr.

Cushion, S., Moore, K., & Jewell, J. (2011). REACH Report, Media representations of black young men and boys. School of Journalism, Media and Cultural Studies Cardiff University.

Division of Counselling Psychology (2015). Black and Asian Counselling Psychologists Group. Proposal to include race, culture and diversity in Counselling Psychology training. https://www1.bps.org.uk/system/files/user-files/Division%20of%20Counselling%20Psychology/public/proposal_to_includerace_culture_and_diversity_in_the_training_of_cops.pdf

Eleftheriadou, Z. (2010). *Psychotherapy and Culture*. London: Karnac.

Fernando, S. (2010). *Mental health, race and culture* (3rd Ed.). Basingstoke: Palgrave Macmillan.

Franklin, Anderson J., & Boyd-Franklin, N. (2000). "Invisibility Syndrome: A Clinical Model of The Effects of Racism on African-American Males." *American Journal of Orthopsychiatry* 70(1): 33–41. doi:10.1037/h0087691.

Glaser, B. G. and Strauss, A. L. (1967). *The discovery of grounded theory: strategies for qualitative research*. New York, NY: Aldine De Gruyter.

Hurd, N. M., Zimmerman, M. A. &. Reischl, T. M. (2010). "Role Model Behavior And Youth Violence: A Study of Positive and Negative Effects". *The Journal of Early Adolescence 31*(2): 323–354. doi: 10.1177/0272431610363160.

Kambon, K. K., & Bowen-Reid, T. (2010). "Theories of African American Personality: Classification, Basic Constructs and Empirical Predictions/Assessment". *The Journal of Pan African Studies 3*(8): 83–102.

Liddon, L., Kingerlee, R. & Barry, J. A. (2017). "Gender Differences in Preferences for Psychological Treatment, Coping Strategies, And Triggers to Help-Seeking". *British Journal of Clinical Psychology 57*(1): 42–58. doi:10.1111/bjc.12147.

Livingston, J. N., & Nahimana, C. (2006). Problem Child or Problem Context: An Ecological Approach to Young Black Males. *Reclaiming Children & Youth, 14*(4), 209–214.

Long, W. (2017). Alienation: A new orienting principle for psychotherapists in South Africa (1st ed., pp. 67–90). Psychoanalytic Psychotherapy in South Africa.

Lu, W., Lindsey, M., Irsheid, S., & Nebbitt, V. (2017). Psychometric Properties of the CES-D Among Black Adolescents in Public Housing. *Journal of The Society for Social Work and Research, 8*(4), 595–619. doi: 10.1086/694791.

Maxime, J. (1986). "Some psychological models of black self-concept". In S. Ahmed, J. Cheetham and J. Small (Eds.) *Social Work with Children and their Families*, London: Batsford.

McInnis, E., & Moukam, R. (2013). Black Psychology for Britain Today? *Journal of Black Psychology, 39*(3), 311–315. doi: 10.1177/0095798413480663.

Memon, A., Taylor, K., Mohebati, L., Sundin, J., Cooper, M., Scanlon, T. & de Visser, R. (2016). Perceived barriers to accessing mental health services among black and minority ethnic (BME) communities: a qualitative study in Southeast England. *BMJ Open, 6*(11). doi: 10.1136/bmjopen-2016-012337.

Mental Health Foundation (2018). *Black, Asian and minority ethnic (BAME) communities*.

MIND. (2013). We Still Need to Talk. A report on access to talking therapies. Retrieved from https://www.mind.org.uk/media/494424/we-still-need-to-talk_report.pdf

Mkhize, N. (2004). Psychology. An African Perspective. In N. Duncan (Ed) *Self, Community and Psychology*, *Chap* 4–1 University of Cape Town Press.

Nazroo, J. (2017). Ethnicity, social inequality and health. Retrieved from https://www.sochealth.co.uk/2017/12/31/ethnicity-social-inequality-health-2/

Nwoye, A. (2015). What is African Psychology the psychology of? *Theory & Psychology, 25*(1), 96–116. doi: 10.1177/0959354314565116.

Office of Nation Statistics. (2016). Suicides in Britain. https://www.ons.gov.uk/peoplepopulationandcommunity/birthsdeathsandmarriages/deaths/bulletins/suicidesintheunitedkingdom/2016registration

Ratele, K. (2017). "Frequently Asked Questions About African Psychology". *South African Journal of Psychology 47*(3): 273–279. doi:10.1177/0081246317703249.

Sweeney, A., Gillard, S., Wykes, T. & Rose, D. (2015). "The Role of Fear in Mental Health Service Users' Experiences: A Qualitative Exploration". *Social Psychiatry and Psychiatric Epidemiology 50*(7): 1079–1087. doi:10.1007/s00127-015-1028-z.

Thompson, C. E., Neville, H., Weathers, P. L., & Poston, W. C., et al. (1990). Cultural mistrust and racism reaction among African-American students. *Journal of College Student Development*, *31*(2), 162–168.

Ward, C. E., & Besson, D. D. (2013). African American Men's Beliefs About Mental Illness, Perceptions of Stigma, and Help-Seeking Barriers. *The Counseling Psychologist*. *41*(3), 359–391.

Watkins, E. C. & Francis, T. (1988). Mistrust level and its effects on counseling expectations in Black client-White counselor relationships: An analogue study. *Journal of Counseling Psychology 35*(2), 194, 1988.

Williams, M. (2011). Why African Americans Avoid Psychotherapy. Retrieved from https://www.psychologytoday.com/intl/blog/culturally-speaking/201111/why-african-americans-avoid-psychotherapy

Williams, M. (2013). How Therapists Drive Away Minority Clients. Retrieved from https://www.psychologytoday.com/gb/blog/culturally-speaking/201306/how-therapists-drive-away-minority-clients

Williams, D. R. (2017). From Disparity to Equity. In A. L. Plough (Ed.), *Knowledge to Actions: Accelerating Progress in Health, Well-Being, and Equity* (pp. 21–30). New York: Oxford University Press.

Williams, S. P. (2018). Why We Don't Talk About Mental Health in the Black Community and Why We Have to Start. Retrieved from https://www.self.com/story/racism-mental-health-in-the-black-community

Woolfe, R., Dryden, W., & Strawbridge, S. (2003). *Handbook of Counselling Psychology* (2nd ed.). Thousand Oaks, California: Sage.

Zimmerman, M., Ramírez-Valles, J., & Maton, K. (1999). Resilience Among Urban African American Male Adolescents: A Study of the Protective Effects of Sociopolitical Control on Their Mental Health. *American Journal of Community Psychology*, *27*(6), 733–751. doi: 10.1023/a:1022205008237.

Chapter 5

Social justice, leadership and diversity

Rachel Tribe

**A version of this chapter was published in the *European Journal of Counselling Psychology*; this version contains minor changes.

Definitions of social justice

There are several definitions of social justice. These include rights to self-determination, a fair allocation of resources, to live in peace, freedom from constraints and to be treated fairly and equitably (Kagan et al., 2011). Whilst few people would argue with these objectives, the reality may be more complex. One individual exercising freedom from constraints may engage in behaviour which impinges on the rights of others, is contrary to the interests of the wider community and society, or may be illegal. For example, an individual may claim the 'freedom' to engage in discriminatory behaviours which ignore or condemn diversity in its myriad forms or, even more extreme, claim the freedom to engage in paedophiliac behaviour. Thus, while freedom from constraints may be a goal, the reality may not be as straightforward as it initially appears.

Chung & Bemak (2012) writing about social justice and counselling psychology take a distributive justice position, emphasising that society must give individuals and groups fair treatment and an equal share of benefits, resources and opportunities.

> …'social justice' implies fairness and mutual obligation in society: that we are responsible for one another, and that we should ensure that all have equal chances to succeed in life. Although in societies where life chances are not distributed equally, this implies redistribution of opportunities, although the shape that such redistribution should take remains contested.
>
> Royal Society of Arts, 2017

Two widely quoted theorists are John Rawls (1999), who views justice as fairness, and David Miller (2003), who, in his Principles of Social

Justice, is more concerned with the actual circumstances based on what people do and why they do it. Social justice is concerned with negotiating a balance between social equality and individual freedom. As stated earlier, this is not always easy as these two goals may be in opposition or tension.

In summary, social justice is one way of thinking about addressing social inequalities and encouraging inclusion. It incorporates a human rights perspective and promotes a just society by challenging injustice and valuing diversity. It accepts that there has not been a level playing field, that power has not been equally distributed and that self-determination and opportunities for some individuals and groups remains an aspiration as opposed to a reality. It attempts to move away from an individualised model of blame or causation, which psychology has often unwittingly followed. For example, mental health has often been seen as an exclusively individual issue, without any relation to the wider context and societal factors which may predispose a person to poor mental health. These include, but are not limited to, poverty (Murali & Oyebode, 2004), homelessness (Cockersill, 2017) and discrimination on grounds of diversity. Discrimination may include racial discrimination (Chakraborty & McKenzie, 2002), gender discrimination (Bondi & Burman, 2001) or age discrimination (Lane & Tribe, 2017). Ratts (2009) has argued that within counselling, social justice is the 'fifth force', after the psychodynamic, cognitive behavioural therapy (CBT), humanistic and multicultural 'forces'.

Social justice and counselling psychology

Kagan, Tindall and Robinson (2010) argue that counselling psychology should move towards social and cultural explanations of distress and psychological interventions at a broader level and away from a focus predominantly on the individual. This might ultimately benefit service users/ experts by experience and may also help raise the issue of inequalities and discrimination in wider society. Goodman et al. (2004) argue that a psychologist may wish to discuss with the service user/expert by experience the option of reframing their experiences or responses to them, as an adaptive response to an oppressive and unfair situation. It has been argued that social justice should take an ethical stance, which has been defined as paying attention to working collaboratively, trying not to take an expert position, talking about prejudice, enquiring about resistance to social abuse, viewing survival of oppression as an ability, respecting resistance in therapy, reflecting on power and privilege and being receptive and open (Afuape & Hughes, 2016). These are important because they not only form the basis of people's lives but will in themselves give rise to distress, and to ignore them is highly reductionist.

It is important also to be cognisant of intersectionality, which is when cultural patterns of oppression are inter-related. So, for example, a gay older woman who has a learning disability might be viewed as suffering multiple forms of discrimination because the different forms of discrimination inter-sect with each other (Crenshaw, 1989). Services are often set up around a single issue and this may not always be in the best interests of service users facing discrimination on several different fronts.

The history of the social justice movement in American counselling psychology can be traced to the 1950s (Chung & Bemak, 2012) and has a much longer history than within British counselling psychology. In the UK, the history is somewhat different, and references to values such as anti-oppressive practice, difference and diversity, and awareness of power issues are frequently made in the literature (Cutts, 2013). However, there are not many explicit references to 'social justice' in UK literature before 2010. This may merely reflect linguistic differences and the integration of the phrase into the language used in Britain. The Division of Counselling Psychology (DCoP) social justice network was established by Laura Winter in June 2015 and provides a newsletter, networking, details of events and organizes two events a year. Social justice and counselling psychology in the USA have been defined as:

> We conceptualize the social justice work of counseling psychologists as scholarship and professional action designed to change societal values, structures, policies and practices such that disadvantages or marginalized groups gain increased access to these tools of self-determination.
>
> Goodman et al., 2004, p. 795

Community psychology, engagement and leadership

If we were to consider anew how to minimise psychological distress from a social justice perspective would the main solution be individual therapy? It may be helpful to consider that psychology/psychiatry/mental health is not synonymous with individual therapy. Within the NHS in the UK, there are incentives to focus on treatment rather than prevention, which might be viewed as perverse. Community psychology is beginning to come of age in the UK and working with groups or communities of people may be something that counselling, and other psychologists are well placed to undertake. It may provide an opportunity for working more holistically and enabling societal inequalities to be challenged and form part of the work. This may require some small changes to the training curriculum, but many psychologists have the necessary transferable skills. The National Institute for Health and Clinical Excellence (NICE) have provided guidelines (NG44) on community engagement, 'improving health and wellbeing and reducing health inequalities' (NICE, 2016). In addition, Lane and Tribe (2010) wrote a practical guide (following the first publication of guidelines on this) for health professionals.

Counselling psychologists may wish to consider what should be the role of community consultation and engagement in their practice? The latter may be more resource-effective, less stigmatising, accessible and appropriate and also in line with social justice principles. It may enable communities to take ownership and leadership and determine their own priorities and move away from the position of passive service recipient, to working in real partnership with psychologists to improve services. It is important to remember that everyone is a member of multiple communities and membership may be fluid and self-defined. Communities, as well as experts by experience, frequently have much to teach psychologists, as they may not be restricted in the way they view, understand or construct psychology or psychological help.

An example of leadership has been the work of counselling psychologist Thompson et al. (2018), who is leading on the writing of 'Guidance on Working with Community Organisations for Psychologists' developed by the London Community Psychology Network (2018). Genuine community engagement offers the opportunity to communities to contribute to the shaping of services. It may also influence those commissioning services and providers to develop services in a dynamic way based on need, and in line with any changes in the population as well as the requirements of the whole community. Among the benefits of community engagement is the fact that it minimises the model of individual psychopathology which may sometimes stigmatise individuals. Community psychology can focus on prevention rather than treatment and be used perhaps before problems have developed. It may provide an opportunity for working more holistically and enabling societal inequalities to be challenged and to form part of our work. It can also address problems that are identified by community members and build capacity within communities leading to more accessible and appropriate services. It can build in support structures and provide a normalising function as well as being cost effective and can work with a range of cultures. It can bring to the foreground the voices of potential service users and communities in line with the principles of social justice. The disadvantages include the fact that evaluation of any work may be less straightforward, access may not be straightforward and confidentiality must be considered, but this is balanced by the importance and richness of the contributions to psychology.

Challenges and barriers

One challenge relates to how to turn social justice values into social justice action given the current training curriculum. Cutts and Hanley (2014) have questioned whether there is a rhetoric-action gap in the UK. Barriers to implementing social justice values have been identified by Bemak and Chung (2008) as being both personal and professional. Personal barriers might include, for example, where there may be worries about being disliked, viewed as a trouble maker or feelings of powerlessness to act. Professional barriers include concerns about job security and systems which are resistant to change or challenge.

Some psychologists have argued that incorporating a social justice perspective is inconsistent with the apparent neutral positioning of psychology, but in reality, psychology is not neutral but reflects the dominant prevailing social arrangements (Fox and Prilleltensky, 1996; Marsella, 2011). Many changes within psychological theory and practice have come about as a result of advocacy by individuals or groups and the need for diversity to be recognized and incorporated into theory and practice. For example, it has come to incorporate a range of perspectives including but not limited to feminist, Black and Asian ethnic minority (BAME), Lesbian/Bisexual/Gay/Transgendered (LBGT), learning disabled and other groups which are frequently marginalised. What appears important is how social justice may change theory and practice and how this change may happen, over and above being a value or valued within the profession. Few counselling psychologists would argue against the values of social justice, but it is the subsequent changes to practice and action that will make a difference, and leadership at the individual, division and BPS level may be important. An example of leadership on this issue is the DCoP booklet, 'Race, Culture and Diversity – A Collection of Articles' (Ade-Serrano et al., 2017).

Using a social justice perspective

Goodman et al. (2004) suggest that reading and teaching about social justice issues, taking a public position on issues—for example, the BPS statement on unaccompanied child refugees (BPS, 2016)—and integrating broader systemic factors into therapeutic interventions are important for counselling psychologists. As stated earlier, it is well known that, for example, poverty and discrimination are detrimental to mental health and well-being (Saraceno & Barbui, 1997). Some psychologists have campaigned and taken a public position against the psychological effects of austerity (Psychologists Against Austerity, 2017, now called Psychologists for Social Change). Other social justice activities might include networking and lobbying at a range of levels. For example, in the UK, it has included input by psychologists into the MIND guidelines for commissioners of services for vulnerable migrants or the psychological impacts of the 'bedroom tax' (McCoy & Winter, 2015). Engaging in advocacy, outreach and prevention may also be important. For a range of examples see Tribe and Tunariu (2018). Attempting to influence public policy making, for example, being signatories to, and supporting the aims of documents such as the 'Bill of Rights for Children and Young People with Mental Illness' (World Psychiatric Association, 2016) and the 'Global Position Statement on Mental Health, Human Rights and Human Dignity, the Careif Magna Carta for people living with mental Illness' is another form of advocating for social justice. It may also be done by choosing to work with groups which may have been labelled 'hard to reach' or marginalized groups and, as mentioned earlier, openly discussing the socio-political aspects of their life and the discrimination they may have been subjected to, as part of our clinical work. Advocating at a wider level is also important. For example, engaging with the media by giving interviews or using social media are other methods of getting a message across. In addition, linking with others can be important and these might be professional groups, charities or pressure groups.

The benefits of promoting social justice

The importance of promoting social justice has been demonstrated through an increasing and diverse array of evidence which shows that creating a more equal society will benefit the entire community. Some of the most widely read works on this include: Thomas Piketty (2014), 'Capital in the 21st Century' (Piketty is an economist); Oliver James (2007), 'Affluenza: How to Be Successful and Stay Sane' (James is a clinical psychologist and analyst); and Kate Pickett and Richard Wilkinson (2009), 'The Spirit Level: Why More Equal Societies Almost Always Do Better for Everyone' (Pickett and Wilkinson are epidemiologists). Psychological theory, clinical work and research could helpfully consider contextual factors in more detail, and psychologists can usefully take a leadership role in campaigning for social justice, whether within the service where they are employed or through theory development, research, speaking out about it or engaging in campaigns around some of the relevant issues.

The positioning of psychology and diversity

The positioning of psychology has a long history of being negotiated and re-negotiated, as well as at times contested (Tribe, 2014). Psychology and psychiatry have existed since time immemorial within a range of cultures and is not solely the preserve of Western thought or philosophy. Psychology has often been presented as being applicable around the world, whilst much of it has been developed in Western high-income countries, with the rich traditions and practices in much of the rest of the world being viewed as folk or cultural practices (Fernando, 2014). For example, mindfulness comes from Buddhism and has been used very successfully within Western mental health services and other contexts. Some people have referred to this as the

'Macdonaldisation' of Buddhism because it fails to take account of the wider context and beliefs of Buddhism, but just takes one aspect of it and places it within another context. Psychology has repositioned itself in relation to LBGT issues, moving away from a position that, alongside psychiatry and the wider society, discriminated based on homosexuality and used treatments such as aversion therapy and invasive drug treatments to 'cure' it. It was not until 1974 that homosexuality was removed from the Diagnostic Statistical manual (DSM II) produced by the American Psychological Society as a psychiatric diagnosis, whilst the 'International Statistical Classification of Diseases and Related Health Problems' (ICD) did not remove it until 1990 (Herek, 1990). Therefore, social justice has a role to play in questioning theory and associated practices particularly in a 'post-truth' world.

Psychology has positioned itself in a range of ways which have included accepting positivism and quantitative methodologies as the only methodological positions for research to the acceptance of qualitative methods and a range of epistemological positions. In addition, topics deemed worthy of interest by psychologists have often reflected the wider society and the inequalities of power found there. Some important areas were viewed as not worthy of study by psychologists, and contextual factors were frequently ignored or seen as not being relevant to the core discipline of psychology, although this is changing, and counselling psychologists can work with others to take a leadership role on this. Sexism within psychology can also be seen through looking at the national profile of psychologists, as most psychologists are women and most managers are men, although this is changing.

Critical and community psychology have much to offer in relation to social justice, because both challenge and deconstruct prevailing theories and practices in psychology, as well as arguing that the individual may not always be the most appropriate or only focus. There is a need to embrace diversity and guard against ethnocentrism (Fernando, 2014), as well as the other isms, if psychology is to be inclusive and maximise its potential contribution, for the benefit of all and be in line with the BPS mission to promote excellence (BPS Statement on Promoting Excellence in Psychology, 2014).

Leadership by counselling psychologists can be shown in a range of ways, many of which have been detailed already. It includes publishing articles and challenging psychological practices, and the theories and assumptions which govern them. These are often based on a white middle class heteronormative perspective which fails to consider adequately issues of diversity. Working with commissioners and other mental health professionals can be very productive and by, for example, linking with psychiatrists, social workers or community activists can lead to a critical mass and bring about change. Psychologists often work in silos and even within the discipline of psychology, in different divisions. Building bridges and raising issues are important. Without these, services offered by counselling psychologists may not uphold the principles of counselling psychology and social justice and thus fail to serve the entire community in the best way possible.

Issues of diversity and organisational, institutional and cultural barriers put in place by health professionals

There is an assumption frequently made that, as people from certain communities don't use mental health services very much, they don't need them, and it becomes self-perpetuating, with appropriate services not being set up (Lane, Tribe & Hui, 2010). Mental health services have been found to be inaccessible or inappropriate by BAME community members (Patel, 2014; Lago, 2011) and usage poor compared to the white community (Bhugra & Gupta, 2011). King et al. (2008), in a meta-analysis of 25 studies investigating mental health issues, including suicide and self-harm, found that there were twice as many LBGT people compared to the straight community involved in suicide attempts as well as higher rates of depression, anxiety and alcohol dependence. Maguen & Shipherd (2010) found that 41% of trans-men and 20% of trans-women reported suicide attempts. The impact of factors such as school and workplace bullying, homophobic attacks and the subsequent use of drugs and alcohol were all mentioned as ways of coping within this study. These worrying patterns are of serious concern, and counselling psychologists may wish to champion and provide leadership around challenging discrimination and working towards a more inclusive society.

Health professionals may not be welcoming to patients whom they view as being different to themselves or as diverse. This may be due to discrimination or because they are seen as being resource intense (even if this is not the case). Perceived discrimination, specifically racism, may adversely affect psychological well-being (Fernando, 2014; McKenzie, 2003). Within mental health frameworks, assumptions that a Western diagnostic system is the only mechanism for understanding distress may be an issue, even though it is culturally located (Summerfield, 2012). Stigma and fear around mental health may be influenced by different cultural formulations and models (Kirmayer & Bhugra, 2009). Should we as psychologists be challenging these and if so how?

More recent forms of psychology which set out to promote social justice and to challenge social inequalities

Critical psychology

This questions the relevance and deconstructs many of the theories and practices of psychology, including challenging the ingrained power and privilege of traditional psychology, which is viewed as aligned with dominant sections of a population. It also acts as a challenging and political protest, concerned with moving psychology to a more holistic position and away from a purely individualist and, on occasions, reductionist position. It moves beyond a purely 'mind-centred' focus.

Positive psychology

Positive psychology has worked to bring together some elements of psychology and related disciplines. Part of its vision is to encourage the recognition of strengths, resilience and focussing on what it labels flourishing, rather than on deficits or illnesses, which has been the predominant model within psychology and mental health and well-being. This can be applied to individuals, families, communities, groups or organisations.

Community psychology

'It is a way of thinking...psychologists who've seen the limitations of simply working with individual people....' They also have concluded that we need to be very careful about approaches that imply blaming people who should be seen as the victims of social arrangements. Community psychology sees individuals in a wider context' (Orford, 2014). A section of community psychology was established within the BPS in 2010, whose underlying values 'Include those of inclusivity, social justice and improvement of health and well-being.... Those who base their work through non-individual intervention' (BPS Community Psychology Section, 2010).

Liberation psychology

Liberation psychology (Martin-Baro, 1994) is oriented to the oppressed majority, the excluded, the exploited. It uses the standpoint/perspective of the oppressed to interrogate psychological theory and practice to de-ideologise .... and to recover and rework approaches for a more adequate psychology for the needs of the population (adapted from www.libpsy.org). Dykstra (2014) has also considered liberation psychology as something which can make a helpful contribution. A British book on liberation psychology and practices was published in 2016 by Afuape and Hughes, which provides a useful overview of using liberation psychology and practices in a range of contexts.

Summary

A range of examples of work which have embodied the principles of social justice work have been described throughout this paper, including innovative work led by counselling as well as other psychologists who have fought for anti-discriminatory practice and for diversity to be recognised and viewed as a central, rich and vital part of life which contributes significantly to society. Many of the examples described in this paper have taken place outside the consulting room, but there is also a role for providing leadership and questioning discriminatory practice and structural inequalities within clinical work. Leadership has been shown and will continue to need to be shown in a range of different ways and in a wide variety of contexts. Some potential psychological theories have been offered which may be useful when undertaking this work.

Finally, the author of this paper would offer a challenge for psychologists to consider: are there things we should be doing to promote social justice and challenge inequalities? Are there places we should be working/researching where we are not and thereby not challenging social inequalities and promoting social justice and inclusion? This relates to all our roles, as individuals, a division, the BPS and as part of the mental health community and wider society.

References

Ade-Serrano, Y., Nkansa-Dwamena, O. & McIntosh, M. (2017). *Race, Culture and Diversity- A Collection of Articles*. BPS Division of Counselling Psychology Black and Asian Counselling Psychologists Group.

Afuape, T. & Hughes, G. (2016). *Liberation Practices Towards Emotional Wellbeing Through Dialogue*. London: Routledge.

Bemak, F. & Chung, R. (2008). New Professional Roles and Advocacy Strategies for School Counselors: A multicultural/social justice Perspective to Move beyond the Nice Counselor Syndrome. *Journal of Counseling Development, 86, 3*, 259–384.

Bhugra, D. & Gupta, S. (eds). (2011). *Migration and Mental Health*. Cambridge: Cambridge University Press.

Bondi, L. & Burman, E. (2001). Women and Mental Health: A Feminist Review, *Feminist Review, 68*, 6–33.

British Psychological Society (2005). *Division of Counselling Psychology Professional Practice Guidelines*. Leicester: BPS

British Psychological Society (2014). Statement on Promoting Excellence in Psychology. Retrieved from: www.bps.org.uk.

British Psychological Society Guidelines for working in partnership with Community Organisations. Thompson, K., Tribe, R., & Zlowitz, S. (eds) (2018). Community Psychology Section. Leicester: BPS https://www.bps.org.uk/sites/bps.org.uk/files/Policy%20-%20 Files/Guidelines%20for%20psychologists%20on%20working%20with%20community% 20organisations%20%282018%29.pdf

British Psychological Society statement on Appropriate treatment and care of unaccompanied minors in Calais (2016). Retrieved from: https://beta.bps.org.uk/news-and-policy/ appropiate-treatment-and-care-unaccompanied-minors-calais

Careif (2016). Global Position Statement: Mental Health, Human Rights and Human Dignity, 'Magna Carta for people living with Mental Illness'. Retrieved from: http:// careif.org

Chakraborty, A. & McKenzie, K. (2002). Does racial discrimination cause mental illness? *British Journal of Psychiatry*, *180*(6), 475–477.

Chung, R. C-Y. & Bemak, F. P. (2012). *Social justice counseling: The next steps beyond multiculturalism*. London: Sage.

Cockersill, P. (2017). Social Exclusion and Anti-Discriminatory Practice: The Case of Older Homeless People in P. Lane & R. Tribe (2017) *Anti-discriminatory practice in mental health for older people*. London: Jessica Kingsley Publishers.

Crenshaw, K. (1989). *Demarginalizing the Intersection of Race and Sex: A Black Feminist Critique of Antidiscrimination Doctrine, Feminist Theory and Anti-racist Politics*. University of Chicago Legal Forum, *14*, 538–544.

Cutts, L. (2013). Considering a social justice agenda for counselling psychology in the United Kingdom. *Counselling Psychology Review*, *28*, 8–16.

Cutts, L. & Hanley, T. (2014). *Counselling Psychology and Social Justice: is there a rhetoric-action Gap?* Counselling Psychology Conference, London.

Dykstra, W. (2014) Liberation psychology - a history for the future. *The Psychologist*, *27*(11), 888–891.

Fernando, S. (2014). *Mental health worldwide; Culture, globalization and development*: Basingstoke: Palgrave-Macmillan.

Fox, D. and Prilleltensky, I. (1996). The inescapable nature of politics in psychology: A response to O'Donohue and Dyslin, *New Ideas in Psychology*, *14*(1), 21–26.

Goodman, L. A., Liang, B., Helms, J. E. Latta, R. E., Sparks, E. & Weintraub, S. R. (2004). Training counseling psychologists as social justice agents: Feminist and multicultural principles in action. *The Counseling Psychologist*, *32*(6), 793–837.

Herek, G. M (1990). The Context of Anti-Gay Violence Notes on Cultural and Psychological Heterosexism. *Journal Interpersonal Violence* 5(3), 316–333.

James, O. (2007). *Affluenza: How to Be Successful and Stay Sane*. London: Vermillion.

Kagan, C., Burton, M., Duckett, P., Lawthorn, R. & Siddiquee, A. (2011). *Critical community psychology*. West Sussex: BPS Blackwell.

Kagan, C. Tindall, C. & Robinson, J. (2010). Community psychology: Linking the Individual with the Community in Woolfe, R., Strawbridge, S., Douglas, B., Dryden. W. *Handbook of Counselling Psychology*. London: Sage.

King, M. et al. (2008). A systematic review of mental disorder, suicide, and deliberate self-harming in lesbian, gay and bisexual people. *BMC Psychiatry*, *8*(1), 1–17.

Kirmayer, L. J., & Bhugra, D. (2009) Culture and Mental Illness: Social Context and Explanatory Models. In I.M. Salloum & J. E. Mezzich (eds), *Psychiatric Diagnosis: Patterns and Prospects* (pp. 29–37). New York: John Wiley & Sons.

Lago, C. (ed) (2011). *The Handbook of Transcultural Counselling and Psychotherapy*: Milton Keynes: Open University Press.

Lane, P. & Tribe, R. (2010). Following NICE 2008: A practical guide for health professionals: Community engagement with local black and minority ethnic (BME) community groups. *Diversity, Health & Care*, *7*(2), 105–14.

Lane, P., Tribe, R., & Hui, R. (2010). Intersectionality and the Mental Health of Elderly Chinese Women Living in the UK. *International Journal of Migration, Health and Social Care*, *6*(4), 34–41.

London Community Psychology Network (2017). *Guidance on Working with Community Organisations for Psychologists*. Retrieved from: https://www.bps.org.uk/news-and-policy/guidance-psychologists-working-community-organisations

Maguen, S., & Shipherd, J. (2010). Suicide risk amongst transgender individuals. *Psychology and Sexuality*, *1*, 34–43.

Marsella, A. (2011). Twelve Critical Issues for Mental Health Professionals Working with Ethno-culturally Diverse Populations. *Psychology International*. Retrieved from www.apa. org/international/pi/2011/10/critical-issues.aspx

Martin-Baro, I. (1994). *Writings for a Liberation Psychology*. Cambridge, MA: Harvard University Press.

McCoy, L. & Winter, L. (2015) *Children and families in context: The psychological implications of the 'Bedroom tax' in the UK*. In 46th Annual meeting of the Society for Psychotherapy Research. Retrieved from: https://www.research.manchester.ac.uk/ portal/en/publications/education-poverty-and-psychological-wellbeing-the-impacts-of-the-bedroom-tax-on-children-and-their-families(f622815d-cb25-482e-98c2-0fdb687047a3).html

McKenzie, K. (2003). Anti-racism is an important health issue, *BMJ*, 326:65.

Miller, K.R & Rasco, L. (2004) *The Mental Health of Refugees: Ecological approaches to Healing and Adaption*. New York: Lawrence Earlbaum.

Miller, D. (2003). *Principles of Social Justice*. Massachusetts: Harvard University Press.

Murali, V., & Oyebode, F. (2004) Poverty, social Inequality and mental health. *Advances in Psychiatric Treatment*, *10*, 216–224.

National Institute for Health and Clinical Excellence (2016). Community engagement: improving health and wellbeing and reducing health inequalities. Retrieved from: www. nice.org.uk/guidance/ng44

Orford, J. (2014) A publicly engaged academic. *The Psychologist*, *27*, 11, 872–873.

Patel, N. (2014). Private communication.

Piketty, T. (2014). *Capital in the 21st century*. Massachusetts: Harvard University Press.

Prilleltensky, I. & Nelson, G. (1997). Community psychology: Reclaiming social justice. In D. Fox & I. Prilleltensky (Eds.), *Critical psychology: An introduction* (pp. 166–184). London: Sage.

Psychologists Against Austerity (2017). Retrieved from: https://psychagainstausterity. wordpress.com

Ratts, M. J. (2009). Social Justice Counseling: Toward the Development of a Fifth Force Among Counseling Paradigms. *Journal of Humanistic Counseling*, *48*(2), 160–172.

Rawls, J. (1999). (Revised Edn). *A Theory of Justice*. Massachusetts: Harvard University Press.

Royal Society of Arts (2017). Retrieved from: www.thersa.org

Saraceno, B., & Barbui, C. (1997). Poverty and Mental Illness. *Canadian Journal of Psychiatry*, *42*, 285–290.

Singh, A. A., Hofsess, C. D., Boyer, E. M., Kwong, A., Lau, A. S. M., McLain, M. & Haggins, K. L. (2010). Social Justice and Counselling Psychology: Listening to the Voices of Doctoral Trainees. *The Counselling Psychologist*, *38*(6), 766–795.

Summerfield, D. (2012) Afterword - Against global mental health. *Transcultural Psychiatry* *49*(3), 1–12.

Tribe, R. (2014). Culture, Politics and Global Mental Health. *Disability and the Global South*, *1*(2), pp. 251–265.

Tribe, R. & Melluish, S. (2014). Special Edition of the International Review of Psychiatry, *Globalisation, Culture and Mental Health*, *25*(2).

Tribe, R. & Tunariu, A. (2018). Psychological Interventions and Assessments in Bhugra, D. & Bhui, K. *The Textbook of Cultural Psychiatry*. Cambridge: Cambridge University Press.

Wilkinson, R. & Pickett, K. (2009). *The Spirit Level: Why More Equal Societies almost always do Better for Everyone*. London: Penguin.

Winter, L. & Hanley, T. (2015). 'Unless everyone's covert guerrilla-like social justice practitioners…': A preliminary study exploring social justice in UK counselling psychology. *Counselling Psychology Review, 30*(2), 32–46.

World Psychiatric Association (2016). *Bill of Rights for Children and Young people with Mental Illness*. [online] Retrieved from: www.wpanet.org

Chapter 6

Ethics and social justice

Tony Wainwright, Lyndsey Moon,
Neha Cattra (née Malhotra),
Tasim Martin-Berg and Simon Toms

Introduction

The world is facing unprecedented challenges including climate change, resource depletion, biodiversity loss and conflict, and the scale of displaced people is growing year on year (Internal Displacement Monitoring Centre, 2017). The pressures that these challenges present are associated with social justice in many ways. Climate change, for example, is already affecting the poorest and most vulnerable people (United Nations, 2015). In Britain, we are not immune to these challenges and it is becoming evident how the effects of the global financial crash, and the austerity that followed it, have been exacerbated by our own unequal society—for example, variations in mortality rates between the north and south of the UK (Buchan, Kontopantelis, Sperrin, Chandola, & Doran, 2017; Wilkinson & Pickett, 2010).

For psychologists, this means that we need to rise to the challenge of addressing issues surrounding social justice—for example, the long-term impacts of child adversity and the continuing impact of discrimination on the basis of identity (such as gender identity and ethnicity). Our knowledge and skills need to be brought to bear in as many ways as possible to prevent or mitigate the worst effects. We hope this paper will go some way to suggesting how we might take forward the goals identified in the British logical Society. (2017). Declaration on Equality, Diversity and Inclusion.

Social justice movements in psychology have gained increasing support over recent years, striving for better recognition of issues related to equality, diversity and inclusion. Within the field of applied psychology in the UK, social justice work can be understood as a scholarly and practical endeavour that emphasises societal concerns, including issues of equity, self-determination, interdependence, and social responsibility, with the goal of decreasing human suffering and inequality. The historical tendency for Western psychology to view people as independent entities with mental health or illness being located and defined within the individual has been challenged by critical, feminist, and community psychologists who argue, and evidence the need to understand human distress by taking into account our social, cultural, and political contexts (Kagan, Burton, Duckett, Lawthorne & Sidiquee, 2011).

Inclusion and exclusion

Part of the social justice agenda requires that we recognize how we exclude and include 'others' in our work. This involves thinking about the way we appraise individuals and groups, how responses to their needs are shaped, and how power is negotiated. Recognizing that power is maintained not only through coercion but through voluntary consent of the very people we recognize as oppressed (Bell, 2007) is essential to fully understand inclusion and exclusion. It is also important that practitioner psychologists are cognizant, socially and in terms of their own practice, of how they are working with clients or with colleagues from marginalised groups and that they are conscious of the contexts which may present as being open to minority groups yet be limited in provision of facilities or understanding. For example, assuming that all clients can read or write can lead to those with limitations in these areas experiencing exclusion, even though the psychologist may be working at including the client in the service. Power in this respect is not always easy to recognise since it is not always top down. As Bell (2007) suggests, power is relational and constantly moving within and through relationships. Therefore, constant vigilance is required, including being reflexive and reflective about the roles we take on because how we shape them to reflect a social justice agenda needs to be at the heart of our thinking and feeling.

Research is central to ensuring that a social justice agenda meets the needs of diverse populations. Assuming that collecting evidence allows us to 'include' because the research reflects 'all people' will only prove correct if we thoroughly consider how research has been conducted and how the research protocols have been established. For example, when thinking about the research question, how has diversity been considered? How is the researcher thinking through issues of intersectionality where multiple characteristics (race, ethnicity, age, gender, sexuality, class, disability, mental health) are understood as important intersecting levels of identity that must be assessed as part of non-oppressive research? Coming to terms with these issues raises recognition and, by raising recognition, we improve understanding of the growing needs of diverse communities. Taylor (1994) highlights the importance of recognition as a social justice imperative. Nonrecognition and misrecognition are, he suggests, forms of oppression that damage and distort how identity is shaped. For example, when working with clients do we recognize 'otherness' or do we fail to 'see' what the client is bringing into session. This leads to research agendas that need to become more fully inclusive in order that they shift theory and practice for future generations of psychologists who will represent these diverse communities, thereby enriching psychological resources and building a more psychologically healthy population.

Turning words into actions: The declaration

The British Psychological Society has recently published a Declaration on Equality, Diversity and Inclusion (2017), which declares a commitment to actively promote an inclusive culture, and to challenge prejudice and discrimination. The Society is a membership organization, which is also a professional body, an education and training body, and a charity, which exists for the public benefit. Thus, to an extent, it is a policy-lobbying body alongside being an employer, and the actions to make the declaration a reality for everyone who interacts with the Society will inevitably be multi-layered.

The Declaration recognizes the need for this multi-layered approach across the stakeholder interests referred to above. For our members, there is a commitment to improved member engagement, which includes focus groups, member surveys (with individual follow-up discussions), and a dedicated Standards and Inclusivity Officer and Project Officer: Structural Review. For the wider public with whom the Society engages, part of the commitment is communicating the psychological knowledge base and evidence related to equality, diversity, and inclusion. For the Society as a professional and educational body, the Declaration will influence policies and processes. As an employer, the Society will place it at the heart of the staff experience.

The Declaration also connects with our role as European and International citizens as we engage with psychological societies on matters of common interest. The international agenda encourages psychologists everywhere to connect with the United Nations (2015) Sustainable Development Goals, which are underpinned by a vision, as it relates to people, of 'universal respect for human rights and human dignity, the rule of law, justice, equality and non-discrimination; of respect for race, ethnicity and cultural diversity; and of equal opportunity permitting the full realization of human potential and contributing to shared prosperity' (p. 4).

It is also important to consider whether the Society knows what stakeholders want and need. The first step is to establish appropriate baselines, from which to fulfil the commitment to measure, assess, and reflect on progress. The next step is to develop specific actions. These will relate to the areas of focus within the Declaration and, in terms of fulfilling its underpinning commitment to culture change, they need also to address the way in which the actions are then carried out.

The gathering of information is one area of consideration, but availability, accuracy, transparency, and openness are indispensable for effective and lasting culture change to occur. Structures and processes are needed to underpin the Declaration. This needs to be seen more broadly in the context of how the Society is organized to deliver its aims. Part of a commitment to equality, diversity, and inclusion is about how the Society is run, which is reflected in our efforts to achieve an overall shift in the focus and balance of our governance. A new Senate, which will launch at the General Assembly in 2018, is designed to foster engagement across the membership, draw on the positive ethics of debate, freedom of opinion, and general and equally representative voting based on fairness, compromise, and equal consideration of all options and different points of view. Proposed reforms to the Board of Trustees, including bringing in non-psychology expertise, will offer the opportunity for broadening the perspectives which input into decision making whilst proposed changes to the structure of member networks will help foster parity of esteem and enhance representation in governance structures.

What might Society procedures look and feel like in response to the Declaration? Their main features might include openness and accessibility, removal of barriers, and fostering an environment in which people feel respected rather than undermined, and where problems will be put right. In order to achieve these goals, the Society will need to provide sufficient resources and to support the members in their work, for example, with dissemination of research and good practice, guidance, conferences, and professional development events, and also support them as their professional body in their work and professional endeavours.

Finally, the Declaration commits to evaluation. This should not just be in terms of measures against targets. As psychologists, Society members are familiar with the concept of reflective practice, and it will be crucial that they are consistently open-minded and proactive in building on success, and that they thoughtfully consider where further engagement and effort are needed.

Ethics and social justice in the Ethics Committee and Code

The question of how social justice concerns should be linked with codes of professional ethics has engaged the BPS Ethics Committee and others over the years (Winter, 2015). How should the Code be written so that it incorporates the necessary principles to guide psychology practice, without covering areas that are beyond its scope? The recent revision of the Code of Ethics (BPS, 2018) continues with the four principles *respect, competence, responsibility, and integrity*, and during the revision process the Committee debated how it could frame the Code so that it did not just focus on individual one-to-one psychological treatments but had a wider frame.

The principle of respect was the one in which ideas that provided this wider frame were incorporated. In the introductory section, the draft

Code refers to 'Respect for the dignity of persons and peoples'. It goes on to say:

> Respect for the dignity of persons and peoples is one of the most fundamental and universal ethical principles across geographical and cultural boundaries, and across professional disciplines. It provides the philosophical foundation for many of the other ethical Principles. Respect for dignity recognizes the inherent worth of all human beings, regardless of perceived or real differences in social status, ethnic origin, gender, capacities, or any other such group-based characteristics. This inherent worth means that all human beings are worthy of equal moral consideration (p. 5).

In the subsequent section, it also refers to how this principle should be applied, namely, consideration should be given to communities and shared values within them, issues of power, and also self-determination.

Using this approach, the Committee hoped to provide a broader reach for the Code to inform practice. However, this does not cover social justice, which leaves the question of how social justice can be related to ethics.

Janel Gauthier has written about some of these issues as part of the work undertaken in developing the Universal Declaration of Ethical Principles for Psychologists (Gauthier &Pettifor, 2012). In a personal communication, he says:

> Ethics codes in psychology pay little attention to social justice, which is in contrast with codes of ethics in some other disciplines (e.g., social work). When working on the development of the Universal Declaration of Ethical Principles for Psychologists (UDEPP), I found that some regions of the world were willing to embrace the concept of social justice whereas it was the opposite in other regions. Given the lack of consensus, it was not possible to include it in the UDEPP. The UDEPP describes ethical principles that are based on shared human values across cultures. Research and broad consultation demonstrated that social justice did not enjoy support worldwide enough to qualify as a 'shared human value across cultures'.
>
> Gauthier, 2017

Nevertheless, the BPS report on social justice noted that the Society is increasingly focused on this area. So how do we put these two issues together? Alfred Allan (2013) discusses whether human rights are needed in codes of ethics, and as social justice might be seen as a subset of human rights, this is very pertinent to this debate. In his view,

> (...) the profession should acknowledge human rights as a separate and complimentary norm system that governs the behaviour of psychologists and should ensure that they have adequate knowledge of human rights and encourage them to promote human rights. (p. 251)

This is the approach that the Ethics Committee has taken and, as well as the report on Social Justice, work that Tony Wainwright has undertaken with the European Federation of Psychologists' Associations' (EFPA) Board of Human Rights and Psychology (see EFPA, 2017a and 2017b) on behalf of the Society has addressed these issues. One particular area is the development of a curriculum and related teaching materials for psychologists (for example, a textbook is in preparation) so that they are more familiar with human rights issues and how they are applied in psychology, but also materials for human rights workers on the psychological insights that can inform human rights practice (EFPA, 2017a and 2017 b).

Social justice, equality, diversity and inclusion within the BPS member networks

In June 2014, at the instigation of the British Psychological Society Board of Trustees, a 'Social Justice, Equality, Diversity and Inclusion Task Force' was jointly created by the Membership and Standards Board and Ethics Committee with the remit of promoting social justice and inclusion and enhancing communication and influence within the organization. Given that the Society's five-year Strategic Plan (2015–2020) explicitly states that social justice, inclusivity, and diversity are integral to the work of its members, it was understood that many relevant activities and practices existed within the BPS. However, in order to develop a formal baseline assessment and a 'central hub' of information about current social justice work within the Society, an audit of Member Networks was carried out between November 2015 and March 2016 (Malhotra, Martin-Berg, & Toms, 2017).

The audit provides evidence that most member networks apply overarching BPS policy and values to various 'network-specific' aims and activities relating to social justice, inclusivity, and diversity, although some report no social justice work specifically. Motivation to engage in social justice work comes from professional values, principles and purpose, and a desire to address and improve knowledge, participation, and awareness. Obstacles exist, such as limited time and resources, BPS bureaucracy, a lack of member or societal awareness, and differences in priorities. Overall, Member Networks saw their social justice work as necessary, integral, and successful, believing it is something to continue building upon.

As reported in *The Psychologist* (April 2017, p. 15):

> This audit provides clear and up-to-date evidence of social justice work within the Society as well as examples of good practice. At the same time the audit confirms the absence of work and explicit policies in this area for certain Member Networks, which is just as valid to acknowledge. There is a great deal to celebrate and build on, and there is a clear basis for change within the Society.

The results of the audit suggest a need for broader, explicit policies relating to social justice, equality, diversity, and inclusion to achieve overall coherence within the organization and its Member Networks. As such, the Social Justice, Equality, Diversity, and Inclusion Task Force continues to promote the social justice agenda within the BPS, including the development of a Standards and Inclusivity Officer position. This role will include policy development, addressing obstacles identified by Member Networks, a focus on training issues relating to diversity and inclusion, and supporting good practice and the pooling of resources for example. Within the BPS, there is also recognition of the need for on-going critical self-examination, given that our own membership is made up of diverse groups with distinct and evolving identities, each with varying frames of reference, representation, and access to power and resources. The mandate to further social justice work is clearly outlined and explicitly reflected in the values, objectives, and operational principles of the Society's Strategic Plan 2015–2020.

Social justice includes not only a moral and ethical imperative for us as psychologists to critically consider the social justice issues related to our profession, but also a practical necessity. We should not be passive bystanders, but active agents who challenge social injustice in all its forms, actively reaching out to those who are experiencing oppression, sharing power, loudly voicing our common humanity, and taking shared responsibility for human rights.

Conclusion: The way forward

What steps do we take to make our Declaration a reality? A recent report from our sister organization in the United States, the American Psychological Association (APA), offers some useful pointers. Following the wide-ranging review that was prompted by the 'enhanced interrogation' programme (APA, 2015), the Association undertook an audit of the organization and its orientation to social justice. In the report, it has made a series of recommendations that focus on how a psychology association can enhance its impact as an agent of social justice in the contemporary world. The first recommendation states 'that the APA [should] revise the APA mission and vision statements and articulate a core set of organizational ethical principles and standards' (APA, 2017; p. 4). The Association proposes that these principles should then inform all aspects of the organization's work.

Since social justice is a key part of the British Psychological Society's vision and, as indicated above, the Society is already undergoing a major transition, the time feels right for this aim to be realized and for the next steps to be taken to effectively address present issues. Having gathered and analysed data on its membership base, the Society will be able to determine how diverse its membership is and establish a baseline for further action. The next stage involves putting in place clear specific plans to ensure that where gaps in and barriers to fair and equal representation have been identified, existing policies are changed, and tools developed which will help bridge the gaps and remove barriers. Simultaneously, adequate and equitable distribution of available resources will be necessary in order to fulfil the Society's pledge, and responsibility, to challenge social injustice in all its manifestations and in all settings.

References

Allan, A. (2013). Are human rights redundant in the ethical codes of psychologists? *Ethics & Behavior, 23*(4), 251–265. doi:10.1080/10508422.2013.776480

American Psychological Association (2015). *Report to the special committee of the board of directors of the American Psychological Association: Independent review relating to APA ethics guidelines, national security interrogations, and torture.* Available at http://www.apa.org/independent-review/revised-report.pdf

American Psychological Association (2017). *Report to APA Board of Directors & Council of Representatives.* Available at http://www.apa.org/ethics/ethics-processes-report.pdf

Bell, L. A. (2007). Theoretical foundations for social justice education. In M. Adams, L. A. Bell & P. Griffin (Eds), *Teaching for Diversity and Social Justice.* London: Routledge.

British Psychological Society (2017). *Declaration on Equality, Diversity and Inclusion.* Leicester: BPS. Available at http://beta.bps.org.uk/news-and-policy/bps-publishes-declaration-equality-diversity-and-inclusion

British Psychological Society (2018). *Code of ethics and conduct.* Leicester: BPS.

Buchan, I. E., Kontopantelis, E., Sperrin, M., Chandola, T., & Doran, T. (2017). North-South disparities in English mortality 1965–2015: Longitudinal population study. *Journal of Epidemiology & Community Health, 71*(9), 928–936. doi:10.1136/jech-2017-209195

European Federation of Psychologists' Association (2017a). *EFPA's role regarding 'Human Rights'.* Available at http://human-rights.efpa.eu

European Federation of Psychologists' Association (2017b). *Expert meeting human rights education for psychologists.* Available at http://www.humanrightsforpsychologists.eu

Gauthier, J. (2017). [Comparing UDHR and UDEPP - Personal Communication].

Gauthier, J., & Pettifor, J. L. (2012). The tale of two universal declarations: Ethics and human rights. In M. Leach, J. M. Stevens, G. Lindsay, A. Ferrero, & Y. Korkut (Eds.), *The Oxford handbook of international psychological ethics.* New York: Oxford University Press.

Internal Displacement Monitoring Centre (2017). *Global report on internal displacement.* Available at http://www.internal-displacement.org/global-report/grid2017/

Kagan, C., Burton, M., Duckett, P., Lawthorn, R. & Siddiquee, A. (2011). *Critical community psychology.* West Sussex: BPS Blackwell.

Malhotra, N., Martin-Berg, T. & Toms, T. (2017). *A report into the social justice, equality, diversity and inclusion audit of the British Psychological Society.* Leicester: BPS.

Malhotra, N., Martin-Berg, T. & Toms, T. (2017). Clear basis for Change on Social Justice. *The Psychologist.* April 2017, p. 15.

Taylor, C. (1994). The Politics of Recognition. In A. Gutmann *Multiculturalism: Examining the Politics of Recognition (pp. 25–73).* Princeton: Princeton University Press.

United Nations (2015). *Transforming our world: The 2030 agenda for sustainable development.* Available at http://www.un.org/sustainabledevelopment/sustainable-development-goals/

Wilkinson, R. & Pickett, K. (2010). *The Spirit Level: Why Equality is Better for Everyone.* New York: Bloomsbury Press.

Winter, L. A. (2015). The Presence of Social Justice Principles Within Professional and Ethical Guidelines in International Psychology. *Psychotherapy and Politics International,* *13*(1), 55–66. doi:10.1002/ppi.1346

Part II

Developing your leadership style

Chapter 7

Power and privilege in psychology: Can we have egalitarian leadership?

Laura Anne Winter

Introduction

When presented with the overarching theme of this collection, 'Leadership and Diversity', I began to reflect upon how we might understand 'leadership' and 'diversity' both separately and when combined. *Diversity*, viewed through a social justice lens which emphasises the importance of equality and the balancing of power structures (Cutts, 2013; Toporek, Gerstein, Fouad, Roysircar & Israel, 2006), is understood as referring not simply to differences and variations between individuals or groups of individuals, but about power imbalances, privilege and oppression (Proctor, 2011; Winter, Guo, Wilk & Hanley, 2016). *Leadership*, to my mind, is commonly understood to involve both leaders and followers: leaders who occupy a special, designated position or role in a group or have a guiding role in a group or society, and followers, whose position or behaviour is to some extent directed by the leader. There therefore exists a social structure or hierarchy inherent to leadership. One person (the leader) holds a degree of power or privilege, and the follower is subject to, and behaves in relation to, that power.

Situated within the social justice perspective noted above, in this article I suggest that there may be some potential issues with ideas of leadership and diversity in psychology when considered from the view that diversity is about power, privilege and equality. To be clear from the outset: I take as my starting point that equality is something to be prized and inequality is problematic. Social inequality and discrimination are negatively associated with health and wellbeing (Allen, Balfour, Bell & Marmot, 2014) and therefore to my mind they are extremely important issues of consideration for psychologists (and indeed, for all members of society!). To mitigate some of the potential problems that I suggest are issues with leadership from such an equality perspective, I suggest that psychologists might usefully consider 'relational equality', understood as treating others as moral equals, as a frame to guide their interventions and communications in leadership (and beyond).

Within this chapter my aim is to provoke and stimulate thinking about equality, power and privilege issues in relation to leadership in psychology.

Unapologetically, in a potentially frustrating move, rather than providing any concrete answers or ways forward, I aim to bring to the surface some potential issues or problems which exist and often go without mention in my opinion. I don't expect that all readers will agree with me that the issues I see are indeed issues or problematic, nor with my tentative ideas about ways forward. Nonetheless, my hope is that whatever perspective you come from, and whether you agree or disagree with my musings, this contribution stimulates deeper thinking about some commonly held ideas and ways of working in psychology and society more broadly.

Diversity, social justice and the importance of equality

We might think of diversity simply as being about differences in society; for example, Johnny has brown hair whereas Steven has blonde hair, or Rachel is from Wales whereas Eda is from Croatia. Nevertheless, diversity is necessarily tied up with power in society, and those who are 'different' or 'diverse' are defined in relation to the majority or what is considered to be the social norm (Lago, 2011). Taking the lead from authors such as Proctor (2011), I suggest that 'diversity' as a term can often confound and obscure the stark reality of inequalities in our society, and focus our attention simply on what is different about particular groups and individuals. For example, when thinking of sexuality in terms of 'diversity' it might be easy for people to simply think about differences between varying sexualities and understandings, rather than thinking about sexuality in terms of power, privilege and oppression. I suggest it is important to ground our understanding of diversity within the wider social justice agenda in psychology (Toporek et al., 2006; Winter & Hanley, 2015). Social justice is understood as follows:

> [Social justice is] both a goal of action and the process of action itself, which involves an emphasis on equity or equality for individuals in society in terms of access to a number of different resources and opportunities, the right to self-determination or autonomy and participation in decision-making, freedom from oppression, and a balancing of power in society.
>
> (Cutts, 2013, pp. 9–10)

Within this broader movement, diversity and difference cannot and should not be divorced from power and privilege (Winter et al., 2016). This is because when we talk about diversity we are always talking about an inequality of some type: there are many individual differences we don't talk about in terms of diversity in society, for example, that Rob has green eyes whereas Jack has brown eyes. Instead we talk about differences such as race, ethnicity, sexuality and social class in terms of diversity: all of these relate back to power differentials and inequality. In this section of the article I will briefly explore these further, before moving on to link these reflections with the topic of leadership in the final section of the article.

David Smail defined power as *"the means of obtaining security or advantage"* and argued that power is the "medium of our social existence, the dynamic which moves the apparatus of our relations with each other" (Smail, 1995, p. 348).

In terms of diversity, power is important because of the imbalance of one's ability to advance, progress or exert an influence (on processes or people) between different groups of society. An individual from a working-class background in urban Manchester may be described as having less power than someone from a middle class background in a wealthy area of London such as Kensington, for example, because they are typically less able to have their voice heard and exert an influence on processes and people around them, and are more likely to struggle to obtain security in terms of things like housing or finances. They are more likely to have decisions made for them by those with more power, influence and ability to exert that power. This may be interlinked with a range of factors such as access to education or secure housing, or it may simply relate to the financial ability to access particular areas. Typical categories of diversity such as gender, race, sexuality, class, religion, all intersect here, as someone is not just working class or middle class, they are both working class, female and atheist, or middle class, homosexual and Muslim, and this intersectionality will also play a role in determining power structures and relations in our society.

As well as this, different types of power may be enacted in relationships: *role power* relates to the influence one has by virtue of the position they occupy; *historical power* relates to that which relates to an individual's personal history of power and powerlessness, and *societal power* to the influence one has with respect to their position in society's social hierarchies (Proctor, 2017). Privilege refers to advantages for individuals on the basis on membership of a dominant group of society rather than earned (Israel, 2012). For example, in the case where someone is able to train as a counselling psychologist by virtue of their class and wealth, rather than because of their ability, knowledge or skills, then they would be said to be privileged (I realise this isn't the case for a whole range of counselling psychology trainees, but use this simply as an example as a *possible* case of privilege).

For me, equality underpins both power and privilege, and we cannot usefully reflect on diversity without reference to equality. Equality is usually thought about as the equal distribution of wealth or income, but we can also think about it in terms of social relations, where equality means treating others as moral equals. In this case, a society has greater relational equality when different individuals or groups of individuals are accorded the same status and treatment as others (Anderson, 1999; Mangan & Winter, 2016; Winter, 2017). These two understandings of equality are interrelated, and may well coincide such that the greater distributive equality you have the greater relational equality you have and vice versa. But they are distinct and may not always coincide entirely (Fraser, 2001). For example, it is likely that if you have greater equality in terms of status in a society you are more likely to also have a system where people are allocated more equal resources; and in a society where money and other resources are unequally distributed, it is likely that people will be treated differently and relate to each other unequally. Nevertheless, this is not evident or certain.

As psychologists, when we talk about power I think we are talking about issues of equality: the types of power differentials and imbalances manifesting in relationships described by Proctor (2017) and seen in the example of class can be at their root, thought of as *unequal status distributions*. Similarly, privilege, in relating to advantages in society (for example, in terms of special rights), boils down to unequal relations between individuals and groups of individuals whereby some are worthy of access to such special rights and some are not, and an unequal distribution for example of access to things like goods and services and other resources. So, when we talk about diversity, power and privilege I think we are commonly talking about equality in society and importantly, within relationships.

Leadership and (in)equality

Building on from this, when we begin to examine the idea of diversity and leadership within this broader context of (in)equality in distributions, systems and relationships, potentially complex issues emerge. Specifically, if leadership entails a hierarchy within a social system and differential power relations, how can leadership in psychology be egalitarian? Commonly we discuss the issue of representation and diversity in leadership, and whether or not our leaders and those in power represent our society more broadly, or whether instead they come from already powerful groups, marginalising those historically or currently oppressed even further.

For example, we reflect upon issues of privilege, and the unequal distribution of advantages in society. Do we have enough leaders from working-class backgrounds, or representation of enough women in powerful positions in society, or are enough young people from Black and Minority Ethnic cultures getting into leadership roles? For example, we might talk about barriers such as discrimination and prejudice (external and internalised), access to opportunities and resources, or structural issues around how we set up our society. But, if we think about equality as being a central concept underpinning diversity, I wonder whether the potential issues with leadership are even more complex than this (and therefore I won't spend much time here reflecting on those barriers, though they are of course fundamentally important to consider). Even if we take out of the equation the issues connected to the inequality in the relationship by virtue that one person is heterosexual and one is bisexual, or that one person comes from a migrant background and the other is a 'local', or finally that one person is male and the other female, and the various historical and current inequalities and privileges being members of those particular groups in our society bestows, there still exists issues of *role power* within systems of leadership. A leader in a work setting (commonly) has the power to hire people, to fire people, to discipline people, to get their own voice (or whoever else's voice they decide) heard, and influence processes and procedures. They will more than likely have access to a higher level of resources and greater pay and opportunities for development. A 'follower' by contrast has no such powers, and typically access to fewer resources (sometimes including financial resources, time and other benefits) and opportunities. There is therefore an inequality which exists in any relationship between leader and follow, before we even get to the historical or social elements of power at play.

Case example 1: Leadership and social hierarchies

Rose has just started her new job as a newly qualified Practitioner Psychologist in a local Improving Access to Psychological Therapies (IAPT) service, after recently completing her doctoral training. During her first week she met several of her new colleagues. She had a meeting with Rebecca, the service director who was also her line manager and who would have responsibility for providing her with managerial supervision. Regularly, Rebecca engages in performance management processes in the service and should any issues arise, has the authority to initiate disciplinary procedures in appropriate circumstances. She monitors the activity of all staff on a monthly basis, looking at how many client contacts they have per week, the clinical outcomes of their work, and how long they are seeing clients for, among other things. She also met Sarah, who works as a trainee High Intensity Cognitive Behavioural Therapist in the service. Rose will be Sarah's clinical supervisor. Sarah has worked in the service for two years on fixed-term contracts in different roles. She doesn't yet know whether she will secure another contract once she has qualified. Rose will be responsible signing off and approving all of Sarah's work in the service to confirm whether or not she passes elements of her training.

In this case example I have purposely not referred to inequalities in relation to one another by virtue of membership of particular groups of society, and yet we can see that inequality of status (role power) remains as a result of the social and relational structures of the service, and these relate specifically to leadership structures. Rebecca, Rose and Sarah all have different degrees of power in the service, and in relation to each other, because of the positions they occupy. Rebecca has a greater amount of power and say in the service in virtue of her management position, and Sarah has very little as well as less security. Simply put, leadership necessarily involves social hierarchies, which adds a layer of inequality beyond issues of power which we might typically think of when we consider diversity in leadership simply in terms of representation of different groups of society.

One response to my musings about the problems with leadership might be to question 'What about good leaders, for example, leaders of social movements and change for good?' However, I do wonder whether even in the case of individuals who could be described as leaders of social movements such as Gandhi or Martin Luther King, Jr. (or perhaps a modern-day example, Jeremy Corbyn), there exist inequalities, commonly both relational and distributive. They exert greater influence and are more likely (than some at least) to advance their goals by virtue of their status. Most certainly those leaders of social movements who come from disadvantaged backgrounds or have been oppressed are not at the top of the social pyramid—but there still exists inequality in my mind by virtue of them 'leading' people. Then we are left with questions about how much leadership is required or needed, and how much it is worth sacrificing some equality to reap the benefits of having leaders. That however is something I won't stray into too much now as I turn to whether or not in a structure of leaders and followers, we can do anything to enhance or improve the level of equality.

Can we enhance equality in leadership?

We have seen so far that diversity is underpinned by understandings of power, privilege and equality, and that, given the negative impacts of inequality and the implication that we cannot remove the problematic role power inherent within systems of leadership, we are left with dilemmas about how to proceed with regards to diversity and leadership. Rather than making an argument that we should abandon leadership entirely, as noted at the outset of this article, my aim in this article has been to simply raise these questions and stimulate thought for those in psychology who care about equality. I do however have some tentative suggestions of ideas we might draw upon when thinking about trying to enhance equality in leadership. Specifically, to mitigate some of the potential problems, I suggest that psychologists might usefully consider ideas of relational equality, understood as treating others as moral equals, as a frame to guide their interventions and communications in leadership (and beyond).

So far I have mostly reflected on relationships in terms of inequality— but how could we make a relationship between a 'leader' and a 'follower' more egalitarian? Social justice literatures often talk about 'giving voice' and 'empowerment' as practices which are unquestionably good; however, I would not be the first to point out that these are not always wholly unproblematic. Smail (1995) reflected on his wariness about the concept of empowerment and the view that power is something which can simply be switched on when one person (typically in a position of power) magically empowers the other. I also worry that there may be a paternalistic element behind such ideas. Whilst not wholly a 'bad' thing, this does not fit with truly egalitarian ideals in every circumstance, as there still exists a power differential and an inequality in the relationship.

I have suggested elsewhere that we can think of relational equality on the micro level (in interpersonal relationships), the meso level (how our families, organisations and communities structure relationships) and the macro level (how our broader society structures relationships, for example, through national policy and laws) (Winter, 2018). Given that relational equality comes back fundamentally to relationships and how individuals treat one another, I would think that as psychologists and therapists we might be able to contribute to ideas of what relational equality might look like, for example, between leaders and followers.

We have spent a great amount of time thinking and talking about, for example, the therapeutic relationship and how we might be collaborative and engage in dialogue which might result in a more democratic relationship. Practising psychologists often fall into the category of 'leaders' by virtue of their role in the therapeutic dyad, and therefore this literature seems wholly appropriate to me to stimulate thinking about creating more egalitarian leadership relationships. So perhaps we can enhance equality between leaders and followers by, for example, drawing on our understanding of the Rogerian core conditions, and as leaders try to communicate empathy, unconditional positive regard and congruence (Rogers, 1957). This is both relevant on the level of interpersonal relationships and in broader level structures: for example, as leaders we might think about how our organisations and communities are structured and whether these conditions are encouraged or not. We might also think about engaging in meta-communication and dialogue in interpersonal relationships, in order to communicate our respect for the other as our equal human being (Cooper & McLeod, 2011), and again work towards having systems which support rather than hinder these processes. Meta-communication involves communicating about our communication; for example, we might ask someone what it was like for them when we said something, or ask them to reflect on how they communicated something to us. The following case example hopefully illustrates some of my thinking on this further:

Case example 2: Working towards relational equality in leadership roles

Rose met Sarah for their first clinical supervision session. The first thing they did was talk about their hopes and expectations from their supervision sessions, as well as each of their responsibilities. Together they came up with a supervision agreement. As part of this, Rose and Sarah explored their understandings of their relationship and in particular the hierarchical and power elements in it and within the broader service. Rose encouraged an open dialogue about how they might ensure that despite the role power in the relationship, other elements were as democratic and equal as they may be. Challenges to this way of working are considered openly and explicitly (for example, Rose's requirements as a supervisor to monitor Sarah's progress in relation to performance targets). An agreement is made that although some elements of power are inherent in their relationship (e.g., role power), Rose will ensure that she communicates clearly and openly about any performance issues for example, and that Sarah is treated as an equal in all possible areas. For example, they talked about making decisions about where, when and for how long to meet collaboratively—taking into account both of their schedules, responsibilities and lives, rather than Sarah having to fit in with Rose's other appointments.

Conclusion

In this short article I have aimed to raise some questions, possible issues and tentative ideas to respond to such issues. These have all been situated within a social justice paradigm in psychology. I have suggested that if diversity is about power, privilege and equality, rather than simply difference, then the concept of leadership in psychology might encounter some problems from a diversity perspective. Specifically, given the inherent role power involved in relationships between leaders and follows, leadership will always involve inequality—even if we can tackle the historical and societal power structures tangled up in the relationships. This left us with the question of how we might respond, and how, if we are to have leaders and followers, we might work towards enhancing equality in psychology. I suggested that although we might not be able to eliminate the role power in leadership relations, we might be able to draw upon our therapeutic and psychological literatures, for example, those which focus on humanistic psychology and relationships, meta-communication, collaboration and dialogue, to guide our communication within leadership structures and improve relational equality.

References

Allen, J., Balfour, R., Bell, R. & Marmot, M. (2014). Social determinants of mental health. *International Review of Psychiatry*, 26(4), 392–407.

Anderson, E. S. (1999). What is the point of equality? *Ethics*, 109(2), 287–337, DOI:10.1086/ 233897

Cooper, M. & McLeod, J. (2011). *Pluralistic Counselling and Psychotherapy*. London: Sage.

Cutts, L. A. (2013). Considering a Social Justice Agenda for Counselling Psychology in the United Kingdom. *Counselling Psychology Review*, 28(2), 8–16.

Fraser, N. (2001). Recognition without ethics? *Theory, Culture & Society, 18*(2-3), 21–42. Retrieved http://www.cridaq.uqam.ca/IMG/pdf/Fraser-1st_lecture_1_Seymour.pdf

Israel, T. (2012). 2011 Society of Counseling Psychology Presidential Address. Exploring Privilege in Counseling Psychology: Shifting the lens. *The Counseling Psychologist, 40*(1), 158–180, https://doi.org/10.1177/0011000011426297

Lago, C. (2011). Diversity, oppression, and society: Implications for person-centeredtherapists. *Person-Centered & Experiential Psychotherapies, 10*(4), 235–247, http://dx.doi.org/10.1080/14779757.2011.626621

Mangan, D. & Winter, L. A. (2017). (In)validation and (mis)recognition in Higher Education: the experiences of students from refugee backgrounds. *International Journal of Lifelong Education*, DOI: 10.1080/02601370.2017.1287131

Proctor, G. (2011). Diversity: The depoliticization of inequalities. *Person-Centered & Experiential Psychotherapies, 10*(4), 231–234, http://dx.doi.org/10.1080/14779757.2011.626618

Proctor, G. (2017). *The dynamics of power in counselling and psychotherapy: Ethics, Politics and Practice.* (2nd Ed) Ross-on-Wye: PCCS Books.

Rogers, C.R. (1957). The necessary and sufficient conditions of therapeutic personality change. *Journal of Consulting Psychology, 21*(2), 95–103. DOI: 10.1037/h0045357

Smail, D. (1995). Power and the origins of unhappiness: Working with individuals. *Journal of Community & Applied Social Psychology, 5*, 347–356, DOI: 10.1002/casp.2450050506

Thompson, N. (2011). *Promoting Equality. Working with diversity and difference.* Basingstoke: Palgrave Macmillan.

Torporek, R. L., Gerstein, L. H., Fouad, N. A., Roysircar, G. & Israel, T. (Eds.). (2006). *Handbook for Social Justice in Counseling Psychology. Leadership, Vision, and Action.* Thousand Oaks, California: Sage.

Winter, L. A. (2017). *Relational equality in education: What, how and why?* Oxford Review of Education, 1–5, https://doi.org/10.1080/03054985.2017.1391761

Winter, L. A., Guo, F., Wilk, K. & Hanley, T. (2016). Difference and diversity in pluralistic therapy. In M. Cooper & W. Dryden. *The Handbook of Pluralistic Counselling and Psychotherapy.* London: Sage.

Winter, L. A. & Hanley, T. (2015) "Unless everyone's covert guerrilla-like social justice practitioners…": A preliminary study exploring social justice in UK counselling psychology. *Counselling Psychology Review, 30*(2), 32–46.

Winter, L.A. (2018). Relational equality in education: what, why and how? *Oxford Review of Education, 44*(3), 338–352, https://doi.org/10.1080/03054985.2017.1391761

Disability and identity: Reflections on my journey as a disabled woman, student and counselling psychologist

Sarah Supple

Introduction

This article evolved through dialogue with colleagues regarding how it is to be a psychologist who also fits into the category of being diverse from the mainstream. One of those colleagues was finding it difficult to voice her thoughts on diversity within the psychological community and experiencing certain barriers. This made me think about the historical frustrations I have experienced throughout my life and more specifically during my journey through academia (studying to be a counselling psychologist and more lately a CAT (cognitive analytic therapy) practitioner). These experiences often included feeling marginalised and excluded due to being registered blind. That is not to say that I have not met kind and helpful individuals along the way, because I have, and I could not function to the level I do without the much-appreciated help of others. However, I find that more entrenched, institutional discriminations are still everywhere, meaning that I have to be more determined and probably more stubborn than my non-disabled colleagues.

When I agreed to write about these experiences here, I was asked to include some reflections on the issue of leadership, and initially this made me feel anxious. This is because I do not see myself that way and it made me feel awkward to do so. However, as I pondered on it, I thought about how I have often been labelled as a 'trail blazer' throughout my life and I realised maybe this is a kind of leadership, that is, developing the courage to overtly tell those around me what I wanted to achieve and what I needed, as well as talking to both individuals and institutions about discrimination and in doing so hoping to ease the way for the next disabled person. Writing this article has also made me think how my own sense of a disabled identity is now more positive and robust than it has ever been (probably a function of being in my 40s as much as anything). However, I also think this is because to survive my lifestyle (i.e., a practising psychologist with young children) I have had to develop courage as well as coping strategies and (perhaps most importantly of all) learn how to be kind to myself. Furthermore, I think I have had to develop the ability to choose the battles that are worth fighting and to know when to accept the limitations that my sight dictates; that is, to realise I do not have enough energy to fight all the barriers I face but have to choose wisely when to challenge stereotypes and assumptions and when to admit defeat.

In this article I will reflect on the journey of developing my disabled identity and how this has related to the other parts of myself, including being a psychologist. An important part of this journey was the research that I undertook for my doctorate and wondering if my disabled identity and my identity as a psychologist are intertwined.

Beginning my journey

I was not born with limited vision, but at some point, during primary school my sight began to deteriorate, so that I failed a compulsory sight test. This resulted in me being sent to hospital where I presented something of a problem for the doctors as they could not find a physical reason for me not being able to see. Because of this they decided it was 'hysterical blindness' and told my parents that my inability to see was psychosomatic. I won't go into all the details, but it is sufficient to say that the way they spoke to me as a 10-year-old girl was not compassionate, kind or helpful and put me off going back to see them again and so after many stressful appointments my parents decided to stop taking me. The fact that the consultants had told me that one day I would wake up and be able to see meant I put increasing effort into having to conceal my diminishing sight. I had to find ingenious ways of hiding the fact I could not see the things my friends could (e.g., blackboards and textbooks). As I now reflect I realise this was during the years when we begin to develop our unique sense of self and our opinions about others and the world. By the age of 15 my sight had decreased to the extent I could not read the exam papers and failing my mock GCSE exams forced me into having to confront what I had been trying so hard to conceal for years. Therefore, I decided I had no choice but to go and see the optician. By this point the damage to my retina was easily visible and I was diagnosed with Stargardt syndrome, also referred to as cone dystrophy, a type of macular degeneration meaning that over the next few years I would lose all my central vision. Much more prodding, poking and testing followed but at least now I had a way of making sense of my experiences.

Looking back, I am rather surprised I chose to persevere with the world of academia but off I went to college to study a B-Tech in Social Care. I followed this with university to study a BSc in sociology and psychology, choosing to move away from home to do this. Although on the whole I enjoyed my time at university, I encountered many types of individual and institutional discrimination and think I only survived this because I had already begun developing a positive sense of self, having experienced a stable, supportive and loving childhood. However, I had to navigate some significant challenges during college and university and had to develop coping strategies based on taking the lead. The academic institutions I went to had not encountered a visually impaired student before and so my learning curve was also theirs. This also meant having to let go of my own old coping strategies of hiding my disability and instead I had to 'find my voice' and learn how to represent myself at meetings and be assertive about what I needed. I found this was essential to avoid being held back by stereotype and the assumed limitations that went with the negative social constructions of blindness. I had to become an expert in my own disability and in how to manage it and began to form my leadership skills, facing a choice of either leading meetings about my needs and my future or if not, having decisions made for me. I felt in order to succeed I had to be determined and was often described as 'fiercely independent'. I think this was because when I could do something for myself that it felt important that I did it. I felt so often I had to rely on the help of others and often this itself created new problems. I am extremely fortunate that I live in this time of technology and a mixture of speech software on my computer, scanners and paid helpers allowed me to pass my degree with success.

However, there was a much harder journey I also went through, that of having to move from concealing my disability to being able to openly talk about it and ask for the help I needed. Often there were lecturers who would repeatedly forget to read out slides from the screen in a large lecture hall and I would sit in a silent room of people who were reading things that I could not. On brave days I would raise my hand and ask them to read it out loud; on less brave days I would not. Making myself stand out as disabled felt hard, as the implicit message I felt I had been given as a child in the hospital was that not being able to see was my fault and in some way something to be ashamed of, something wrong with me and to be hidden.

Developing a positive disabled identity

After university I travelled for a while, living in Canada working with homeless people, and then worked in various mental health settings, including a children's home. Looking back, I think I was determined not to let my disability limit me and wanted to find adventure and independence. After this I applied to train as a psychologist and retrospectively, it is not a surprise that I chose to go into a profession that is about understanding others' emotional experiences and perspectives, after having had mine so badly misunderstood when they told me it was 'hysterical blindness'. I was lucky enough to get a place on the Doctorate in Counselling Psychology at Guildford and began training when I was 25. When it came to choose a subject for our research we were told to choose something that had meaning for us and so I chose disability, and I wonder if this was again an example of taking a kind of leadership role, that is, becoming increasingly knowledgeable about the experiences of disabled people and then sharing this with others through my research.

My doctoral research began by undertaking a literature review, considering psychological research pertaining to disability between 1999 and 2001. It reviewed the work included on the database 'PsycINFO' and literature concerning physical impairments was focused upon. I explored what representations and expectations were embedded in the literature and a social model of disability was adopted. This differentiates physical impairment from disability (Shakespeare, 1993) and asserts that the former comprises the embodied restrictions of a certain physical state whilst the latter stems from social and physical barriers, which inhibit personal choice (Oliver, 1996).

This enabled me to think about how the literature constructed and/or perpetuated certain representations of disabled people. I concluded at the time that disability was still perceived as a largely negative phenomenon within the psychological literature. I chose to adopt a material discursive stance (see Yardley, 1997), as it enabled a consideration of the language and representations embedded in the research and enabled me to consider the role that psychological perspectives play in this.

I found the majority of the literature included presumptions stemming from the traditional view of disability based on an individualised medical model, which sees disability as a personal tragedy caused by a physical state (Burman, 1994; Oliver, 1989). Also, I found that throughout the literature 'disabled people' were treated as a homogeneous group, distinct from the 'non-disabled', although the criteria for inclusion or exclusion was rarely attended to and never clearly defined.

I felt that the way much of the research was done did not make space for disabled people's own perspectives and so my next piece of research thought about how disabled people speak about themselves, considering how, if at all, disability features in their identities.

In this I found that none of the participants seemed to have a sense of a positive disabled identity, as defined by Gill (1997). He asserts that there are four stages involved in developing a positive disabled identity. These are integrating into society, integrating with the disabled community, internally integrating our sameness and difference, and integrating how we feel and how we present ourselves. Regarding my own journey, joining ABAPSTAS (Association of Blind and Partially Sighted Teachers and Students) as an undergraduate was liberating and meant I could identify with other disabled people who I could also respect for their academic achievements. It was so lovely to meet others without having to go through the whole 'sight story' and to be with people who knew what the challenges really were, that is, other people's attitudes and practical things, like navigating an unfamiliar kitchen when on placement. Meeting with other visually impaired teachers and students may also have helped me define my disabled identity as positive, in the way Gill (1997) describes, that is, identifying with a disabled community as part of building one's own identity. Connecting with others who experience being perceived as 'other' has remained important to me, from being in touch with the disability movement when a post-grad student, to being part of a disabled psychologists e-mail network after qualifying.

However, despite my own revelations, none of the participants in my research seemed familiar with this idea of a disabled cultural identity or community, and therefore did not identify with it. It seemed that the participants' voices served to silence their experiences of disability, instead speaking about how they hide or minimise their physical impairments. This seemed to imply that disability as an identity was not integrated into their self-concepts. Furthermore, few of the participants had adopted a social model of disability. This may have been because they had never encountered this perspective and so instead they may have coped with the negative stereotype of disability inherent in our culture by denying that part of themselves.

As I began to mature and develop my adult identity I increasingly noticed the ongoing institutional discrimination around me, both in terms of the world of academia but also in the world more broadly: People unwittingly making assumptions such as the nurse when I went to get my vaccinations thinking I needed help getting undressed and pulling my top off. I began to become aware that people either put me in a 'tragic' category, telling me what a shame it was 'that I was like I was' or conversely telling me what 'an amazing inspiration' I was, somehow making me special. However, at the time I was unable to reflect on this much and despite the three years of therapy I had during training, I felt stuck in this dichotomous choice of either being 'tragic' or 'amazing'. Given this choice I tried very hard to be 'amazing' which was exhausting and kept me stuck in a striving pattern, struggling to admit when things were tough and overwhelming, soldiering on regardless. I remember in one of the therapies I had wondering why the therapist kept going on about my sight, feeling I did not need to keep talking about it. Now when I look back at this time I realise that I was not ready to acknowledge how the striving concealed an underlying sense of shame and feeling in some way less than others.

As I finished my doctoral training my attitudes toward disability consolidated and I co-wrote an article called 'Seeing is Believing' with one of my former lecturers, Sarah Corrie (Supple & Corrie, 2004). This reflected on the issue of adapting Cognitive Therapy for visually impaired people and maybe another example of how wanting to combat discrimination put me back in a leadership type role, that is, in an educating stance. At the time I felt that psychology, as a discipline, still had a complex and not always positive relationship with disability. I held the belief then (and still do) that psychology should hold at its centre an awareness of diversity, within both practitioners and clients alike. I feel in some respects the field of psychology attends to the idea of diversity and differing perspectives but also feel it is essential that as part of this, notions of normality and abnormality should be considered and scrutinised. By doing this, psychologists can consider what assumptions and beliefs may be integral to such constructs. That is to say, it may be easy to overlook certain types of diversity, including disability, and in doing so unwittingly perpetuate the dichotomy of normal and abnormal that is arguably embedded in much of traditional psychology.

My time of study left me concluding that historically disability had come to be perceived as negative and tragic. French, Gilson and Depoy (2000) and Burman (1994) suggest that developmental psychology has contributed to such negative perceptions of disability by participating in the creation and perpetuation of a dichotomy of ill/well or able/disabled. It does this by defining and measuring mental qualities, classifying abilities and establishing norms (Burman, 1994). In doing so, it has sought to define normal development and thus has also defined 'abnormal' development. Moreover, traditionally, disability has been understood using a medical model, which means that physical impairment has been viewed as something to be treated and cured (Oliver, 1989). However, as disability is likely to be untreatable in the conventional sense, disabled people came to be seen as tragic and lesser than those who could recover from illness (French, Gilson & Depoy, 2000). As a result, disability became viewed as a tragic loss and psychology focused on the guilt and shame associated with such a loss (Lindemann, 1981). It was theorised that the trauma of disability would result in the development of maladaptive personalities and behaviours (Hersen & Van Hasselt, 1990).

Such an individualised conception of disability causes problems. First, if disability is located within an individual, no consideration needs to be given to how environment or socio-cultural context and meaning impact upon levels of ability or the experience of disability. Shakespeare & Watson (1997) suggested that psychology, as a discipline, was largely unaware of social explanations of disability. They asserted that psychology often adhered to traditional models and overlooked contextual and experiential issues. Secondly, psychology has always played a central role in the diagnosis, treatment and rehabilitation of disabled people (Burman, 1994) and thus, the representations and expectations held by psychologists and the institutions that train them will directly affect the lives of disabled people.

As a newly qualified psychologist I felt concerned about this, particularly as I began adopting Zola's (1989) definition of disability. This suggests that disability will affect all people at some stage either through illness, injury, congenital impairment or old age and thus it applies to a huge range of people.

Attitudes now

I am aware that the original work I did to look at how psychological research constructs disabled people was over 15 years ago now and so I wanted to take a more up-to-date look. Ironically, the electronic systems that I need to search literature are inaccessible to me due to my visual impairment and so I had to rely on the help of a trainee I had on placement who kindly did a 'PsychINFO' search. We searched from 2014 until the present, looking at articles that mentioned physical disability. We could only take a superficial look and were not able to spend enough time on this to do any in-depth analysis. It seemed from what we saw that there was still an overall negative bias toward disability in the research. When we searched for articles about physical disability we found 1528 articles, but when we specifically looked for the phrase 'social model' we only found 24 articles, and when we searched for the term 'social model of disability' we found 15 articles. I assume this means that over 1000 articles on disability have not mentioned the social model of disability, and so I wonder if old, more medicalised perspectives still dominate.

However, it did seem something had changed; that is, rather than investigating what the negativity was (measuring how much more depressed disabled people are, for example), it instead seemed to explore what barriers disabled people face or what stereotypes or stigma they face, for example, 'Framing disability amongst young adults with disabilities and non-disabled young adults, an exploratory study' by Soffer and Chew (2015). Similarly, we found research reflecting on the evolving social construction of disability and how this may impact on disabled people's lives (e.g., 'Disability models affect disability policy support through awareness of structural discrimination' by Dirth and Branscombe (2017)). Also, we found a book review of 'Disability Studies, a students' guide' edited by Collin Cameron (2014), which looks at how society has become less prejudiced but there is still an underlying assumption that impairment is considered a tragedy and that we all strive for normalcy.

In the research which did not explicitly mention social models, there were reflections about barriers faced by disabled people (e.g., 'We don't know, we've never had anyone like you before, barriers to perinatal care for women with physical disabilities' by Tarasoff (2017)).

However, there were still some that leant toward the negative construction of disability (e.g., 'Associations between depression, chronic physical health conditions and disability in a community sample: a focus on the persistence of depression' by Deschenes, Burns & Schmitz (2015)).

When we searched for disability and depression 222 articles came up, markedly more than mentioned the social model. However, a lot seem to be thinking about associations, predictors or effects of depression on disabled people. So again, indicating a subtle shift, rather than measuring how much more depressed disabled people are, they are thinking about what may improve or worsen the depression.

As I did not have time to look in great detail it was hard to explore the constructions of disability in any depth and I may have missed important information. However, I notice that I did not stumble over research looking at positive integration of a disabled identity or any strengths or skills-based work around experiences of being disabled or any overtly positive accounts of disabled people. I hope future students will be able to look in greater detail at psychology's relationship with the construction of disability and that over time our discipline will begin to reflect on how disability, like any other aspect of a person, has positives and negatives, builds strengths and creates fragility.

CAT and my developing disabled identity

I then had a bit of time out from being a psychologist to develop another part of my identity, that is, becoming a mother. Up until then I had resisted using 'the stick' but when I became pregnant I felt it was no longer just my safety at stake. Whereas previously I ventured out and about alone, being pregnant meant I had someone else's safety to think of, so a white stick was obtained. Immediately I noticed people treated me differently, curving a wide arc around me on the pavement or offering help. I do not mean to sound unfair to those who were just trying to be kind, but I felt in this gesture was an assumption that I needed help even if it was not asked for. The white stick was a very immediate and public symbol to all who saw me that I could not see and made me feel self-conscious to begin with, feeling open to others' assumptions and interpretations.

Since having my children, who are now both at primary school, many people have tentatively asked me how I coped, presuming it must have been difficult being a visually impaired mum. In fact, breast feeding, changing nappies and playing are all tactile and did not pose a problem. What causes me the biggest problem is the school run and negotiating bikes, toddlers, dogs, buggies and other children! Also, assumptions are made that my husband is my carer, and this is definitely not the case. We are a very egalitarian couple. Also, it is surprising how many people ask me if my husband is visually impaired too, and I will let you draw your own conclusions on what assumptions may be buried in that question!

Following maternity leave, I trained as a CAT (cognitive analytic therapy) practitioner and part of this involved engaging in my own CAT therapy. Here is where I was finally ready to reflect on that striving pattern and how I often felt pushed into trying to stay in the 'amazing, coping' place to avoid the 'tragic, overwhelmed' place. It clarified to me that many people cannot tolerate competency and incompetency in the same individual. They cannot comprehend you are both strong and weak, independent and in need of help and always want you to choose one or the other. The CAT therapy I had as part of this training helped me move on from feeling I had to compensate for being 'lesser' in some way and thus begin to be more kind to myself and admit there are some things I need help with and some things I cannot do. This felt very liberating although the striving pattern still lurks, and I still need to be mindful of it. However, as much as the CAT therapy helped me address some of my personal struggles, the experience of going back into the world of academia presented me with the same barriers as it always had.

Although I encountered a real enthusiasm for flexible approaches within CAT, I also found myself feeling excluded due to my disability. I knew I would have to give some thought to how to deal with the visual aspects of CAT, such as diagrams, but I did not expect to find myself experiencing such negative reciprocal roles (RR). From my first dealings with the Association of Cognitive Analytic Therapists (ACAT) I experienced barriers which left me in the reciprocal role of excluding/dismissing to excluded/dismissed. This has been on an institutional, rather than individual basis. For example, when I first joined the training course I found materials were not in an accessible format and were not easily made available to me.

I found myself feeling I had to again work harder than my peers to access what I needed, sometimes relying on the kindness of friends to help me, playing out an RR of disempowering to dependant/crushed and also in danger of falling into the RR of excluding/excluded that Crowley, Field, Lloyd, Morrison and Varela (2014) discussed when thinking about disability. They describe being disabled as 'lacking the ability to join in and connect with' (p. 8) and suggest that like all reciprocal roles both positions can be experienced by either client or therapist.

I found myself reflecting on what reciprocal roles could potentially be played out within CAT with clients for whom the written word is inaccessible. Therefore, I chose to write an essay on how CAT therapists have thought about how to work with diversity and disability. I wonder if again this put me in the reluctant leadership position that by now was becoming familiar, taking on a role of naming and then exploring the issue of exclusion within CAT and using my own experiences to share and explore these issues with my colleagues.

When writing this essay, I discovered within CAT many creative adaptations which left me feeling that inclusion is not only possible but sought and enjoyed. This made me feel optimistic that RRs of curious/encouraged and creative/flexible to accessible/included are possible. Personally, I felt most included and connected with CAT when being able to experiment with using objects or the body in exploring procedures and RRs. Another idea I found interesting whilst writing my essay was that raised by Crowley et al. (2014). They discuss when the therapist feels disabled by their inability to understand or communicate with a client for whom mainstream speech and understanding is not available. They suggest that not being able to utilise traditional approaches and tools can leave the therapist feeling disempowered, de-skilled and stupid, leading them to feel that to pursue therapy with this client would be pointless. They suggest the therapist's reaction and relationship to disability is itself a reciprocal role and thus this can be reflected on as part of the therapy. I think this is an important point and that CAT is a good approach for reflecting on RRs within the therapist/client relationship, enabling this to be worked with as part of the therapy. I again concluded, as after my doctoral training, that it is essential that issues of disability and diversity are reflected upon within the psychological community so as to avoid colluding in an RR of silencing/silenced which could be perpetuated due to social taboos or a fear of offending.

Ongoing identity and institutions

That leads me to the present and, as I said in the introduction, I now feel more comfortable with my disabled identity, drawing on the social model of disability and the belief we all have limitations, which helps me avoid feelings of not being good enough or lesser in some way. However, it is much harder to avoid feelings of exclusion and being marginalised. I find our culture of computer technology both a blessing and an arduous trial. In some ways it is what enables me to work independently (e.g., having a laptop that speaks, having an adapted mobile phone, etc.). However, in other ways it is a huge barrier. Increasingly, systems become more complex and this adds layers of barriers within the software. Programmes that are designed to be used by a sighted person with a mouse are often inaccessible to me. So I increasingly get left behind as improvements in software move on suddenly, just as I had caught up with them.

As previously stated, I have to choose my battles as I do not have energy for all of them and unfortunately the NHS still has ingrained institutional discrimination in terms of accessing its systems and I am unlikely to win that battle. I now work with social care teams and I feel that this setting is, on the whole, more accepting of my disability and I feel I am just accepted in my role as 'the psychologist'. The challenges I face daily still relate to the bureaucracy and the electronic systems. However, if I expend too much time on raising awareness about this and lobbying for increased accessibility, I would run out of time to do my actual job.

Conclusion

In conclusion I think studying constructions of disability and finding the social model of disability and being able to reflect on my own identity, inclusive of disability, has been extremely helpful to me. It has enabled me to own my disability and integrate it into a positive sense of self, although at times the old fear of embarrassment and shame still lurks. It has been very helpful to me to connect in some way with others who take this view of disability and to be able to make sense of my own internal struggles of not feeling good enough during my CAT training. This has allowed me to find compassion and kindness toward myself. Using these perspectives to make sense of my own experiences has allowed me to own my disability without shame but also has given me the strength to voice how it is to feel 'other' and 'lesser' and I think this helps me as a psychologist. That is, it helps me empathise with clients in a therapy setting but it also helps me take that reluctant leadership position when I need to, having the courage and strength to name discrimination and exclusion when I find it. However, I am not sure if psychology's relationship with diversity and disability has evolved in similarly positive ways. Although I think our discipline is beginning to be more thoughtful about how it constructs disability I think it still has some way to go in avoiding historical assumptions, based on dichotomous patterns of normal and abnormal. Also, institutions, whether they be academic or the NHS, still hold ingrained barriers that continue to exclude and marginalise those who are not within the 'norm', and I feel, sadly there is still a long way to go in changing this.

References

Burman, E. (1994). *Deconstructing Developmental Psychology*. New York: Routledge.

Cameron, C. (2014). *Disability studies: A student's guide*. London: Sage.

Crowley, V., Field, B., Lloyd, J., Morrison, P., & Varela, J. (2014). When the therapist is disabled. *Reformulation*, Summer, 6–9.

Deschenes, S. S., Burns, R. J., & Schmitz, N. (2015). Associations between depression, chronic physical health conditions, and disability in a community sample: a focus on the persistence of depression. *Journal of Affective Disorders, 179*, 6–13.

Dirth, T. P. & Branscombe, N. R. (2017). 'Disability models affect disability policy support through awareness of structural discrimination'. *Journal of Social Issues*.

French Gilson, S. & Depoy, E. (2000) Multiculturalism and disability: a critical perspective, *Disability & Society, 15*, pp. 207–218.

Gill, G. (1997). Four types of integration in disability identity development, *Journal of Vocational Rehabilitation, 9*, 39–46.

Hersen, H. & Van Hasselt, V. V. (1990) *Psychological Aspects of Development and Physical Disabilities. A Casework*. London: Sage.

Lindemann, J. (1981). *Psychological and Behavioural Aspects of Physical Disability*. London: Plenum Press.

Oliver, M. (1989) Disability and dependency: A creation of Industrial Societies. In L. Barton (Ed), *Disability and Dependency*. Lewes: Falmer Press.

Oliver, M. (1996). A sociology of disability or a disablist sociology? In L. Barton (Ed.), *Disability & Society: Emerging Issues and Insight*. Harlow: Longman Publishing.

Soffer, M., & Chew, F. (2015). Framing disability amongst young adults with disabilities and non-disabled young adults, an exploratory study. *Disability and rehabilitation: an international multidisciplinary journal, 37*(8), 171–178. Doi: 10.3109/09638288.2014.913701

Shakespeare, T. (1993) Disabled people's self-organisation: a new social movement? *Disability Handicap and Society, 8*, 249–64.

Shakespeare, T., & Watson, N. (1997). Defending the social model. *Disability & Society, 12*(2), 293–300.

Supple, S. & Corrie, S. (2004). Seeing is believing: Adapting cognitive therapy for visual impairment. *Counselling Psychology Review, 19*(3).

Tarasoff, L.A. (2017). We don't know, we've never had anyone like you before, barriers to perinatal care for women with physical disabilities. *Disability and Health journal, 10*(3), 426–433. Doi: 10.1016/j.dhjo.2017.03.017

Yardley, L. (1997). *Material Discourses of Health and Illness*. London: Routledge.

Zola, I. (1989). Towards a Necessary Universalising of Disability Policy. *Millbank Quarterly, 67*(2), 401–428.

Chapter 9

Dyslexia: Shackles far beyond the written word

Ute Liersch

Introduction

This awareness piece aims to invite you not only into the world of dyslexia, but also into my world as a person who lives with it. I will offer views of this phenomenon from various angles: first, with a definition of dyslexia and its translation into a lived experience; secondly, the genesis of dyslexia and my personal history. Thirdly, I invite the reader to undertake an experiment so as to become aware of how we tend to judge a "book by its cover": a socialisation process that is discussed thereafter. I conclude with a personal account of overcoming challenges, with a summary of suggestions.

What is Dyslexia?

"Dyslexia is an alternative term used to refer to a pattern of learning difficulties characterized by problems with accurate or fluent word recognition, poor decoding, and poor spelling abilities" (American Psychiatric Association, 2013, p. 67). *The Guardian* headlined that dyslexia costs the UK £1bn annually, as those who are undiagnosed are more likely to be excluded from schools, be unemployed for a longer period of time, and may experience periods of imprisonment (Curtis, 2004, September 24). Dyslexia occurs in more than 700 million children and adults worldwide, with at least one in ten people being dyslexic: a prevalence of at least 10% in any given population (Dyslexia International, 2014). Various theories are proposed to understand the causes of dyslexia, such as cognitive, brain, and genetic reasons, but a discussion of the same would exceed the scope of this essay. Interested readers are referred to Elliott and Grigorenko (2014) for an overview and discussion of current ideas.

The UK's National Health Service (NHS choices, 2015) insists that this learning difficulty does not affect intelligence, in contrast to a learning disability. It is reasoned that those with lower IQs should have learning difficulties across cognitive abilities, whereas the dyslexic shows a mismatch between measured intelligence and reading skills (Ramus, 2014). It is, however, not so clear-cut. I perform significantly below the level of my verbal comprehension, perceptual organisation, and mathematical calculation. I have difficulties with written expression and find the mechanics of writing difficult, but I also have difficulties with memory, organisational, and sequencing skills, together with poor gross-motor management. All of this indicates that I am experiencing a range of difficulties. Moreover, lower academic achievement and increased behavioural problems have been observed in dyslexic students (Lawrence, 2009). Such qualities are commonly associated with intelligence and these difficulties could indicate that intelligence is affected. This discrepancy perhaps highlights the complexity of the phenomenon called dyslexia and its link to intelligence. Furthermore, intelligence is not an isolated, deterministic, biological ability: rather, it should be understood as a quality that arises out of the interaction of nature and nurture (Gopnik, 2009). Yet the NHS's explanation of dyslexia seems to assume and distribute a deterministic ontology.

Children who consistently struggle with school work might be given less trust to solve problems, less praise when achieving "the norm", and might be less likely to be chosen as team leaders, all of which significantly affect the developmental trajectory. An early diagnosis of dyslexia is seen as advantageous for these children and their families (Dyslexia International, 2014), allowing it to be managed proactively. At best, this could create a flexible scaffolding of help to develop the person's ability. At worst, however, it could manifest a belief in inability, teaching children not to try. The latter can be problematic. For example, should I adhere to the belief that my spelling mistakes are due to my dyslexia, only to fail to acknowledge that there are words I have not yet learned how to spell? "Onomatopoeia" is hard to write, with or without dyslexia. In short, categorisation could reduce the agency I have over my own life and hinder the development of my abilities.

The label "dyslexia" might disguise the phenomenon's idiosyncrasies. Any evaluation needs to be phenomenological, and needs to recognise and recommend help according to the person's particular needs (Miles & Miles, 1999). For example, a child who struggles with learning to read might benefit from a structured multisensory teaching program, and a student who struggles to spell may benefit from text-to-voice software. Yet, another layer of complexity should also be considered. Dyslexia does not necessarily present homogenously in the person. I often read, for example, what is not actually there. When reading, I change syntax whilst keeping the sentence's message intact, and do so more fluently in German (my mother tongue) than in English. This indicates that I grasp the meaning through something different than the written word alone. I can hear, but not see, my mistakes, yet I am quite good at spotting yours. Even more puzzling for me is that once I allow my writing to rest, my spelling mistakes seem to emerge from the page. My word-blindness thus seems to be time-sensitive. This is bewildering for me and my environment. To this day, my mother suspects laziness, at best, concerning my writing, and stupidity at worst.

This problem calls for bespoke support. Yet, society-funded and tailored resources are scarce and many argue that the struggle has become worse over time. Is more money for early diagnostics and tailored interventions the solution? I would argue that it is not. Diagnosis—society's triage service of human conditions—can allow for "conveyor-belting" into treatment so that we can function on the playing-field of the non-dyslexics. This might not foster curiosity for differences and can nurture ignorance. It allows those who are not dyslexic to avoid thinking about changing the playing-field itself. Counselling psychology is not immune from such behaviour. During my doctorate, for instance, I was asked to speed read questions in a "quiz" and to hit the buzzer and "win" for my team. Such fun! What the counselling psychologist was asking me to do was to run with shackles against Nike Air Max. This inequality was artificially created and put into place before engaging with the actual exercise. From then on, my expertise became insignificant, as I simply could not grasp text that quickly. Do I need to say that this fed the perception I had of myself, as nurtured by my mother?

How can this happen in times when resources are spent on dyslexia coordinators, student support agreements, specialist technology, and one-to-one support? In my experience, these support processes can allow the notion of outsourcing the problem. In the three years of my doctorate, only three of the twelve tutors who acted as module leaders actually asked me what would be helpful. However, I also bought into a power-dynamic, waiting to be asked by those who are perceived experts in their profession. Now what? What we can—or rather should—do is to cultivate communication so that the phenomenon can be brought into the open. We need to be curious. We need to ask questions. I am happy to "take one for the team" and run with shackles when everyone knows that I wear them.

Today's dyslexics can struggle to access help, struggle with the environment's deliberate and non-deliberate ignorance, whilst nursing the wounds that such behaviour can inflict. I suppose this echoes across many minority communities. The person of the past struggled with the recognition of dyslexia altogether. Thus, it might be that the kinds of difficulties have changed, rather than the difficulties themselves.

The genesis of dyslexia and my dyslexic history

At the end of the twentieth century, when I was in mainstream German education, dyslexia did not exist—at least, not in the heads of the teaching community, and hardly in the social discourse. My inability to produce words following German orthography (the conventional spelling system of a language) was taken as evidence for my inability to master higher education.

Consequently, I was regarded as unsuitable and removed from this trajectory, despite my teachers' unawareness that people with reading problems had been described since the nineteenth century. At first, sufferers were labelled with "Wordblindheit"—word-blindness—by Adolph Kussmaul, a German neurologist, and very soon afterwards, with "absence of language" or dyslexia, by the ophthalmologist Rudolf Berlin (Hallahan & Mercer, 2002). As the discovery, observation, research, and reporting of dyslexia was driven by members of the medical community, it was positivistic in nature and explained dyslexia as a disease:

> ...cases of word blindness are always interesting, and this case [a young boy] is.... particularly so...in that it follows upon no injury or illness, but is evidently congenital, and due most probably to defective development of that region of the brain, disease of which in adults produces practically the same symptoms...
>
> Morgan, 1896, p. 1378

Education made no significant contribution to children's learning difficulties before the twentieth century and those who exhibited "such symptoms" were considered as poorly motivated, disabled, medically challenged, or unteachable (Lawrence, 2009). Psychology was indifferent at best; at worst, Freud's concept of the "slips of the pen...which are in agreement with those of the tongue" (Freud, 1920, 2011, p. 57) questioned the existence of spelling difficulties but implied the existence of correct spelling as an ontological truth, and errors as a possible expression of interfering intentions and a revelation of the inner psychic.

At the end of the twentieth century, dyslexia started to be considered in less pathological terms (Lawrence, 2009). The thought arose that the dyslexic could be a person with a difference rather than one with a defect. Gardner's work on multiple intelligences seemed to have been instrumental in this shift, advocating that intelligence might not be uniquely expressed through competent linguistics but rather through multiple skills (Lawrence, 2009). Yet, today we still "diagnose" those who illustrate reading and spelling difficulties (NHS choices, 2015), implying pathology. This could foster the assumption that a cure is possible, or even needed. Such categorisation might kindle binary discussions about the existence of my experienced difficulties, as showcased by Graham Stringer (British Member of Parliament from 1997–2010): "The education establishment, rather than admit that their eclectic and incomplete methods for instruction are at fault, have invented a brain disorder called dyslexia" (BBC, 2009, para. 7).

I did not have Stringer's mentioned "brain disorder" until I was diagnosed at the age of thirty-nine, and the teaching I experienced was, and indeed still is, incomplete in its methods. Since then, I have clawed my way into academia, often without the support of my educational and family environment.

This was sometimes a very hard and painful experience, but one which has also taught me invaluable lessons: persistence, organisation, and the value of working hard and taking pride in what I do. My writing and spelling have doubtless improved. What it did not do, Mr Stringer, was to enable me to remove my otherness: my idiosyncratic expression of dyslexia. Having come to terms with my dyslexia, I like to believe that it gives me a unique way of approaching the world. Indeed, a dyslexic's right brain hemispheric preferences are supposedly linked with heightened creativity and visual processing (Vlachos, Andreou, & Dellliou, 2013): a claim that is, however, also contested (Lawrence, 2009).

Nonetheless, such discussions highlight that this phenomenon is taken seriously by researchers. Collaboration between psychology, education, biology, and medicine started to take a prominent role in managing this childhood learning difficulty. In the UK, the Warnock Report (1978) is deemed instrumental in stimulating this change (Lawrence, 2009). In Germany, notable work was published as early as 1951 explaining the phenomenon and its link to a child's ability (Leopold Ludwig, 2015). Yet, attitudes changed slowly. In 1993, my teacher reported on my poor motivation: "15 spelling mistakes! Make sentences! A hasty piece of work!" The academic feedback I received thirty-three years later could imply the same: "You need to check and be careful of spelling mistakes in presentations as, in conferences, those who read it might not take what you say seriously."

Dyslexia is now accepted as a learning difficulty for which provisions are made (Lawrence, 2009). As Snowling (2015, p. 7) says: "…a great deal is known about its [dyslexia's] nature, aetiology and assessment…it should be possible for educators to recognise the signs…such early identification should allow interventions…" Parents who believe that their child has special educational needs and disabilities can contact their special educational needs and disabilities co-ordinator at nursery, school, or their local council (BBC, 2009; Gov.UK, n.d.). From here on in, children can be supported by health visitors and receive special learning programs and help from assistant teachers, to name but a few available services (Gov.UK, n.d.). Today's dyslexics are not automatically deemed unsuitable for education. Society has come a long way. We are given support. I am given extra time in exams, am allowed to use a computer, and "sensitive marking criteria"[1] can be applied by tutors. I firmly believe that without those provisions, I would not have been able to stay at university. Equally important is the funding of research, as the acquired knowledge can be an informed learning style (Godwin, 2012): for instance, I change the background colours when writing, and since last month I have been using a special font for dyslexics. Both seem to enable my brain to process the letters somehow differently. The computer's read-back function and a special grammar and spell-checker software also help to reduce (but not eliminate) mistakes. I dare not think where I would be without them and feel utterly grateful to be living in a time when they exist. Yet, I cannot stop feeling like an academic fraud because I rely on such aids. I wonder whether others who have also found themselves deviant from the norm would agree that the notion of being less worthy is imprinted upon us. The long-standing negative judgement of teachers and the like has certainly become part of my self-narrative.

Being told, persistently, how mediocre you are can feed the intrusive voice of deprecating self-judgement. Cognitive research has long evidenced that "the problem of anxiety is, to a significant extent, a problem of intrusive thoughts that interfere with task-focused thinking" (Sarason, 1984, p. 929), reducing good outcomes. This can lead to "a downward spiral of underachievement, lowered self-esteem and poor motivation" (Snowling, 2015, p. 7). In my case, and despite the deprecating voice in my head, society's initial resistance to acknowledge my abilities has kindled incredible persistence and high levels of self-motivation. This could elucidate that it is not whether you have dyslexia, but how you work with it which is important for performance: for example, by having access to and engaging with help, by refusing to buy into the diagnostic lure of inability, and by changing language—I am not the dyslexic, but the Ute who has it.

However, I am aware that I engage with these aids to keep up and assimilate with the performance of people without dyslexia. The race is still on. The shackles are less heavy, but I am still competing on a playing-field that is made by, and for, those who have no difficulties with spelling and reading. This can be difficult when tight and multiple deadlines simply do not allow repeated listening to and checking my written pieces. A way forward could be to rethink the configuration of the playing-field, starting by bringing awareness to the negative bias towards bad spelling in the assumption that such awareness allows for change.

Can we stop judging the book by its cover?

Please engage with a little experiment and read the quotes of the following two writers:

Writer 1[2]:

> "Because of picture thinking, intuitive thought, multi-dimensional thought, and curiosity, the dyslexic's creativity is greatly enhanced. Creativity allows us to conceive of things which don't actually exist. From that experience, we can bring new things into existence."

Writer 2[3]:

> "Becose of picture thinking, intuitive thought, multi-dimensional thought, and curiosity, the dyslexic's creativity is greatly enhanct. Creativity allows us to conceive of things which don't actually exist. From that experience, we kan bring new things into existance."

Now answer the following questions:

- Who do you think is the more trustworthy writer?
- Who is more knowledgeable?
- Who is the better decision maker?
- Who would you ask for advice?

What were your initial thoughts when reading the misspelt text, which is dyslexic writing? If you found yourself trusting Writer 1 more than Writer 2, attributed more knowledge and skill to the first, or assumed that the second lacks ability or effort, you are in good company. It is not uncommon that society equates dyslexia with a lack of intelligence (Lawrence, 2009). Roslyn Petelin, an Associate Professor in Writing at the University of Queensland in Australia, points out that "nothing can make you lose credibility more quickly and seem uneducated than a spelling mistake, and that includes apostrophes" (Morrison, 2017, para. 13), a caution that is echoed by the editor of the journal "Counselling Psychology Review", who knows that spelling mistakes weaken the writer's voice (Richards, 2017), and by my peers, who have argued against the quality of a paper on the grounds of spelling mistakes. Here comes to light the fallacy of the "sensitive marking criteria". Markers are not living in a vacuum. They are part of our society and may be unable to trust that dyslexic writing can be the written work of knowledge. But these arguments, which are made in the realm of academia, might not apply to the world beyond. Thus, one might argue that those who do not spell could still show their capability in other realms. Even if we agree with this argument and therefore vote for exclusion from academic thinking on the grounds of spelling, market research suggests otherwise.

Consumers doubt a website's credibility when seeing a single spelling mistake (Coughlan, 2011). The online dating site Match.com provided evidence that users ranked the importance of correct writing more important than the candidate's smile or dress sense (Morrison, 2017). Here, it is not the eagle eye of an editor or academic scrutiny, but the clicks of the many that withhold trust. In other words, those who want to be taken seriously should know how to spell. The German magazine *Der Spiegel* is frank: "Orthogarfie ist eine Grundfähigkeit, dies das Tor in die Welt jedweder Bildung offnet. Wer sie nicht beherrscht, versagt", meaning that "Orthography is a fundamental skill, which opens the door to any education. Those who do not master it will fail" (von Bredow & Hackenbroch, 2013, para. 26). The more indirect English discourse is equally bleak in predicting a failing future for bad spellers: "56% of employers rate proficiency in English as a top priority when recruiting.... at times when one in every eleven young people (ages 18–24) is currently out of work.... good spelling...has never been more important in improving job prospects" (Dürre, 2000).

Despite evidence that knowing how to spell is not a deterministic developmental process (Dürre, 2000), we still seem to position orthography as a basic skill, implying that it is a capability that comes naturally to everyone. Correct spelling further seems to be linked to credibility. It appears that misspelling signals misinformation. From this perspective, our possible mistrust towards Writer 1 in the exercise above is understandable. It does not, however, tackle the prejudice that those who can spell are more trustworthy than those who cannot. We need to become aware of the socialization process we underwent to shake off the binary oppression.

Dr Samuel Johnson, an English writer in 1755, and later Noah Webster defined English orthography anew, abolishing the previously common practice of spelling "by ear" (Essinger, 2006). Whether writing "skool" or "scool", both were correct. When reading aloud, words made sense. Yet silent reading, as Baldus (2015) knows, could take time to process. The inconsistency in writing further complicated printing. Discontented English booksellers commissioned Johnson to tame spelling, leading to the authoritative "Dictionary of the English Language" (Essinger, 2006). Not only did the English language became standardized, but in 1788, Germany's Johann Christoph Adelung, an editor and librarian, published "Das Grammatisch-kritisches Wörterbuch der hochdeutschen Mundart" (the grammatic critical dictionary of the high German dialect; Bayerische StaatsBibliothek, 2009). The written word, which catered to the uniqueness of the user, was on its way to becoming a mass product.

This, perhaps, helped with the dissemination of printed texts to the many rather than to an exclusive few, making book production more efficient and affordable. Yet, Johnson soon realised that language had a changing nature (British Library, n.d.). Nonetheless, by recording "laugh' as the only spelling possible, he manifested that "laff" is wrong, possibly planting a new idea that good and credible writing must come with correct spelling.

Three centuries later, this idea bore strange fruits; the application of the APA style (American Psychological Association, 2013) is one example. Nobody argues against the importance of referencing. Giving credit to the original author and ensuring that their work can be found is of undisputed academic value. However, it could be questioned whether today's obsession with italics and bold, commas, semicolons, and brackets, truly serves its value, or whether it makes it harder for people with dyslexia to become the counselling psychologists they aspire to be. For somebody who has difficulties seeing the difference between "p" and "b", noticing the difference between "," and ";" is even harder. Nonetheless, my proficiency in, for example, working with diversity and differences in the therapy room is also judged by how I conform with such APA pettiness, as it is a significant marking criterion.

To pass any assignment, I must not only show "clear referencing and citation", a duty beyond dispute, but also "in accordance with APA style"

(Regent's University School of Psychotherapy and Psychology, 2017, p. 25). The reason for such rules was primarily to create standards for communication (American Psychological Association, 2013), as in Johnson's times. I would, however, argue that a problem arises out of our community's obsessive adherence to rigorous application of these standards, as demanded by the APA. One might want to argue that I could make an effort to learn them, and to update myself on the frequent changes, of which some are due to societal movements, such as the internet, while others are arbitrary. Yet we seem to overlook that the APA has a financial interest in such changes, as their "strong financial footing" is sourced mainly from "the sale and licensing of APA publications" (Anderson, 2014, p. 9). When I engage with the APA style manual, the pages very quickly become a space with scattered signs, and much energy must be employed to comply with it.

The British psychologist Edward B. Tichener was concerned that APA "analism" would supersede the craft of academic argumentation (Almeida, 2012, para. 2): "This bashing of spelling and punctuation takes out all the joy of writing as aesthetics. How can you expect people to write decently when you put their treasures through a mangle and turn them out all machine-made products?" Yet, APA—the "sound and rigorous standards for scientific communications" (American Psychological Association, 2013, p. xiii)—is now widely adopted in psychology's academic writings, including for BPS (British Psychological Society) research journals (Barker & Pistrang, 2010).

Eimer (2018) advises that the currency of academia is publications, on which suitability for academic positions is judged. Yet my psychological narrative can only be published by adhering to orthography and submitting to the APA style. Lacking such style precludes publication, and a lack of publication precludes the possibilities of senior positions in academia. Just as in Johnson's time, we are streamlining language and bowing once again to the editor's desire for a neat and consistent product (Almeida, 2012), possibly leaving behind those who can stare at a piece of writing for hours without seeing the difference between "," and ";". I do not advocate a different set of publication rules for those who suffer with dyslexia; rather, I advocate levelling the playing-field through the retention of a reasonable set of rules but with greater freedom in style.

Finding a balance

Our present society relies on the written word to acquire and convey meaning in a fast, effective, and reliable way; yet correct and consistent spelling is not a prerequisite for pulling people into a narrative. Acquiring good grades and credibility seems to be inevitably linked with spelling and style, but nonetheless, the list of successful people with dyslexia is long and not all have received special educational aids. Dyslexia seems to be a problem too complex to resolve, yet I would like to offer some insight and idiosyncratic suggestions learnt from my life with dyslexia.

For those with dyslexia: Work it!

I alluded earlier that a diagnosis can have the lure of believing in our inability. Even though my diagnosis of dyslexia, dyspraxia, and dyscalculia came as a relief, by confirming my difference and disconfirming stupidity, it never changes the fact that writing, reading, note-taking, studying, and statistical analysis are difficult. Yet, I do not ponder whether being dyslexic or having to function in ignorant settings is fair. To me, this is a waste of time: time that I put to better use to organise my projects so that I finish promptly, allowing time for proofreading. I avoid procrastination and extension, as this can increase the stress and put extra pressure on timelines because we still engage with old materials whilst being involved with the demands of the next. I have seen too many peers with dyslexia entering a vicious cycle of assignment extension. I have seen some swallowed up by it.

Nobody else can do my work, yet I cannot read, focus, and write as quickly as people without dyslexia. Once I faced up to this, my behaviour changed. I started to train skills like awareness, focusing, and organisation. Today my non-dyslexic peers attest that I am often more skilled in these qualities than they are. I also decided to stop attempting to read every paper, but allowed myself to read fewer, more deeply. I now deconstruct what I read, with lots of annotations, colours, and pictures. When writing, I play around with background colours, read-back functions, grammar and spell checkers, and different fonts (Open Dyslexic, 2018). I am not concerned about the style, the look, the spelling, or conventions when pouring thoughts out onto paper, as this can be fixed later, but ideas are fleeting and need to be written out before they disappear.

Believe in yourself. If you love to write—write. If you love to read—read. If you love maths—do it. I regret that I did not allow myself to see my writing as golden because I could not spell. Guess what—I was wrong. Speak up for yourself; take the lead. I am now asking people whether they can help me, rather than being apologetic for having dyslexia. This leads towards assertiveness. I have started to call people out, challenging whether they judge me on my content or on its word-representation. I forewarn people that my writing style is that of a woman with dyslexia. Years of being put down have made me feisty: you do not want to judge my book by its cover.

For the non-dyslexic community: Learn to look beyond the written word!

Rethink oppressive styles such as the APA and engage in discourse around the freedom of word representations. As long as you foster social discourse that sees the current orthography as a positivistic truth, we will always run shackled:

- "It was with great regret that I didn't do better at school. People just thought I was thick. It was a struggle. I never really understood dyslexia and who could bring out my strengths" (Slipper, 2014, para 12).
- "Writing and spelling were always terribly difficult for me. My letters were without originality. I was… an extraordinarily bad speller and have remained so" (Slipper, 2014, para 8).
- "When I was a kid they didn't call it dyslexia. They called it… you know, you were slow or retarded or whatever" (Slipper, 2014, para 7).

Jamie Oliver, Agatha Christie, and Whoopi Goldberg (names in order of the above quotes) have become leaders in their fields, and they are no exception. The list of highly accomplished people with dyslexia is long, fostering the genius idea. Yet I do not agree with the theory that "their genius didn't occur in spite of their dyslexia, but because of it" (Davis & Braun, 2010, p. 3). This could undervalue luck, socioeconomic status, and such important skills as self-belief: a skill that can be consistently undermined, especially in educational settings, which look unkindly upon "outside the norm" writing. This is a look that can be challenged. After all, we still extol Shakespeare's "the most unkindest cut of all" (Shakespeare as cited in Bryson, 2007, p. 110), a double superlative that would certainly need to be deleted from any contemporary submission. We celebrate Shakespeare's genius for throwing 600 new words at Hamlet's audience (Bryson, 2007), but discredit contemporary writers for the use of 'theatr' or 'womanning' because they are against norms. This can hold great danger.

"The way we feel about ourselves and the way we think other people feel about us has a huge impact on our well-being", warns Welford (2012, p. xvii), who advises that how we value ourselves impacts our success. This can certainly affect whether we put ourselves forward for leadership roles. Creating self-value or self-compassion is, at best, difficult, and at worst, impossible, especially when consistently failing in educational settings: for example, when a "first" cannot be reached because of spelling; and when the marker and editor have bought into the concept of orthographic truth and lost the ability to see beyond it. Yet to function well in life, we need to learn to support ourselves (Welford, 2012), and educational settings have an obligation to teach these skills too.

The dyslexic support my university has provided to me was by luck, thanks to the arrival of a pragmatic director of study. He was able to see my potential rather than the dyslexia, advising me to obtain assistance from a proofreader. Suddenly my academic competency was separated from my inability to spell. It felt as if, at last, somebody had said: "You are intelligent, you can write, and you are where you belong." My shackles have changed.

Notes

1. Marking that aims to avoid penalizing the student for their spelling.
2. Davis & Brown (2010).
3. Davis & Brown (2010).

References

Almeida, P. (2012, July 10). The origins of APA style (and why there are so many rules) [Blog post]. Retrieved from http://blog.efpsa.org/2012/07/10/the-origins-of-apa-style-and-why-there-are-so-many-rules/

American Psychiatric Association. (2013). *Diagnostic and statistical manual of mental disorders* (5th ed.). Washingotn, DC: American Psychiatric Association.

American Psychological Association. (2009). *Publication Manual of the American Psychological Association Paperback* (6th ed.). Washington: American Psychological Association.

Anderson, N. B. (2014). APA's strong financial footing. *Monitor on Psychology, 45*, 9.

Baldus, H. (2015). History's paper trail: What handwriting & spelling reveal about early America. Retrieved from https://livesandlegaciesblog.org/2015/07/29/historys-paper-trail-what-handwriting-spelling-reveals-about-early-america/

Barker, C., & Pistrang, N. (2010). *Basics of APA Citation and Referencing Style*. Retrieved from London: https://www.ucl.ac.uk/dclinpsy/docs/res_docs/Apastyle.doc

Bayerische StaatsBibliothek. (2009). Adelung, Johann Christoph: Grammatisch-kritisches Wörterbuch der hochdeutschen Mundart (1811). Retrieved from http://lexika.digitale-sammlungen.de/adelung/online/angebot

BBC. (2009). MP brands dyslexia a 'fiction'. *BBC*. Retrieved from http://news.bbc.co.uk/1/hi/england/manchester/7828121.stm

British Library. (n.d.). 1755 - Johnson's dictionary. Retrieved from http://www.bl.uk/learning/langlit/dic/johnson/1755johnsonsdictionary.html

Bryson, B. (2007). *Shakespeare: the world as stage* (1st ed.). New York: Atlas Books/HarperCollins.

Coughlan, S. (2011). Spelling mistakes 'cost millions' in lost online sales. Retrieved from http://www.bbc.co.uk/news/education-14130854

Curtis, P. (2004, September 24). Dyslexia 'costs UK £1bn annually'. *The Guardian*. Retrieved from https://www.theguardian.com/education/2004/sep/24/schools.uk1

Davis, R. D., & Braun, E. M. (2010). *The gift of dyslexia: why some of the smartest people can't read—and how they can learn* (Updated; rev. and expanded; Updated Perigee trade pbk. ed.). New York, N.Y.: Penguin Group.

Dürre, R. (2000). *Legasthenie: Das Trainingsprogramm für Ihr Kind*. Freiburg, Basel, Wien: Herder.

Dyslexia International. (2014). *Dyslexia International: Better training, better teaching*. Retrieved from http://www.dyslexia-international.org/wp-content/uploads/2016/04/DI-Duke-Report-final-4-29-14.pdf

Eimer, M. (2018). [The Birkbeck psychological society: Careers event].

Elliott, J., & Grigorenko, E. L. (2014). *The dyslexia debate*. New York, NY: Cambridge University Press.

Essinger, J. (2006). *Spellbound: The improbable story of English spelling: The true story of man's greatest invention*. London: Robson Books.

Freud, S. (1920, 2011). *A general introduction to psychoanalysis*: PDF Books World.

Godwin, J. (2012). *Studying with dyslexia*. Basingstoke; New York, NY: Palgrave Macmillan.

Gopnik, A. (2009). *The philosophical baby: What children's minds tell us about truth, love, and the meaning of life* (1st ed. ed.). New York: Farrar, Straus and Giroux.

Gov.UK. (n.d.). Children with special educational needs and disabilities (SEND). Retrieved from February 12, 2018, https://www.gov.uk/children-with-special-educational-needs/print

Hallahan, D. P., & Mercer, C. D. (2002). Learning disabilities: Historical perspectives. In R. Bradley, L. Danielson, & D. P. Hallahan (Eds.), *The LEA series on special education and disability. Identification of learning disabilities: Research to practic* (pp. 1–67). Mahwah, NJ, US: Lawrence Erlbaum Associates Publishers.

Lawrence, D. (2009). *Understanding dyslexia: A Guide for teachers and parents.* Maidenhead: Open University Press.

Leopold Ludwig. (2015). Geschichte der Legasthenie: Forschungsarbeiten von 1945-70 [Blog Post]. Retrieved from https://geschichtederlegasthenie.wordpress.com/

Miles, T. R., & Miles, E. (1999). *Dyslexia: A hundred years on.* Buckingham, Philadelphia: Open University Press.

Morgan, P. (1896). A case of congenital word blindness. *The British Medical Journal, 2,* 1378.

Morrison, L. (2017, August 8). The true importance of good spelling. *BBC Global News.* Retrieved from http://www.bbc.com/capital/story/20170807-the-true-importance-of-good-spelling

NHS choices. (2015, September 15). *Dyslexia.* Retrieved from https://www.nhs.uk/conditions/dyslexia/

Open Dyslexic. (2018). Free, open source dyslexia typeface. Retrieved from https://opendyslexic.org/

Ramus, F. (2014). Should there really be 'dyslexia debate'? *Brain a journal of neurology, 137*(12), 3371–3374. doi:10.1093/brain/awu295

Regent's University School of Psychotherapy and Psychology. (2017). *DPsych Assessment Handbook 2017/18*: Regent's University.

Richards, C. (2017). *How to write for publication.* Paper presented at the DCoP Annual Conference, Stradford Upon Avon.

Sarason, I. G. (1984). Stress, anxiety, and cognitive interference: Reactions to tests. [10.1037/0022-3514.46.4.929]. *Journal of Personality and Social Psychology, 46*(4), 929–938.

Slipper, D. (2014). The dyslexia factor. *BBC.* Retrieved from http://www.bbc.co.uk/ouch/features/high_achieving_dyslexics.shtml

Snowling, M. J. (2015). Early identification and interventions for dyslexia: a contemporary view. *Journal of Research in Special Educational Needs, 13*(1), 7–14. doi:10.1111/j.1471-3802.2012.01262.x

Vlachos, F., Andreou, E., & Dellliou, A. (2013). Brain hemisphericity and developmental dyslexia. *Research in Developmental Disabilities, 34*(5), 1536–1540. doi:10.1016/j.ridd.2013.01.027

Von Bredow, R., & Hackenbroch, V. (17.06.2013). Die neue Schlechtschreibung. *Der Spiegel, 25,* para 26.

Warnock, H. M. (1978). Report of the committee of enquiry into the education of handicapped children and young people. London: Her majesty's stationery office.

Welford, M. (2012). *Building your self-confidence using compassion focused therapy.* London: Robinson.

Chapter 10

Managing self, managing others: What does owning one's perspective add to leadership when you are a black woman in the NHS?

Lorraine Gordon

Introduction

Emotional intelligence is an established pre-requisite for effective leadership (Goleman, 2000). This key characteristic inherently involves managing aspects of oneself and others in relation to the demands of the situation. A keen knowledge of ourselves, our self-concept and identity, and how we manage interactions with others undoubtedly is advantageous in the complex process of negotiating and taking up authority. This gives counselling psychologists a leadership vantage point providing a platform from which vision and values can be seen and heard. Effective leadership is the ability to influence, drive for results, manage crisis and manage change. All of these transactions and transformations happen within relationships and are dependent on enhanced communication skills. As scientist-reflexive practitioners, counselling psychologists are well-positioned to embody a rigorous and authentic personal leadership style. The level of awareness achieved through engagement with psychological theories of human development and distress, the application of theory in research and clinical practice, alongside exploration and challenge in personal therapy, make it possible for a robust individual to emerge from training. Learning is, by necessity, continuous. Leadership, of course, happens at every stage of a counselling psychologist's journey. From the first conversation with a colleague on placement, to the lonely heights as a consultant heading up an NHS multidisciplinary psychological therapies team, leadership can shine through. For some, the 'lonely heights' of leadership are difficult to contemplate and to articulate. In reality, it is about being careful whom one confides in, knowing there will be other political agendas. It is a relatively isolative position; middle managers can feel they are between a rock and a hard place with pressures from the executive being metered down on them whilst the anxiety of staff in the team they are leading also needs to be managed.

Although beset with a focus on ever more demanding targets and the harsh dogma of austerity, the National Health Service (NHS) is viewed internationally as a model of excellence (Schneider, Sarnak, Squires, Shah & Doty, 2017). An NHS 'free at the point of use' speaks to the value of nationwide equality of access for potential service users regardless of protected characteristic (Equality Act, 2010), social class, or economic status. Ethnicity, the self-determined, psychological essence of who we are as a people with shared history and a sense of belonging (Eleftheriadou, 1994), is one such defining feature. Catastrophically, however, even with the stated aim of equity, inequalities persist for service users (Joannou, Fernando, Harrison-Read & Wickramasinghe, 2011), carers and staff (West, Dawson and Kaur, 2015). When it comes to representation of diversity at the board level across organisations, people from black and minority ethnic groups are few and far between (McGregor-Smith, 2017). To the despair of a few, the great institution that is the NHS fares no better (Shaw, 2010; Kalra, Abel & Esmail, 2009; Kline, 2014). Those of us who are awake to this reality will be able to surmise that the cultural context within which we operate privileges some to the detriment of others. This is not a conclusion designed to induce guilt, although it may, but rather to allow for a realisation; a minor provocation to effect social change for the good of all. This being 'awake' involves a reflexive process of acknowledging one's own perspective and the impact of social construction. Further, it incorporates an awareness that the inherent biases and assumptions based on experience, theoretical orientations, personal anticipations and beliefs, necessitates flexibility allowing for the possibility of the alternative perspectives of others (Elliott, Fischer & Rennie, 1999).

We may discover that despite often hostile working environments, it is possible for a black woman to own her perspective and lead in the NHS. In this reflective piece any insights we gain would serve a useful purpose to future leaders. This section invites the reader to open themselves to the possibility that black women can lead effectively. This begs the question whether it is only possible for a black woman to lead if others in power allow it. Indeed, others with privilege can facilitate or allow black women to take up positions of leadership, as much as they can directly or indirectly work against it. The leadership displayed by others in the system is crucial. The kind of leadership that seeks the approval of other powerful figures or placates those with perceived power in order to maintain the status quo can have deleterious effects, stifling black would-be leaders. This chapter will go on to propose that the quality of service delivery, where service users are at the centre of our concern, with their needs as the highest priority, ought to be what drives us all. Sadly, I have found too many times that it is not. What follows throughout this chapter are further reflections of the author's own perspective and leadership style.

Leadership, diversity and the NHS

Diversity at all levels in an organisation such as the NHS is of paramount importance (West, Dawson & Kaur, 2015). Let us explore what it takes to become a leader in the NHS if you are of African or Caribbean heritage in Britain. As a British-born, Black-Caribbean, Consultant Counselling Psychologist Head of an adult mental health secondary care, borough-wide psychological therapies service in London, cultural identity development (Patel, Bennett, Dennis, Dosanjh, Mahtani, Miller & Nadirshaw, 2000) has had a key role to play along the journey. Imagine being eight years old and a kind teacher from Mauritius telling you, 'You know in order to do well you're going to have to work ten times harder than everyone else.' She saw something that others found it difficult to reconcile, acknowledge and validate. She saw potential, and articulated the struggle in that one sentence. The angry child side of me (Artnz & Jacob, 2012) railed against this injustice, and still does. Many individuals of African or Caribbean heritage may experience this same sense of having to work harder than others just to plateaux in their careers whilst the more fortunate flourish and thrive. One view that goes some way to expand on the reason black people may internalise this sense of 'not being good enough' is that they face unconscious bias, prejudice, the legacy of multiple stereotypes and discrimination by the majority with power and privilege which puts individuals from black and ethnic minority groups at a disadvantage. Perhaps the stage of identity development the black person has achieved as they interact within an environment that appears hostile, disapproving of them as a holistic person, determines their response to the unrelenting demands placed on them to conform. At times one may find themselves compensating for doubts about their self-worth and coping by overachieving. Others, or indeed the same individual at a different moment in time, may withdraw into themselves or surrender to the negative invalidating messages. We continue to ask ourselves how it is that in the Department for Education publication on Pupil Exclusions (2017) we see the following:

- 'Black Caribbean pupils were permanently excluded at three times the rate of White British pupils.
- For the broad ethnic groups, Black and Mixed pupils were the most likely to be permanently excluded and to have a fixed term exclusion'.

There are no definitive answers as to what makes this so; much more needs to be done to understand this phenomenon and its effects. Assuming acquiring an education is advantageous to developing the knowledge, skills and abilities necessary to obtain leadership positions within the NHS, we note that black children are often denied this right which extends the privilege of others. There is little published on this area in counselling psychology in the UK. A rare and visionary black female leader in the field asserts that, 'it is often apparent', 'that people of colour and also other ethnic minorities are underrepresented at different levels, especially high roles within the psychology profession' (McIntosh, 2017, p. 19). Although not all counselling psychologists gravitate towards the NHS on completion of their training, the BPS website careers page suggests there are, 'good prospects' for counselling psychologists in the NHS. This begs the question of whether prospects are better for some than they are for others.

On examination of the Workforce Race Equality Standard (Equality and Diversity Council, 2017) it becomes clear that although improvements are being seen in terms of an increase in nurses and midwives at Bands 6–9, between the years 2014 and 2017, and an increase in representation of people from black and minority ethnic groups as very senior managers between 2016 and 2017, in addition to a growing number of NHS Trusts with three or more BME board members, there is still much that needs to be done. Whilst shortlisted applicants from white backgrounds are 1.6 times more likely to be appointed than BME shortlisted applicants and BME staff are 8% more likely to experience discrimination at work from their colleagues and managers as white staff, we cannot conclude that there is race equality for staff in the NHS. Further, BME staff are reported to be 1.37 times more likely to enter the formal disciplinary process than white staff, depicting an environment or NHS culture that is hostile to BME staff.

We may well be all too familiar with the barriers for black women in leadership in the NHS, a series of micro-aggressions if you will. A dark-skinned middle-aged black woman with kinky curly hair who does not see her image reflected at the top of the organisation she works for may feel pressured to conform to white European ethnocentric views of how a 'professional' might appear. This often internalised authoritative, demanding narrative becomes part of the self-talk that perpetuates hypervigilance, heightened arousal and a constant state of threat for the individual like a punishing, demanding parent wielding unrelenting, unobtainable standards against a fearful vulnerable child (Arntz & Jacob, 2012). There have been accounts elsewhere of black women finding that those with light skin or straight hair are given preferential treatment (Robinson, 2011). Kalra et al. (2009) discuss how institutional racism is linked to the NHS discriminating against certain sections of its workforce. According to Kalra et al. (2009), direct management interventions are required to overcome barriers to promotion for black and minority ethnic staff. The next section is dedicated to expounding some of the competencies that might be exhibited by an effective leader and to the demonstrating the difference this can make.

Leadership competencies and reflexivity

According to Goleman (2000), self-awareness, self-regulation, motivation, empathy and social skill are vital leadership competencies. Reflexivity—acknowledging one's own perspective—is required as we interact with others and position ourselves within organisational cultures. For a black woman in leadership it is fundamental to centre herself in the Venn diagram (see Figure 10.1) of holding full knowledge of one's own culturally informed beliefs, values, verbal- and non-behaviour as well as her physical appearance

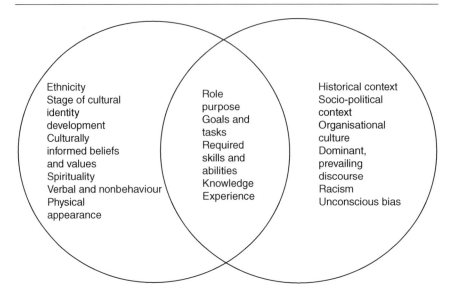

Figure 10.1 A black woman in leadership.

superimposed onto the socio-political/cultural context within which inter-actions with those we seek to lead take place.

There are established self-assessment tools utilised in programmes designed to enhance learning to manage and lead (REACH, 2017). For example, leadership can be demonstrated through competency in the following areas shown in Table 10.1 below:

Table 10.1 Leadership competencies (REACH, 2017)

1. **Self-awareness** – the ability to be aware of and manage one's own emotions, awareness of strengths and blind spots
2. **Communicating and influencing** – communicating complex information clearly, the ability to influence others
3. **Managing self** – self-motivated and self-confident, copes under pressure, demonstrates presence and poise
4. **Continuing self-development** – committed to one's own self-development, seeks feedback from others and makes changes to behaviours as a result
5. **Acting with integrity** – models and promotes a commitment to the principles of public life including: selflessness, objectivity, being open, and inclusive in behaviour
6. **Drive for results** – plans effectively, anticipates and prioritises, clear focus on results
7. **Change and improvement focus** – fully committed to service improvement, thinks and acts creatively and innovatively
8. **Managing the business** – manages financials and risk, establishes and delivers on plans, analyses data to reach sound decisions
9. **Building and maintaining relationships and networks** – builds effective relationships with others, adopts a collaborative approach, manages conflict effectively

Let us consider an example of the leadership competency of self-awareness. Clearly, it is possible to be aware of one's emotions, able to feel them in the body, accurately label, and use them in a positive way. An example of this is, through the vehicle of self-disclosure, highlighting frustration around the limitations in the system associated with financial constraints whilst outlining the consequences of deficits in service provision. Disclosing in this way brings attention to an unmet need which can then be analysed further leading to a shared understanding of the problem and an opportunity for resolution with all involved. A blind spot might be following through on implementing recommendations and reviewing solutions. Open discussion regarding blind spots would facilitate accountability and potentially also growth.

Let us now turn our attention to the leadership competency around communicating and influencing. Taking part in research such as randomised controlled trials being both on a steering group and as a trial therapist provides an opportunity to communicate complex information in a skilled, clear manner, disseminating information also through publishing articles in peer reviewed journals. Teaching and training psychologists and other professional groups, co-producing and delivering courses with peer trainers are some of the ways in which competency in communicating and influencing might be displayed. From this position, it is possible to, for example, give lectures, workshops, events on culture and diversity whilst regularly applying principles based on theory to one's own clinical practice in this area. This may involve playing a lead role in developing, coordinating and supervising psychologically informed training delivered within community mental health teams by psychologists and therapists as part of an approach to disseminating psychological theory. The strategic development of the training would necessitate that senior leaders and key decision-makers received a presentation about what this would involve and that a funding application to support the training was made.

Whilst managing change, demonstrating robust leadership is essential. Ahead of a service or directorate redesign, an effective leader would use skills in diplomacy to listen to the views of those affected by the change, bearing in mind the likelihood that there will be fear of the unknown. Providing information about the givens allows for a structural framework on which to hang uncertainty so the process of transformation can begin to take shape. Then follows engagement workshops where the relative merits of each option can be scrutinised. In one instance, a leader might present the strengths, weaknesses, opportunities and threats of a number of proposed models. A noble aim would be to do this in a balanced way whilst also working to positively influence a wide audience of stakeholders, possibly including commissioners, service users, carers, managers and staff. The delicate balance that must be struck in such a situation relates to positioning oneself in order to be a positive influence without appearing biased whilst acknowledging any conflicts of interest. Subsequently, organising team away days and using these opportunities to translate complex issues into meaningful actions, communicating the direction and strategic vision for the psychological therapy service could be beneficial.

Here, we consider an example of the leadership competency of managing self. Following change, the pressures on time can escalate along with the expectation of ever more 'efficiency' with ever fewer resources, a commonplace expectation in the NHS at the present time. Responsibility may increase without a corresponding rise in authority or reward. Determination, motivation to continue to drive for improvement in these circumstances cannot be imposed externally although the threat of cost improvement savings looms, motivation comes from the positive reinforcement achieved by striving for a resolution that is congruent with one's belief system. What is required is persistence, a consistently visible presence, reorganising priorities and choosing battles strategically. There may well be an expectation that an effective leader continuously adapts to anticipate and respond to changes which are out of her control whilst remaining true to the values she holds, with tension and the ability to recognise that and let it go.

A quality we might expect to see in an effective leader is continuing self-development. In our work with service users, as part of a collaborative approach it is an inherent part of the process that one regularly requests feedback. Through supervision and an organisation's appraisal system it is possible to gain regular feedback from supervisees and managers. Attending courses and conferences relevant to the leadership role assists with keeping knowledge and skills up to the required standard. Service user involvement through the coordination of service user for a where feedback on the service is gathered and developments are put in place in response to their comments/suggestions is essential. This is where members of staff meet with service users, facilitated by service user consultants on an involvement register, remunerated for their time, with the aim of driving quality improvement. An effective leader in the NHS puts the voices of service users at the heart of any improvement project.

Here we see an example of leadership incorporating acting with integrity, driving for results whilst maintaining a focus on change and improvement. Conducting an audit on the implementation of a directorate psychology supervision policy; quality improvement and service evaluation projects such as auditing against NICE guidance; supporting pre-qualified and qualified staff in their research and audit work are exercises demonstrating a focus on change and improvement. Completing assigned projects and meeting deadlines demonstrates leading from the front. This driving for results occurs whilst the leader pays attention to business financial risks, performance, outcomes and national strategic initiatives such as the Five Year Forward View for Mental Health (NHSE, 2016). Managing oneself by prioritising tasks and engaging in time management facilitates responsiveness to urgent requests. Providing deadlines for projects allows individuals within one's domain of influence to prioritise their work. An ability to utilise highly developed listening, verbal and written communication skills including communicating complex, highly technical and sensitive information to colleagues, clients and families is essential. The appropriate exchange of information with co-workers through honest and direct communication builds credibility. An ability to encourage others to share their ideas and suggestions enables multiple perspectives to be considered and makes innovation more of a possibility. On occasion, creating a space that facilitates a whistle-blowing culture within an organisation can be a catalyst for meaningful growth. A consistent message shared with staff about the evaluation framework of a service, emphasising the importance of demonstrating the quality of the work, develops a shared narrative and shared purpose.

Lastly, we turn our attention to the leadership competence of building and maintaining relationships and networks. Differing perspectives within a service are a strength, a resource which, when debated, synthesised and amalgamated forms an entity stronger than the sum of its parts. This requires one to be proactive about how informal meetings with peers are used to facilitate staff engagement and maintain meaningful networks. Supervising and managing others involves using knowledge of codes of conduct for people from diverse clinical backgrounds such as the expectations of regulatory bodies (e.g., the Health and Care Professions Council, the British Psychoanalytic Council, the United Kingdom Council of Psychotherapy, the General Medical Council and the Royal College of Psychiatry) whilst liaising with senior managers around appraisals and job planning to ensure resources are used to the maximum benefit of the service and organisation.

Compassionate leadership is possible even though the concept might at first be abhorrent to some. Many with privilege would rather a black woman did not have any influence over them at all and reject compassion expressed towards them. They are bound to be suspicious of her good intentions. For some, it is inconceivable that the agenda of a black female leader would be to improve the quality of life for people using the service. Indeed, the leader's intentions are at odds with the agenda of those she leads for a time. When there are strong personalities within an organisation, it is essential to use the awareness of one's own and others' emotions to empathise, collaborate, negotiate with and influence people and often most importantly, to set and enforce limits (Arntz & Jacob, 2012). A black female leader is able to be visionary and inspire others whilst appropriately receiving clinical, professional and managerial supervision as part of her continued professional development. Managing conflict effectively so that there is respect for each party throughout is an important objective requiring the support of strategic leaders and clear lines of accountability. It is possible to both value the contributions of others and to promote a sense of a shared purpose in delivering quality care to service users and carers.

Conclusion

We have seen that emotional intelligence is an essential component of effective leadership (Goleman, 2000). This relates to the central theme discussed here around managing aspects of oneself and others in relation to the demands of a particular situation. This chapter considered the notion that effective leadership is the ability to influence, drive for results, manage crisis and manage change. These complex interactions occur within relationships which require skilled communication. Counselling psychologists as scientist-reflexive practitioners are equipped with the skills, knowledge and experience which positions them well as leaders. In recent times, the NHS has faced an increasing demand on services with the pressure to meet efficiency targets. Within this context, inequalities persist for staff (West, Dawson & Kaur, 2015). Notably, when it comes to the visibility of diversity at board level across organisations, people from black and minority ethnic groups are underrepresented (McGregor-Smith, 2017). However, diversity at all levels in an organisation such as the NHS is of paramount importance (West, Dawson & Kaur, 2015).

We have discussed how the prevalence of prejudice and discrimination impacts the education system such that it disadvantages black children and privileges others. This was seen as a limiting factor on the development of black leaders who might otherwise take up positions in the NHS. This theme in the education system appears to mirror the institutional racism experienced by many within the workforce in NHS (Kalra et al., 2009; Rao, 2014). There is a chance this paper will be read by people being led by a black woman in the NHS. The intention is not to engender hopelessness or seek sympathy. Rather, to allow for the possibility that direct management interventions designed to overcome barriers to promotion for black and minority ethnic staff (Kalra et al., 2009) will be realised more often for more people.

We have seen examples of how it is feasible for a black woman in leadership to centre herself in the Venn diagram (see Figure 10.1) holding full knowledge of her culturally informed beliefs, values, verbal- and non-verbal behaviour as well as her physical appearance, superimposed onto the socio-political/cultural context within which interactions with those she seeks to lead take place. Despite micro-aggressions against black female leaders, this reflective piece reveals it is possible for a black woman to own her perspective and lead in the NHS.

References

Arntz, A. & Jacob, G. (2012). *Schema Therapy in Practice - an Introductory Guide to the Schema Mode Approach (1ˢᵗ Ed)*. West Sussex: Wiley-Blackwell.

Department of Education (2017). Pupil Exclusions. Statistics and Exclusions. Retrieved from: https://www.ethnicity-facts-figures.service.gov.uk/education-skills-and-training/absence-and-exclusions/pupil-exclusions/latest

Eleftheriadou, Z. (1994). *Gateways to Counselling: transcultural counselling*. London: Central Book Publishing.

Elliott, R., Fischer, C.T. & Rennie, D. L. (1999). Evolving guidelines for publication of qualitative research studies in psychology and related fields, *British Journal of Clinical Psychology, 38*, 215–219.

Equality Act (2010). c. 15. *Retrieved from*: https://www.legislation.gov.uk/ukpga/2010/15/contents

Equality and Diversity Council (2017). NHS Workforce Race Equality Standard: 2017 Data Analysis Report for NHS Trusts.

Goleman, D. (2000). *Leadership that gets results*. Boston, Massachusetts: Harvard Business School Publishing Corporation.

Independent Mental Health Taskforce (2016). *Five Year Forward View for Mental Health*. NHS England.

Joannou, D., Fernando, M., Harrison-Read, C. & Wickramasinghe, N. (2011). Impacting on diversity in practice in an outer London borough. *Ethnicity and Inequalities in Health and Social Care, 4*(2) pp. 71–80.

Kalra, V. S., Abel, P., & Esmail, A., (2009). Developing leadership interventions for Black and minority ethnic staff A case study of the National Health Service (NHS) in the UK *Journal of Health Organization and Management, Vol. 23 No. 1*, pp. 103–118.

Kline, R. (2014). The 'snowy white peaks' of the NHS: a survey of discrimination in governance and leadership and the potential impact on patient care in London and England. Middlesex University Research Repository: an open access repository of Middlesex University research http://eprints.mdx.ac.uk

McGregor-Smith, B. (2017). *The Time for Talking is Over Now is the Time to Act: Race in the Workplace*. The McGregor-Smith Review.

McIntosh, M. (2017). Making sense of idioms of distress and cultural expression in psychotherapeutic practice. In Y. Ade-Serrano, O. Nkansa-Dwamena, & M. McIntosh (Eds.), *Race, culture and diversity: a collection of articles*. DCoP (Division of Counselling Psychology, British Psychological Society).

Patel, N., Bennett, E., Dennis, M., Dosanjh, N., Mahtani, A., Miller, A. Nadirshaw, Z. (2000). *Clinical Psychology, 'Race' and Culture: a training manual*. BPS Books (The British Psychological Society).

REACH (2017). *Learning to Lead programme (personal communication)*. South London and Maudsley NHS Foundation Trust (SLaM) Partners.

Schneider, E. C., Sarnak, D. O., Squires, D., Shah A., & Doty, M. M. (2017). Mirror, Mirror 2017: International Comparison Reflects Flaws and Opportunities for Better U.S. Health Care. Commonwealth Fund.

Rao, M. (2014). 'Inequality rife among black and minority ethnic staff in the NHS'. Guardian article. Retrieved from: https://www.theguardian.com/healthcare-network/2014/aug/01/inequality-black-ethnic-minority-rife-nhs

Robinson, C. L. (2011). Hair as Race: Why "Good Hair" May Be Bad for Black Females, *Howard Journal of Communications, 22*(4), 358–376.

Shaw, P. (2010). Diversity training: a DVD resource showcasing BME roles. *Community Practitioner, 83*(12), 30–33.

West, M., Dawson, J. & Kaur, M. (2015). *Making the difference: diversity and inclusion in the NHS*. The Kings Fund. NHS England.

Part III

Leadership in organizations

Chapter 11

The challenges of authenticity: Leadership as a lesbian

Daisy Best

Lesbian, Gay, Bisexual and Transgender (LGBT) issues are frequently fused together within research and literature. Research within the context of leadership and career development is not distinct from this, wherein lesbians are usually incorporated as part of the broader gay and lesbian community rather than seen as distinct entities of their own (Fisher, Gushue & Cerrone, 2011; Gedro, 2010). Furthermore, research tends to place particular emphasis upon gender, sex and sexual orientation rather than on the skills or attributes of lesbian leaders. Such attributes are, therefore, difficult to define due to the lack of research in this area (Gedro, 2010). Consequently, it seems judicious to consider the 'L' as separate from the 'B, G and T' in order to identify specific issues and to illuminate the challenges that may be present for this distinct group. For example, Gedro (2010) identified four themes which she labelled as 'pressures' for lesbians; managing the heterosexism within organisations, how visible we are about our sexuality, how we express ourselves and the roles that are expected of us as women. It was refreshing to read about the pressures she had identified as they very much resonated with my own experience including questions such as 'am I being treated like this because I am a woman or because I am a lesbian or both?' For example, on occasions when I have been side-lined within a conversation that is dominated by men, I have wondered if I am viewed as 'less than' because I am a woman or because they do not understand me as a lesbian and therefore view me as difficult to tolerate or see as an 'equal other'. Perhaps I am viewed as less of a leader because I am a woman who does not fit the cultural stereotype of a 'masculine' lesbian and therefore, viewed as not having 'masculine' qualities in which the tasks of leadership are favoured over the relational aspects (Gedro, 2010). As a lesbian with leadership responsibilities, this chapter is a reflection of my own experiences synthesised with some of the relevant literature in this field.

Preparation for this chapter began with reflections of my own experience, wondering if I was fraudulent to write about some of the challenges lesbian leaders face when I personally do not face overt discrimination within the workplace. Discrimination does not need to be directly experienced in order for us to express a view on it and yet, I wanted this to be much more than a view. I wanted it to be a reflective, personal account that links with the current literature and affirms those with similar experiences whilst enabling a space for reflection for those with different experiences. I work with a diverse and inclusive team and have some dynamic, lesbian role models within my institution. Therefore, the imposter syndrome crept in and reminded me that I should feel grateful for what I have, concluding that what I have to offer to the leadership and diversity series is limited. However, I then began to remind myself of the subtleties of 'being different' that have a daily presence in my life, described by deLeon and Brunner (2013, p. 179) as 'the small acts of discrimination'. The assumptions others make about my sexuality (most people appear surprised when I tell them I am a lesbian) and the decisions I am faced with including whether or not I 'out myself' are all too common. The frequent normative references to heterosexuality can add to the 'social stress' that pervades as a minority in society and contributes to the 'felt stigma' even when not directly targeted towards the individual (Fassinger, Shullman & Stevenson, 2010). Such 'micro-aggressions' that have been identified in mental health clinicians, for example, can include assumptions that the client is heterosexual, attempts to understand why they are a lesbian and seeing homosexuality as a cause of any current difficulties (Moleiro & Pinto, 2015). These experiences are global and inherent yet I, and undoubtedly others, just want to live my life without my sexuality or gender being an issue or even being something that matters (deLeon & Brunner, 2013). Heintz (2012), however, found most of her fifteen participants within a study, which qualitatively explored lesbian executives' narratives, experienced negative responses from others about their sexuality. Thus, sexual identity remains an issue for others and can present a multitude of challenges for lesbian leaders.

Heteronormative world

It is pertinent to acknowledge the issue of the broader, environmental context. As psychologists, we usually work within environments that would be expected to abide by anti-discriminatory practices; of course, this does not always mean that they do. We should be protected by the law and the ethics/culture of the organisations within which we work compared to some of our lesbian peers within and outside of the UK, where disclosure can be risky for psychological, physical and career security (deLeon & Brunner, 2013; Fassinger, Shullman & Stevenson, 2010). Internalised stigma, often referred to as 'internalised homophobia' or 'internalised homonegativity', which is 'the internalisation of negative attitudes and assumptions concerning homosexuality' is likely to be a part of our identity living in a heteronormative world (Szymanski, Chung & Balsam, 2001, p. 27). This identity can include self-loathing of our bodies (Myers, 2013), hiding our sexuality from others and experiences of shame, anxiety and an overall depreciation of who we are (Frost & Meyer, 2009). Despite the protection of UK law and professional ethics, it is ingrained in the fabric of our heteronormative UK society and subtle in the way it is communicated and experienced.

Some of the studies here focus upon sexual minority people overall (Collins, 2012; D'Augelli, 2006, deLeon & Brunner, 2013; Fassinger, Shullman & Stevenson, 2010) and on gender specifically (Eagly, Johannesen-Schmidt & van Engen, 2003; Fisher, Gushue & Cerrone, 2011; Kim & Shim, 2003), yet by doing so they fail to acknowledge the unique perspectives of lesbians. Such differences are highlighted by Gedro (2010), who states that lesbians may be a triple minority which includes sexual identity, gender and gender expression, not to mention other aspects of intersectionality. Gedro (2010) considers the pressure on women to wear make-up and to dress in order to feel attractive suggesting that the sexuality of women continues to be viewed as important and therefore led by a male dominated, heteronormative agenda.

Invisibility versus authenticity

Lesbianism is mostly a perceptually ambiguous identity (Wilson, Remedios & Rule, 2017). In other words, it is an invisible trait. It is also clear that the paucity of literature on gay women and leadership serves to add to this invisibility. Lesbians in leadership roles may choose to maintain this aspect of invisibility for a number of reasons including to avoid any potential discrimination from those they are leading or who they are approaching for promotion. In addition, sexual identity minorities vary in the way they allow their personal and professional lives to overlap or remain distinct from each other (Masterson, 2011) and many lesbians will choose to hide their sexual identity in order to maintain this distinction. Albeit based upon experiences in the USA, Masterson acknowledges that previously, hiring someone gay for a senior position would be less likely as this challenged the institutional status quo, yet now it would be seen as less controversial and almost a fashionable choice to make. The author suggests that this is a reflection of the changes to the philosophy of organisations which may include a statement of equality and diversity within the mission or stated values. This is also likely to be influenced by changes in law including The Equality Act (2010) and The Criminal Justice Act (2008). I personally would prefer to be hired on the basis of my knowledge and skills rather than as part of fulfilling a diversity agenda. Additionally, lesbians may not wish to take the risk to expose their sexuality for fear that it will influence promotional prospects versus living with the incongruence of not feeling like an authentic leader if they hide who they are. Incongruence can have a profound impact upon emotional experiences, as highlighted by deLeon and Brunner (2013), who developed a model for understanding the experiences of lesbian/gay educational leaders in response to the action and attitudes of society. Within the theme of 'Fear-Losses' the authors identified 'Life Without Emotion' and captured this as follows: 'One can argue that anytime an individual lives a life contrary to their convictions and in direct opposition to their inner-most desires and feelings, they are living lives without, or stifled, emotions' (p. 177). Gedro (2010) acknowledges that 'lesbian leaders must determine if, when, where, and how to self-identify their sexual orientation status' (p. 558), a decision that lesbians and lesbian leaders are consistently confronted with.

Heintz (2012) identifies the potential or perceived choice of a lesbian leader: to be either her authentic self by letting people know or not telling anyone thus, minimising judgement/criticism and ultimately keeping her job. Consequently, a risk assessment or cost benefit analysis is continuously being undertaken. The decision to remain invisible is likely to have psychological consequences for her. For example, detachment from emotion (when we are not being our authentic self), shame, anger and anxiety are all associated with lack of disclosure (Heintz, 2012; deLeon & Brunner, 2013). Furthermore, acceptance is important to most people and this fundamental need for acceptance and a sense of belonging often results in silence and incongruence (deLeon & Brunner, 2013).

'Coming out' (informing others of our sexual identity) can be very difficult for LGB people, but as D'Augelli (2006, p. 204) highlights 'LGB people "come out" to others throughout their lives' and lesbian leaders are no different. According to Heintz (2012), the anxiety that 'coming out' can provoke in those who have made the choice to do so can be considerable. Conversely, 'coming out' also enables lesbian leaders to provide a positive role model to others, and this has certainly been the case within my institution. The openness of others about sexual identity can be affirming and reassuring and it has provided me with the confidence to see those in higher leadership positions who are lesbians use their 'privileged' leadership position of power to enable others to do the same.

Recently, I had a conversation with a self-identified heterosexual psychologist who was surprised by my delight to discover that an internationally recognised professor, researcher and therapist has been in a long-term relationship with a woman. In response, the psychologist asked me 'Why are you so pleased about that? Why does it matter?' I paused for a moment and then said, 'It feels affirming'. Meyer (2003) highlights how being part of a group and having a sense of cohesiveness with another can mitigate against mental health deterioration. This experience of being part of a collective or sharing identity as a lesbian is very important when living in a heteronormative society and when those in leadership positions are visible with an opportunity to become positive role models for others. Described as 'comradely love', deLeon and Brunner (2013) frequently refer to the word 'connection' when describing the experience and importance of belonging to a wider collective for LGBT people, in particular for those in leadership positions.

Personal support

Social Cognitive Theory (Bandura, 1986 as cited in Fisher, Gushue & Cerrone, 2011, p. 443), which was adapted to form Social Cognitive Career Theory (SCCT), implies that personal characteristics, including gender and lesbian identity, are likely to influence the contexts that we live within and the associated barriers or support mechanisms which, ultimately, inform our direction in life. Thus, it has been asserted that a lesbian with minimal support from family or the lesbian community is less likely to be career focused and therefore less inclined to work towards a leadership position. Fisher, Gushue and Cerrone (2011) conducted research informed by the SCCT model to ascertain if external support, sexual identity and career aspirations were causative for women who self-identified as a 'sexual minority'.

Interestingly, they found that women who had support with their careers from family and friends and those who were in a committed relationship were more inclined to have career aspirations. A negative sexual identity was linked to the overall relationship between support from family and friends towards her career and her career aspirations. Thus, women who have fewer career aspirations than their counterparts are unlikely to have support from family and/or friends. It is possible that they will prefer to hide their sexual identity, need acceptance from others regarding their sexuality, experience 'homonegativity' (negative thoughts towards being a lesbian) and have had a difficult time coming out and coming to terms with their sexual identity.

Fassinger, Shullman and Stevenson (2010) identified that stigma from within society is disempowering and can impact all levels of leadership progression due to internalised stigma which in turn pervades the individual's self-worth. As highlighted above, internalised stigma is the level of prejudice and discrimination that exists in society towards sexual identity minorities and which pervades the very being of the lesbian herself. This can result in 'minority stress' which is associated with poor perceived social support, mental health problems and substance use and abuse (Lehavot & Simoni, 2011). The discrimination and prejudice from others can range from a lack of belief in her capability to be a leader, structures that minimise opportunities and the perception of others that she is incapable based upon her sexual identity. Paradoxically, the authors highlight that the skills developed from the experience of stigma can become useful leadership attributes such as resilience, an appreciation of privilege and power for those she leads, self-care and ability to cope with criticism. Described by deLeon and Brunner (2013) as a 'warrior of the heart' (p. 183), the lesbian leader can be courageous and strong yet empathic and aware and utilise her challenging experiences to help develop leadership skills.

Leadership approaches

Much of the literature that focuses upon leadership approaches is based upon studies that were initially influenced by models of the 'great man' theories of leadership that were later applied to women (Chin & Sanchez-Hucles, 2007, p. 609). Issues of diversity have commonly been neglected and Chin and Sanchez-Hucles (2007) identify this bias in a commentary to the *American Psychologist* on their special edition on leadership which excluded attention to diversity issues. They report that the biases 'have placed increased burdens on women, racial/ethnic minorities, and others with multiple identities to behave according to stereotyped leadership characteristics while at the same time being expected to behave according to their gender and/or racial/ethnic minority role characteristics' (p. 609). They suggest that many studies which focus upon characteristics of leaders are based upon those already in leadership positions. They argue that leaders are predominantly white men so those from minority groups may be expected or may expect to lead with a similar style (i.e., masculine traits, as an example). However, research has also suggested that women are more likely to be accepted as leaders when they operate from within their 'expected role' such as kind and selfless rather than authoritative or dominant (Eagly, Johannesen-Schmidt & van Engen, 2003). This, Chin and Sanchez-Hucles (2007) suggest, has also impacted upon the ability for minority groups to gain and effectively sustain leadership positions. The following section aims to provide an overview of leadership approaches for lesbians within the context of minimal research in this area, much of which is focused upon women as leaders rather than lesbians as leaders.

The transformational approach

Gedro (2010) has acknowledged that the leadership style of women differs from men, as they tend to be less hierarchical, more sharing of power and more inclusive with a focus upon relationships. Despite this, Gedro has identified that researchers have found that people would rather be led by a man than a woman regardless of the woman's leadership style. This appears to be linked to gender stereotypes in which men are viewed as credible leaders because their masculinity provides them with the traits required. Thus, because they are male, they are automatically viewed as having the required competencies (Eagly, 2007). She also highlights the results of polls in America that asked respondents about their preferred choice of boss, which showed consistently higher responses for male over female bosses between 1975 and 2006. This prejudice is likely to impact upon the lesbian leader in terms of confidence and it is important to note that the perceptions of the leader are as influential as the experiences of the leader.

Transformational approaches to leadership have been described as a way in which the leader engages the follower(s) by being an authentic role model that provides 'inspirational motivation and intellectual stimulation', demonstrating 'individualised consideration' (Kearney & Gebert, 2009, p. 79). Team outcomes are enhanced via optimism and effectiveness based upon the goals and values of individuals and the shared aims and objectives of the wider team. It can be inferred that this approach to leadership is likely to be favoured by lesbian leaders because LGBT leaders as marginalised groups have a preference for and are more likely to elicit this type of leadership (Fassinger, Shullman & Stevenson, 2010) as are women (Eagly, Johannesen-Schmidt & van Engen, 2003). This was also supported by Kim and Shim (2003) in their study into the gender-based approach to leadership among retail managers in which female managers preferred a style which encourages a work environment that is interactive, including offering support, being persuasive and developing people, characteristics often identified as 'feminine'. However, this study, as many others, focused upon female rather than specifically lesbian leaders.

Eagly (2007) has acknowledged that women are often placed at one of two opposite ends of a stereotypical continuum of what it takes to be a good leader: viewed as being either 'not tough enough or not taking charge' or not demonstrating sufficient feminine qualities and thus being viewed as 'just like a man or like an iron lady' (p. 4). It can be assumed that the same narrow view is associated with lesbian leaders who may already struggle to justify their gender, sexual identity and gender expression within the given context.

In all instances, it is important to consider the context within which leadership is taking place (a military environment versus a health care setting for example), where preferences of gender are often very explicit. The context needs to be 'amenable' to the female leader who engages in behaviours deemed to be transformational (Yoder, 2001, p. 825).

The context

One of Heintz's (2012, p. 129) participants questioned how accomplished others would regard her once they knew she was a lesbian: 'Am I now going to be perceived as my sexuality versus my capabilities, and would that take away from what I am trying to accomplish from a professional standpoint?' Furthermore, sixteen out of seventeen participants in deLeon and Brunner's (2013) qualitative study identified feeling inferior in their professional and/or personal lives and lacking in equality to those in heterosexual relationships. The negative impact upon self-worth is difficult to quantify and can often lead to lesbian leaders overcompensating and having to 'prove' their worth in order to feel good enough; 'these leaders felt the pains of subordination and turned to over-compensation as a vehicle to validate and be *normal*' (deLeon & Brunner, 2013, p. 177). Alternatively, in a different study, lesbians who identified as 'butch' were conflicted between applying for a job that they wanted and doubts that their identity performance (how they dress, behave) would be acceptable when considering the interview process and beyond (Woodruffe-Burton & Bairstow, 2013).

Yoder (2001) states that 'leadership does not take place in a genderless vacuum' (p. 815) and therefore leadership for women and men may differ considerably, particularly within what is described as 'uncongenial contexts' (p. 817). Equally, we cannot ignore that leadership also does not take place in a sexual identity vacuum. Thus, the ability for women to be more effective within the context is dependent upon their own leadership abilities, the support offered by the organisation and the contextual ethos, and therefore such influences will also influence the efficacy of lesbians in leadership. Where support is lacking within an organisation, lesbians may need to work closely with human resources departments to 'help create equitable structures and opportunities for all by dismantling the sexism, heterosexism, homophobia, and silence that stifles the full range of opportunities for lesbians who are, or who want to become, leaders' (Gedro, 2010, p. 561). However, the author acknowledges that the paucity of published research in the area of lesbians and leadership has resulted in limited knowledge of the experiences of lesbian leaders and how they respond to the challenges highlighted here.

In summary, women who are more likely to be effective in 'masculinized settings' are those who value cooperation between themselves and those that they lead, (rather than a focus upon self-interest), gain acceptance from the group before influencing change and demonstrate their competence in their role (Yoder, 2001, p. 820). However, the author identifies that sole responsibility should not be on the female leader but also on the organisational context in terms of support and validation (legitimisation and awareness of skills). Such considerations are likely to apply to lesbian leaders although the limited research in this area results in applying the knowledge from the research to female leaders rather than relying upon a robust evidence base for this diverse population. Furthermore, how lesbian leaders can help to influence the culture of the organisation also requires further investigation.

Implications for lesbian psychologists in leadership roles

Personal reflection and therapy can enable us to explore internalised stigma and the way that this may influence our career choices. Additionally, identifying a support system (allies) within and external to the organisation can support us to develop our confidence, levels of authenticity and the space to reflect upon the difficulties and challenges that are part of our lived experience.

Where possible and if we feel able to take the risk to 'reveal' (Heintz, 2012, p. 123) our sexuality within the workplace, we can be role models to those that we lead and influence. A recent discussion with a very experienced lesbian academic focused upon when and how we 'out' ourselves to our students. Her approach (to display a picture of herself and her wife) in the first lecture felt very affirming for all students who may identify as LGBT and evidence of her own secure base within her sexual identity. I also choose to tell my students and colleagues who I work most closely with in order that I can be honest in those relationships and invite this reciprocity in them. This has been identified as 'demonstrating strength and personal power' by deLeon and Brunner (2013, p. 182) which enables a more congruent self as well as an affirming role model. However, LGBT people 'should be allowed and encouraged to lead without a significant amount of emphasis placed on their personal sexual orientation, unless it is appropriate and necessary to have such emphasis' (Collins, 2012, p. 369). Equally, he identifies that 'those who can be out *must* remain out as the voice for those who cannot speak up' (p. 369). Therefore, as lesbians who feel able to communicate their sexual identity to others, we may be able to advocate for those whose identity remains hidden.

We can encourage and influence others to conduct research that reinforces the skills and abilities of lesbians as leaders, particularly in the UK where research in this area is limited (Collins, 2012; Woodruffe-Burton & Bairstow, 2013) and mostly undertaken from a human resource rather than a psychological perspective. Furthermore, we can contribute to programmes that develop leaders. Fassinger, Shullman and Stevenson (2010) highlight the importance of feminist epistemology which promotes the development of leadership from the experiences and insights of minority groups rather than the privileged groups only.

Conclusion

Those in a senior position are in the limelight of the organisation which can also result in an increased interest in their personal and private lives (Heintz, 2012). Therefore, this can create a number of dilemmas and challenges to authenticity and acceptance. D'Augelli (2006, p. 205) suggested that 'Those of us with social power take risks'. This resonates with me as a middle class, white woman employed in a well-paid role which provides me a degree of social power within an institution that includes the importance of diversity within their vision. Thus, it is safe for me to be a lesbian within this context from a legal and professional perspective but more importantly from a personal perspective. The issue of safety will always influence how 'out' a lesbian leader can be within an environment and ensuring support both within and outside of work is more likely to enable this. As psychologists we can influence the training of leaders, the research into the leadership needs and experiences of lesbians and be role models in supporting lesbians either as a representative or friend.

References

Bandura, A. (1986a). *Social foundations of thought and action: A social cognitive theory*. Englewood Cliffs, NJ: Prentice-Hall.

Chin, J. L., & Sanchez-Hucles, J. (2007). Diversity and leadership. *American Psychologist, 62,* 608–609. DOI:10.1037/0003-066X62.6.608

Collins, J. C. (2012). Identity Matters: A Critical Exploration of Lesbian, Gay, and Bisexual Identity and Leadership in HRD. *Human Resource Development Review 11*(3) 349–379. DOI: 10.1177/1534484312446810

deLeon, M. J. & Brunner, C. C. (2013). Cycles of Fear: A Model of Lesbian and Gay Educational Leaders' Lived Experiences. *Educational Administration Quarterly 49*(1) 161–203.

D'Augelli, A. R. (2006). Coming out, Visibility and Creating Change: Empowering Lesbian, Gay and Bisexual People in a Rural University Community. *American Journal of Community Psychology 37*: 203–210. DOI 10.1007/s10464-006-9043-6

Eagly, A. H., Johannesen-Schmidt, M. C., & van Engen, M. L. (2003). Transformational, transactional, and laissez-faire leadership styles: A meta-analysis comparing women and men. *Psychological Bulletin, 129*, 569–91. DOI:10.1037/0033-2909.129.4.569

Eagly, A. H. (2007). Female leadership advantage and disadvantage: Resolving the contradictions. *Psychology of Women Quarterly, 31*, 1–12. DOI:10.1111/j.1471-6402.2007.00326.x

Fassinger, R. E., Shullman, S. L., & Stevenson, M. R. (2010). Toward an Affirmative Lesbian, Gay, Bisexual, and Transgender Leadership Paradigm. *American Psychologist. Vol. 65*, No. 3, 201–215. DOI: 10.1037/a0018597

Fisher, L. D., Gushue, G. V., & Cerrone, M. T. (2011). The Influences of Career Support and Sexual Identity on Sexual Minority Women's Career Aspirations *The Career Development Quarterly, September, Vol 59*.

Frost, D. M. & Meyer, I. H. (2009). Internalised Homophobia and Relationship Quality Among Lesbians, Gay Men and Bisexuals. *Journal of Counselling Psychology, Vol. 5*, No.1, 97–109.

Gedro, J. (2010). Lesbian presentations and representations of leadership, and the implications for HRD. *Journal of European Industrial Training, Vol. 34 Issue: 6*, pp. 552–564. DOI: 10.1108/03090591011061220

Heintz, P. A. (2012). Work-Life Dilemmas Emerging From Lesbian Executives' Narratives. *The Career Development Quarterly. June, Volume 60*.

Kearney, E. and Gebert, D. (2009). Managing Diversity and Enhancing Team Outcomes: The Promise of Transformational Leadership. *Journal of Applied Psychology, Vol. 94*, No. 1, 77–89. DOI :10.1037/a0013077

Kim, H.-S. & Shim, S. (2003). Gender-based approach to the understanding of leadership roles among retail managers. *Human Resource Development Quarterly, 14*, 321–342.

Lehavot, K. & Simoni, J. M. (2011). The Impact of Minority Stress on Mental Health and Substance Use Among Sexual Minority Women. *Journal of Consulting and Clinical Psychology, Vol. 79*, No. 2, 159–170.

Masterson, K. (2011). Leadership Spots Opening Up for Gay and Lesbian Academics. *Chronicle of Higher Education, Vol. 57, Issue 30*.

Meyer, I. H. (2002). Prejudice, social stress and mental health in lesbian, gay and bisexual populations: Conceptual issues and research evidence. *Psychological Bulletin, 129*(5), 674–697. DOI: 10.1037/0033-2909.129.5.674

Moleiro, C. & Pinto, N. (2015). Sexual orientation and gender identity: review of concepts, controversies and their relation to psychopathology classification systems. *Frontiers in Psychology*. https://doi.org/10.3389/fpsyg.2015.01511

Myers, J. (2013). *Historical Dictionary of the Lesbian and gay Liberation Movements: historical Dictionaries of Religions, Philosophies and Movements Series*. New Jersey: Scarecrow Press.

Szymanski, D. M., Chung, Y. B., & Balsam, K. F. (2001). Psychosocial Correlates of InternalizedHomophobia in Lesbians. *Measurement and Evaluation in Counseling and Development, Volume 34, Issue 1*.

Wilson, J. P., Remedios, J. D., & Rule, N. O. (2017). Interactive Effects of Obvious and Ambiguous Social Categories on Perceptions of Leadership: When Double-Minority Status May Be Beneficial. *Personality and Social Psychology Bulletin, Vol. 43*(6) 888–900. DOI: 10.1177/0146167217702373

Woodruffe-Burton, H. R. & Bairstow, S. (2013). Countering heteronormativity: Exploring the negotiation of butch lesbian identity in the organisational setting. *Gender in Management: An International Journal, Vol. 28 Issue: 6*, pp. 359–374. DOI: 10.1108/GM-01-2013-0015

Yoder, J. D. (2001). Making leadership work more effectively for women. *Journal of Social Issues, 57*, 815–828. DOI:10.1111/0022-4537.00243

Social justice, leadership and multi-cultural competency amongst applied psychology trainees

Tony Ward

Introduction

This chapter discusses the notion that it is important for applied psychology trainees to have a deep awareness and knowledge about their own and other peoples' cultures. It is argued that this is essential not only in terms of their competence in working with clients, but also in terms of their development as future leaders and champions for social justice. There is a brief review of current accreditation standards in relation to this area, and suggestions in the literature for developing multi-cultural competency (MC) are discussed. Finally, suggestions are made as to how the profession could make further advances in relation to the MC of trainees.

Why is this important?

The United Nations (UN) (1948) declaration of human rights declares "all human beings are created free and equal". The majority of people in the contemporary United Kingdom (UK) would agree with the sentiments of this relatively recent statement of the ideal of human equality. However, for thousands of years human societies have not been organised with such principles in mind. For example, it was not until 1928, with The Representation of the People Act, that all women in the UK were able to vote in parliamentary elections on the same terms as men.

Almost seventy years after the UN declaration, the evidence remains that many structures in western society are not ordered according to principles of freedom and equality. Brammer, Millington and Pavelin (2007) report that typical boardrooms in the UK corporate sector are significantly lacking in terms of gender and ethnic diversity. Similarly, Kalra, Abel and Esmail (2009) point out the lack of Black and Ethnic Minority (BEM) representation at senior levels of the National Health Service (NHS).

Given the human propensity to discriminate against each other based on even minimal characteristics (Diehl, 1988), it is sadly not surprising that recourse to law has been necessary to protect people from discrimination based on perceived differences. In the UK, The Equalities Act (2010) protects people who have a number of specified characteristics. These are gender, race, age, sexual orientation, religion or belief, disability, pregnancy, marriage and civil partnership and being or becoming transgender.

We live in an increasingly diverse society. For example, a report by Bristol City Council in 2016 suggests that BEM representation in the city stands at 14%, up from 7% at the 2001 census date. Furthermore, psychological services are developing and reaching out to these diverse groups. Applied psychologists will therefore find themselves increasingly working with clients with one or more protected characteristics, as defined by the Equalities Act. It is therefore incumbent on training providers to ensure that all applied psychology trainees are comfortable and competent in working with the diverse clients they may come into contact with (Constantine et al., 2007).

However, it is not just because it will have an impact on the clients that use our services that we need to ensure that trainees are comfortable and competent in working with all aspects of diversity. There is also the argument that applied psychologists should be active champions of social justice (Constantine et al., 2007). This implies fair and equal access to resources for all. This includes not only our clients, but also ourselves as we strive to have our voices heard within the organisations within which we work. As already mentioned, the NHS is not immune from the lack of diversity evident in its senior echelons. This is an issue for us all, if we are serious about social justice, and becoming champions for diversity (notwithstanding the debate evident in the literature about the extent to which members of privileged groups can be champions for diversity—see Owen, 2009).

Thus, this topic of how we ensure a strong awareness of diversity amongst our applied psychology trainees is important because it impacts upon service delivery and clients, but also because it impacts upon us as professionals playing a role within our organisations. We want our trainees to aspire to become leaders in their turn, and to champion equality and fairness in their services and within management structures. It is good in this respect that our accreditation standards now typically require trainees to become familiar with aspects of leadership (e.g., see BPS accreditation guidelines for both Clinical and Counselling Psychology, both 2017). However, key texts on leadership frequently fail to deal with the issue of equality and diversity, even when written by psychologists (e.g., see Pendleton & Furnham, 2016—clearly not everything you need to know, despite the title!). Thus, we would hope that our trainees will be comfortable and competent in working with all aspects of diversity and will see the link from this to social justice. We would hope that in time they will become positive role models and champions as they take up leadership positions within their work places.

There is a burgeoning literature on all aspects of diversity, and it seems invidious to focus on one aspect at the expense of others. However, given the length of this piece, it will necessarily focus on one area, that of race and culture. There are many other important areas of diversity which trainees should be aware of, for example, sexuality (see, for example, Richards & Barker, 2013). These are just as important, but it is hoped a focus on the area of race and culture may also allow some general points and principles to be drawn out.

The origins of racial prejudice

The precise origins of prejudicial attitudes towards BEM groups in the UK is complex, but to some degree it can be traced back to colonial times (Lawrence, 1982). For example, in his controversial "History of Jamaica", written in 1774, the slave owner Edward Long described people of African descent in highly negative terms. Despite his lack of any academic or scientific training, this work was seen as quite authoritative at the time due to his personal experience of living in Jamaica.

Negative views of Africans undoubtedly served to justify slavery in the minds of European colonists. However, such negative attitudes, along with the physical realities and consequences, continued to pervade colonial societies long after the end of slavery (Ward & Hickling, 2004). Fanon and Sartre (1963) documented the highly negative consequences of colonialism, and reflected at some length on the consequences of European colonialism for people of African descent living under colonial rule (Fanon, 1970). A recent take on these issues was provided by the Martinician writer Edouard Glissant (1989), who detailed the rich irony of the local press on his island of birth, Martinique, in each year announcing the "first day of spring", this on an island where the ambient temperature rarely falls below 20 degrees Celsius. Fanon (1970) detailed the profound culture shock of moving from an overseas colony to the metropolitan centre (in his case, France), to discover that one would be subject to prejudice and discrimination, having being raised to see oneself as French, and being steeped in French culture. Hickling and Hutchinson (1999) detail how they see such processes unfolding in modern day British society, where young people develop an identity consistent with Britishness but then experience a shock where through prejudice they are treated differently. This then leads to the high incidence of mental health issues observed amongst Afro-Caribbean youth.

Modern day UK society seems to be in deep denial of the negative impact of the colonial past, which has implications for all elements of society, not just BEM groups (Ward and Hickling, 2004). A common personal white British response to the subject of racism is to deny personal prejudice, and espouse a "colour blind attitude (i.e., "I see all people as the same, no matter what their colour"). However, such a response fails to acknowledge the existence of privileged groups within society, and ignores the reality of prejudice and discrimination with which BEM groups have to contend every day (Gushue and

Constantine, 2007). The risk is that such "colour blind" attitudes may temper peoples' willingness to move towards a more activist position and champion social justice within their roles. Increasing awareness and acceptance of the reality of the persistent inequalities within society may encourage people to move towards the more active position.

Thus there are deep historical roots of prejudicial attitudes within Western society, and these have continuing consequences for everyone in our societies. It therefore seems imperative that psychologists should seek to ensure that the trainees they are responsible for are as well informed, insightful and competent as possible in dealing with all aspects of diversity.

Accreditation standards and diversity

In terms of applied psychologists working within health contexts, it is positive to note that the accreditation standards for both clinical and counselling psychologists in the UK refer to knowledge of issues around diversity.

The accreditation standards for clinical psychology state (BPS, 2017) as one of the overall programme goals that trainees should have:

> The skills, knowledge and values to work effectively with clients from a diverse range of backgrounds, understanding and respecting the impact of difference and diversity upon their lives. Awareness of the clinical, professional and social contexts within which work is undertaken and impact therein.

This statement is very close to what in the United States of America (USA) has come to be termed multi-cultural competence (MC), which is encouraging.

In the standards for the accreditation of Doctoral programmes in counselling psychology (BPS, 2017), there is a whole section of the programme content specification which deals with diversity. This is a very thorough specification, which covers all important aspects of The Equality Act as well as touching on themes related to social justice, for example:

- value social inclusion and demonstrate a commitment to equal opportunities;

  and

- understand issues of power, discrimination and oppression, the psychological impact of these, and how to work with these issues psychologically.

The counselling psychology specification can also be seen as covering MC, but is more detailed and also as noted leans towards social justice. Again, this is encouraging.

Thus, we can see that current BPS accreditation standards for the two main groups of applied psychologists that work in health settings, specify that trainees should have knowledge, values and competence around the area of diversity and to some extent, social justice. What such guidelines do not do is help trainers to think about best practices in achieving this. Nor does it necessarily encourage trainers to join up different aspects of the training agenda, though this is something we would undoubtedly wish to encourage. Whilst both clinical and counselling standards refer to knowledge and an initial competence around leadership, an explicit link between leadership, diversity and social justice is less apparent. Furthermore, such standards set minimum expectations, but they don't tell us what the best possible practice looks like. At this point in time it's probably also fair to say we don't know how effective programmes are in meeting these objectives.

The psychology profession has been regulated in the UK since 2009 by the Health and Care Professions Council (HCPC). The standards of conduct, performance and ethics require registrants to protect the interests of service uses and individuals, and to challenge discrimination (HCPC, 2016). The HCPC standards of proficiency for psychologists also require practitioners to be aware of the impact of culture, equality and diversity on practice, and to practice in a non-discriminatory manner (HCPC, 2015).

Raising awareness of diversity

In the USA, this aspect of training has come to be known as multi-cultural competence (MC). This is defined as being self-aware and having relevant knowledge and skills around diversity and culture (Constantine et al., 2007; Kim & Lyons, 2003; Daniel et al., 2004). The question then is, how do we instil MC in applied psychology trainees?

One source of inspiration might be the literature on diversity training. Such training has been carried out over many years in many different types of organisations and contexts, including hospitals and universities. Bezrukova, John and Spell (2012) carried out a comprehensive review of 178 studies, and concluded that integrated training is better than stand alone. This may be relevant to applied psychology training programmes, where specific courses or modules are devoted to diversity, whereas this review would suggest that MC competencies should be integrated across the programme. The challenge then, however, may be in ensuring that this embedding does actually happen and is effective. Kulik and Roberson (2008) make the point that despite the huge amount of diversity training now going on, it rarely gets evaluated. This may explain why change is so slow in this area, in that no one seeks evidence that interventions have been effective and made a real difference. This is perhaps a good point for UK based trainers, who might consider the impact of the training on MC. This is also relevant to a point made by Sanchez and Medkik (2004), that there can be unintended consequences of diversity training. They had in mind the observation that some managers behaved less well after training, due to a perception that they had been "sent for training". In relation to trainee psychologists we might wonder how trainees react to such training, and with what subsequent consequences? For example, do trainees assume that they have awareness and don't need to act, or that this part of the curriculum does not really apply to them? Whereas at a deeper level most people would acknowledge some degree of implicit bias.

High self-awareness is defined as part of the constellation of MC. It has also been suggested (Richardson and Molinaro, 1996) that self-awareness is a pre-requisite in the development of MC. There is evidence from the USA that white undergraduates in general are less aware of issues facing BEM groups than their Afro-American peers (Ancis, Sedlacek & Mohr, 2000). Several authors (Gushue & Constantine, 2007; Constantine, 2002; Ancis & Szymanski, 2001) have used the concept of racial identity as one area in which trainees need to develop their awareness. For example, in white trainees, the identity of "disintegration" is linked to higher racist attitudes (Constantine, 2002), whilst "autonomy" is linked to an acceptance of white identity, the existence of oppressive societal structures and a tendency towards a more activist stance (Gushue & Consantine, 2007). Racial identity is also linked to awareness of white privilege (Ancis & Szysmanski, 2001; Hays, Chang & Havice, 2007). From this it would seem that good programs should provide ample opportunities for trainees to reflect on themselves in relation to cross-cultural issues, and the topic of racial identity could be an area for fruitful exploration. The changing nature of racial identity could be one interesting aspect of the topic for discussion with trainees (e.g., see Perez & Hirschman, 2009).

In terms of strategies for raising levels of self-awareness in trainees, there are a number of ideas in the literature. Hill (2003) gives a comprehensive overview of this topic with many useful suggestions. For example, she suggests that it is useful for trainees to share their own experiences of diversity and culture with each other. This fits with McKenzie-Mavinga's (2005) suggestion that there should be a dialogue within training around cultural issues, but there is often a fear amongst trainees in initiating this. Black trainees welcome the opportunity to share their experiences with white peers. However, they may be wary of becoming the "black expert", which in turn may detract from their learning as they expend their energies in facilitating others. Kim and Lyons (2003) suggest a range of games and activities which can be used in training, whilst Thompson et al. (2002) suggest it can be useful to foster openness to aesthetic diversity. Roysircar et al. (2005) report a strategy for bringing trainees into contact with other cultural groups, for example, through mentoring students with English as a second language. Roysircar (2004) makes the link with psychology practice, for example, by suggesting that trainees should explore their relationship responses when working with clients from other cultures. Thus, there are many ideas in the literature, many originating in the USA. It would be good for trainers to take some of these up and evaluate their application within the UK context.

In terms of helping trainees to increase their knowledge of other cultures and perspectives, there are now a number of useful texts which can be recommended. As previously mentioned, Fanon and Sartre (1963) and Fanon (1970) writes about the experience of growing up in a French colony, and the impact of colonial regimes in Africa. Glissant (1989) gives a more recent take on the French colonial perspective, reflecting on his experiences of growing up and living in Martinique. FakhryDavids (2011) writes from a psychodynamic perspective on the phenomenon of racism, from both the perspective of the racist abuser through to the person experiencing the racism. Hickling (2007) talks about the experience of doing therapy in a former English colony and the long term impacts this can have on individuals and society. This led him to develop "psychohistoriography", a novel form of psychotherapy designed to help people reflect on the impact of their culture and history. Lago (2005) discusses the issue of race and culture in relation to counselling, and such perspectives are further expanded upon in a comprehensive edited handbook (Lago, 2011). Laungani (2004) discusses in detail Asian perspectives on counselling and psychotherapy, whilst the book by McKenzie-Mavinga (2009) is a similar work from the Black cultural perspective. Parham, White and Ajamu (1999) discuss psychological perspectives from a Black African USA-centric point of view. All of these texts are useful in helping trainees to think about other cultures and backgrounds, and there are many others, from personal accounts such as Dabydeen's (2005) "The Intended", through to sociological texts such as Griffin's (1961) "Black Like Me" (in this somewhat controversial study, Griffin took medication to make himself appear black, and describes his experiences as he then made his way across the southern USA).

Whichever strategies are used to raise MC in trainees, courses should consider carefully the extent to which opportunities are provided in this area. There is evidence that trainees that have more exposure to relevant opportunities and courses tend to have higher MC. Pope-Davis et al. (1995) found in a sample of trainees in the USA, counselling psychologists had higher MC than clinical psychologists, and one possible factor which might account for this is the increased number of courses in the area which the counselling psychologists had been exposed to.

Becoming champions for social justice

Social justice is the valuing of fairness and equity in accessing treatment, resources and rights (Constantine et al., 2007). There is evidence that trainees would like increased emphasis on this in their courses (Beer et al., 2012; Singh et al., 2010). As previously indicated, social justice may be a theme which links across a number of areas of the curriculum in applied psychology, from work with individual clients, through to service structures and delivery, and on to representation with organisational hierarchies. This is not currently made explicit in our accreditation standards, but it may be something which the profession can actively consider for the future. The notion of "core professional competencies" from the USA, where MC is specified as a central dimension across aspects of applied psychology, could be something we consider in the UK (Fouad et al., 2009).

There is some discussion in the literature about how training programmes should go about making their values explicit (Mintz et al., 2009) and operationalising them (Winterowd et al., 2009). Mintz et al. (2009) make the point that there can be problems where values are not fully made explicit and articulated. They suggest that all applied psychologists need to be able to sign up to the core values of the profession and put them into practice. The initial level at which this arises for most trainees is in their practice with clients. All applied psychologists need to be able to work with all sections of their community, in a way which respects them as individuals. An example of where this can lead to difficulties is where a trainee's religious values appear to be in conflict with the diversity characteristics of a particular client (e.g., their sexuality). Whilst psychologists are free to exercise their rights to religious belief, they are not free to then treat clients differently as a result. Courses need to make provision for trainees to fully explore their values and the consequences, so that they can arrive at a place where they have fully developed MC. Strategies for doing this are discussed by Winterowd et al. (2009).

Recommendations for future directions

Although the accreditation standards for the two main health related areas of applied psychology, clinical and counselling specify in detail the need for cultural awareness and skills, the extent to which this is fully actualised by courses remains unclear. There is evidence that greater awareness and competency is linked to the amount of time dedicated to this area, and also that integrated training can be more effective in some contexts. There clearly have been times when questions have been raised about the extent to which cross-cultural issues are covered in depth in training (McKenzie-Mavinga, 2005). It would probably therefore be a positive step for all training programmes to keep under review the extent to which they cover this area, and the extent to which that coverage allows trainees to engage in deep learning and reflection, around such topics and their own racial identities. It would be a very positive move if trainers were to devote some of their research time and energy to looking at how we currently deliver training in this area, and how we could improve such endeavours in the future. Questionnaires for gauging MC in trainees are readily available for such work (Hays, 2008; Hays, Chang & Decker; 2007).

As noted above, training programs might want to consider the extent to which they develop an explicit statement of values which can be presented to potential and current trainees. This then allows all of the implications of our professional values to be fully and transparently drawn out, including the sometimes thorny debates which can be thrown up where values and characteristics appear to be in conflict.

Courses should also continue to reflect to what extent training in this area is connected to all areas of professional development and competence, for example, around leadership. In the current author's view, we should encourage our trainees to see themselves as champions and advocates for social justice.

As a profession, we should also find ways to ask ourselves questions about our own organisations, structures and training. To what extent do we attract and retain trainees from the range of cultural groups within our society? To what extent are different groups represented within the body of staff in our training institutes? What about leadership positions in our professional bodies, services and training institutes? If we find deficiencies in any of these areas, what are our strategies for changing this? The answers will differ from one institution to another and across the profession, but my own anecdotal impression is that there remains much to be done.

Finally, this article has focussed on the area of race and culture in its discussion of diversity. Trainers and course teams will need to consider in similar levels of depth the extent to which courses provide trainees with opportunities to reflect at length on all aspects of diversity. There is undoubtedly a need for greater research and knowledge around trainees' attitudes and competence in relation to these.

Summary of suggestions for ways forward in increasing trainee awareness of diversity and multi-cultural competence:

- Review the course curriculum to ensure there is adequate coverage of the area.
- Develop an explicit statement of values which the course adheres to, and discuss this with applicants at interview.
- Review recruitment and selection methods, to ensure these promote and encourage future diversity within the profession.
- Encourage research on this topic.
- Encourage staff and students to become diversity champions.
- Ensure that trainees, as future leaders of the profession, are aware of the role of managers in changing organisational cultures and in promoting diversity.

- Give trainees the opportunity to share and reflect on experiences, both personal and in training.
- License a full and frank dialogue around these issues through the creation of a safe, supportive and contained space.
- Use games and activities to encourage learning (e.g., role plays around challenging discrimination).
- Use the trainee group as a resource to share experience as much as possible.
- Bring in other people and groups from outside the course to share their reflections and experiences.
- Encourage aesthetic appreciation of different cultures and expressions.
- Encourage reading from a wide range of relevant texts.
- Ensure this aspect of the curriculum is reflected in the assessment strategy (e.g., by encouraging reflections on diversity in case studies).

References

Ancis, J. R., Sedlacek, W. E., & Mohr, J. J. (2000). Student perceptions of campus cultural climate by race. *Journal of Counseling and Development: JCD, 78*(2), 180–185. Doi: https://doi.org/10.1002/j.1556-6676.2000.tb02576.x

Ancis, J. R. & Szymanski, D. M. (2001). Awareness of White privilege among White counseling trainees. *The Counseling Psychologist, 29*(4), 548–569.

Beer, A. M., Spanierman, L. B., Greene, J. C., & Todd, N. R. (2012). Counseling psychology trainees' perceptions of training and commitments to social justice. *Journal of Counseling Psychology, 59*(1), 120–133. doi: https://doi.org/10.1177/0011000001294005

Bezrukova, K., Jehn, K. A., & Spell, C. S. (2012). Reviewing diversity training: Where we have been and where we should go. *Academy of Management Learning & Education, 11*(2), 207–227. Doi: https://doi.org/10.5465/amle.2008.0090

Brammer, S., Millington, A., & Pavelin, S. (2007). Gender and ethnic diversity among UK corporate boards. *Corporate Governance: An International Review, 15*(2), 393–403. Doi: https://doi.org/10.1111/j.1467-8683.2007.00569.x

Bristol City Council (2016). The Bristol City Population, 2016. Bristol City Council.

British Psychological Society (2017). Standards for the accreditation of doctoral programmes in counselling psychology. British Psychological Society.

British Psychological Society (2017). Standards for the accreditation of doctoral programmes in clinical psychology. British Psychological Society.

Constantine, M. G. (2002). Racism attitudes, White racial identity attitudes, and multicultural counseling competence in school counselor trainees. *Counselor Education and Supervision, 41*(3), 162–174. Doi: https://doi.org/10.1002/j.1556-6978.2002.tb01281.x

Constantine, M. G., Hage, S. M., Kindaichi, M. M., & Bryant, R. M. (2007). Social justice and multicultural issues: Implications for the practice and training of counselors and counseling psychologists. *Journal of Counseling & Development, 85*(1), 24–29.

Dabydeen, D. (2005). The Intended. Peepal Tree Press.

Daniel, J. H., Roysircar, G., Abeles, N., & Boyd, C. (2004). Individual and cultural diversity competency: Focus on the therapist. *Journal of Clinical Psychology, 60*(7), 755–770. Doi: https://doi.org/10.1002/jclp.20014

Diehl, M. (1988). Social identity and minimal groups: The effects of interpersonal and inter-group attitudinal similarity on intergroup discrimination. *British Journal of Social Psychology*, *27*(4), 289–300. Doi: https://doi.org/10.1111/j.2044-8309.1988.tb00833.x

Equality Act (2010). c. 15. *Retrieved from:* https://www.legislation.gov.uk/ukpga/2010/15/contents

Fakhry Davids, M. (2011). *Internal racism: A psychoanalytic approach to race and difference.* Palgrave Macmillan.

Fanon, F. (1970). *Black Skin, White Masks (by) Frantz Fanon.* Paladin.

Fanon, F. & Sartre, J. P. (1963). *The wretched of the earth* (Vol. 36). New York: Grove Press.

Fouad, N. A., Grus, C. L., Hatcher, R. L., Kaslow, N. J., Hutchings, P. S., Madson, M. B., … & Crossman, R. E. (2009). Competency benchmarks: A model for understanding and measuring competence in professional psychology across training levels. *Training and Education in Professional Psychology*, *3*(4S), S5-22. Doi: http://dx.doi.org/10.1037/a0015832

Glissant, E. (1989). *Caribbean discourse: Selected essays.* Charlottesville: University of Virginia Press.

Griffin, J. H. (1961). *Black Like Me.* San Antonio, Texas: Wings Press.

Gushue, G. V., & Constantine, M. G. (2007). Color-blind racial attitudes and white racial identity attitudes in psychology trainees. *Professional Psychology: Research and Practice*, *38*(3), 321–328. Doi: http://dx.doi.org/10.1037/0735-7028.38.3.321

Hays, D. G. (2008). Assessing multicultural competence in counselor trainees: A review of instrumentation and future directions. *Journal of Counseling and Development: JCD*, *86*(1), 95–101. Doi: https://doi.org/10.1002/j.1556-6678.2008.tb00630.x

Hays, D. G., Chang, C. Y., & Decker, S. L. (2007). Initial development and sychometric data for the privilege and oppression inventory. *Measurement and Evaluation in Counseling and Development*, *40*(2), 66–79. Doi: https://doi.org/10.1080/07481756.2007.11909806

Hays, D. G., Chang, C. Y., & Havice, P. (2008). White racial identity statuses as predictors of white privilege awareness. *The Journal of Humanistic Counseling*, *47*(2), 234–246. Doi: https://doi.org/10.1002/j.2161-1939.2008.tb00060.x

Health and Care Professions Council (2016). Standards of conduct, performance and ethics. Health and Care Professions Council.

Health and Care Professions Council (2015). Standards proficiency- practitioner psychologists. Health and Care Professions Council.

Hickling, F. W. (2007). *Psychohistoriography: A post-colonial psychoanalytic and psychotherapeutic model.* London and Philadelphia: Jessica Kingsley.

Hickling, F. W. & Hutchinson, G. (1999). Roast breadfruit psychosis: disturbed racial identification in African-Caribbeans. *Psychiatric Bulletin-Royal College of Psychiatrists*, *23*, 132–134. Doi: https://doi.org/10.1192/pb.23.3.132

Hill, N. R. (2003). Promoting and celebrating multicultural competence in counselor trainees. *Counselor Education and Supervision*, *43*(1), 39–52. Doi: https://doi.org/10.1002/j.1556-6978.2003.tb01828.x

Kalra, V. S., Abel, P., & Esmail, A. (2009). Developing leadership interventions for black and minority ethnic staff: a case study of the National Health Service (NHS) in the UK. *Journal of health organization and management*, *23*(1), 103–118. Doi: https://doi.org/10.1108/14777260910942588

Kim, B. S. & Lyons, H. Z. (2003). Experiential activities and multicultural counselling competence training. *Journal of Counseling and Development: JCD*, *81*(4), 400–408. Doi: https://doi.org/10.1002/j.1556-6678.2003.tb00266.x

Kulik, C. T. & Roberson, L. (2008). Common goals and golden opportunities: Evaluations of diversity education in academic and organizational settings. *Academy of Management Learning & Education*, 7(3), 309–331. Doi: https://doi.org/10.5465/amle.2008.34251670

Lago, C. (2005). *Race, culture and counselling*. McGraw-Hill Education (UK).

Lago, C. (Ed.). (2011). *The handbook of transcultural counselling and psychotherapy*. McGraw-Hill Education (UK).

Laungani, P. (2004). *Asian perspectives in counselling and psychotherapy*. Routledge.

Lawrence, E. (1982). Just plain common sense: the 'roots' of racism. *The Empire Strikes Back: Race and Racism in 70's Britain*. Hutchinson.

Long E. (1774). *History of Jamaica*. Lowndes.

McKenzie-Mavinga, I. (2005). Understanding black issues in postgraduate counsellor training. *Counselling and Psychotherapy Research*, 5(4), 295–300. Doi: https://doi.org/10.1080/14733140500492581

McKenzie-Mavinga, I. (2009). *Black issues in the therapeutic process*. Palgrave Macmillan.

Mintz, L. B., Jackson, A. P., Neville, H. A., Illfelder-Kaye, J., Winterowd, C. L., & Loewy, M. I. (2009). The need for a counseling psychology model training values statement addressing diversity. *The Counseling Psychologist*, 37(5), 644–675. Doi: https://doi.org/10.1177/0011000009331931

Owen, D. S. (2009). Privileged social identities and diversity leadership in higher education. *The Review of Higher Education*, 32(2), 185–207. Doi: 10.1353/rhe.0.0048

Parham, T. A., White, J. L., & Ajamu, A. (1999). *The psychology of Blacks: An African-centered perspective*. Pearson College Division.

Pendleton, D. & Furnham, A. F. (2016). *Leadership: All You Need To Know 2nd edition*. Springer.

Perez, A. D. & Hirschman, C. (2009). The changing racial and ethnic composition of the US population: Emerging American identities. *Population and Development Review*, 35(1), 1–51. doi: 10.1111/j.1728-4457.2009.00260.x

Pope-Davis, D. B., Reynolds, A. L., Dings, J. G., & Nielson, D. (1995). Examining multicultural counseling competencies of graduate students in psychology. *Professional Psychology: Research and Practice*, 26(3), 322–329. Doi: http://dx.doi.org/10.1037/0735-7028.26.3.322

Richards, C. & Barker, M. (2013). *Sexuality and gender for mental health professionals: A practical guide*. Sage.

Richardson, T. Q., & Molinaro, K. L. (1996). White counselor self-awareness: A prerequisite for developing multicultural competence. *Journal of Counseling and Development: JCD*, 74(3), 238–242. Doi: http://dx.doi.org/10.1002/j.1556-6676.1996.tb01859.x

Roysircar, G. (2004). Cultural Self-Awareness Assessment: Practice Examples From Psychology Training. *Professional Psychology: Research and Practice*, 35(6), 658–666. Doi: http://dx.doi.org/10.1037/0735-7028.35.6.658

Roysircar, G., Gard, G., Hubbell, R., & Ortega, M. (2005). Development of counselling trainees' multicultural awareness through mentoring English as a second language students. *Journal of Multicultural Counseling and Development*, 33(1), 17–36. Doi: https://doi.org/10.1002/j.2161-1912.2005.tb00002.x

Sanchez, J. I., & Medkik, N. (2004). The effects of diversity awareness training on differential treatment. *Group & Organization Management*, 29(4), 517–536. Doi: https://doi.org/10.1177/1059601103257426

Singh, A. A., Hofsess, C. D., Boyer, E. M., Kwong, A., Lau, A. S., McLain, M., & Haggins, K. L. (2010). Social justice and counseling psychology: Listening to the voices of doctoral trainees. *The Counseling Psychologist*, 38(6), 766–795. Doi: https://doi.org/10.1177/0011000010362559

Thompson, R. L., Brossart, D. F., Carlozzi, A. F., & Miville, M. L. (2002). Five-factor model (Big Five) personality traits and universal-diverse orientation in counsellor trainees. *The Journal of Psychology*, *136*(5), 561–572. Doi: 10.1080/00223980209605551

UN General Assembly (1948). 'Universal Declaration of Human Rights', Resolution 217 A (111), 10 December.

Ward, T. & Hickling, F. (2004). Psychology in the English-speaking Caribbean. *The Psychologist*, *17*, 442–444.

Winterowd, C. L., Adams, E. M., Miville, M. L., & Mintz, L. B. (2009). Operationalizing, instilling, and assessing counseling psychology training values related to diversity in academic programs. *The Counseling Psychologist*, *37*(5), 676–704. Doi: https://doi.org/10.1177/0011000009331936

Reflective leadership in a multi-disciplinary team

Nicola Massie

The context for this discussion is working for thirteen years as a senior psychologist in the Health Service in Wales. I work in a service that supports individuals with intellectual disabilities, where good quality service is frequently supported by working as a team around individuals or small groups of clients. It is acknowledged that similar ways of working are taking place in other services and the themes and ideas discussed in this paper could be generalised across settings and services.

During my working life as a psychologist I have reflected on my experience as a member of a multi-disciplinary team and my responsibility as a practitioner psychologist to demonstrate and model leadership. As a senior member of a team, and as a reflection of psychology training, it often falls to the psychologist, in my case a counselling psychologist, to demonstrate leadership, particularly clinical leadership in a team which may be made up of several disciplines within the health and allied health professions.

Leadership and the skills required by a psychologist can be found in the Professional Practice Guidelines published by the British Psychological Society (2017). It is defined as:

> Leading in this way demands high levels of skill in developing, managing and maintaining professional relationships. This may include communicating complex and sensitive information, and reflexivity to enable individuals and teams to co-formulate around difficulty and challenge.
>
> British Psychological Society, 2017

Reflecting on my own experience and the lack of specific leadership skills in my doctoral level training, I developed my own ideas about the leadership style that best suits me and my working context. I observed the leadership skills in others which varied, and so I became curious about the different leadership styles and whether they were representative of training or of individual values and personality. I reflected upon myself and my 'way of being' in clinical settings both with clients and colleagues. My natural way of being in these settings is a combination of training and personal values. It is to be supportive of individuals to enable them to develop their own solutions and the same in systems, although I am more likely to be assertive in offering an opinion in a meeting.

I was fortunate to complete a leadership training in 2015, which I found stimulating and informative. Although training helpfully provided some practical tools on reflection it didn't fit with me and my context. I was constantly challenged by the results of my psychometric assessments on my existing skills during the leadership training that analysed my competence as a leader. This led me to experience a low point in the value I placed on my skills as a leader. I became less confident about my ability to hold a leadership position and experienced a sense of not being good enough. However, I further reflected on the way I felt and weighed my feelings against evidence that I was successfully chairing a group within the British Psychological Society, working and leading in a busy multi-disciplinary health team and receiving good feedback from colleagues. The specific findings of the assessments based on the answers given by me that I found most perplexing suggested that I did not appear to be systematic in the way I worked and not committed to following plans to a pre-agreed end-point, which suggested that I left things unfinished. There was also a suggestion that I placed more value on developing others than myself and that I was more reflective than dynamic. Again, thinking about my skills and working context, I acknowledge that I am reflective but can draw on a more dynamic leadership style particularly in meetings. These comments set me off on a path of reflection about how to work with this feedback and so since 2015 I have had time to reflect in more depth on whether this is a deficit in skills or whether alternative ideas and possibilities around what leadership can be should be considered One thing I am clearer about is that the leadership training I undertook was of high quality but probably didn't fit my context, working with complex situations and clients in a multi-disciplinary health and social care setting.

Leadership models were experienced as more focussed on a business model that valued strategy, operational plans, time constraints and achieving exactly what was planned essentially being a 'starter finisher'. Whilst this type of model is relevant to psychology and areas of health particularly in development of services, much of my experience has been working in contexts where the client is a co-contributor to care. If protocols and pathways lack flexibility and willingness to change direction, it becomes problematic when working with complex health presentations in complex systems of care. In the context of the highly complex system of health and social care, the psychologist as a leader is required to be skilled in offering an alternative formulation to explanations that are often medical and can be dominant, offering a formulation that focuses on a biopsychosocial model and includes a combination of biological factors alongside cultural and psychological factors.

The psychologist as a leader in this process supports constant reflection and adaptation and possibly changing pre-planned interventions based on bringing together dynamic sources of information and thereby modelling and facilitating effective and reflective leadership that is open to flexibility and change. When working in a multi-disciplinary team with clients in health-care systems, we know where the intervention starts, but the point at which the intervention will end is not always certain. We aim to meet the planned outcomes, but working with people whose needs may change means that although the outcomes can be evaluated and measured, the client journey may change according to the developing needs of the client. An example of this would be a client referred to the service requiring an intervention in response to behaviour which challenges, and the assessment and observation produces evidence that trauma and response is at the root of the behaviour. It would be appropriate to continue with the production of a Positive Behaviour Support plan, but it would also be imperative to offer a psychological intervention to address the trauma. Within this setting, reflective leadership is an essential component. In response to these positions my most important thoughts lead me back to my core training and identity as a psychologist.

My core training and identity is one that embraces reflection particularly about relationships and this is one which crosses all the systems and boundaries that I work within and includes a willingness and ability to reflect upon myself, which I will return to later. I am proposing that reflective leadership is required to enable formulations to be constructed from complex sources of information and achieve values that I will refer to in the context of health and social care. This approach is systemic in nature, bringing the parts of a system or team together to understand, formulate and think about possibilities for change whilst reflecting on the process throughout.

The importance of context

My current context and that of many other psychologists in the health service across the UK will be similar. The question is what is our current context? The context in health in Wales will be similar in other areas of the United Kingdom, and this context and these ideas generalise across other systems. In very general terms, the context is one of redesign of services to focus on person-centred care, effectively meeting the needs of an increasing number of clients. This is during a period when the experience is of resources becoming increasingly scarce. The focus is for more effective use of current resources to enable efficacy and effectiveness.

The context of Health and Social Care

Alongside the continuing challenges of working with individuals with complex health needs and the dynamic situations that can emerge from working with clients and teams, more recently the recognition of the need to develop more person-centred, efficient and effective models of care in the health services has resulted in a drive to redesign models of care across the UK. This has resulted in '1000 lives plus' (2017) within which sit the principles of 'Prudent Healthcare'.

The four principles of Prudent Healthcare as set out by The Bevan Commission are:

- Achieve health and wellbeing with the public, patients and professionals as equal partners through co-production.
- Care for those with the greatest health need first, making the most effective use of all skills and resources.
- Do only what is needed, no more, no less; and do no harm.
- Reduce inappropriate variation using evidence-based practices consistently and transparently.

'Co-production' has become the focus of the way 'teams' work and is described as a way of working in which clients are experts on themselves and their lives and experience and are therefore the best consultants to developing services. This is described in 'A Co-production model Five values and seven steps to make this happen in reality' (NHS England Coalition for Collaborative Care, 2016). The values described are:

- Ownership understanding and support of co-production by all
- A culture of openness and honesty
- A commitment to sharing power and decisions with citizens
- Clear communication
- A culture in which people are valued and respected

These points are highly relevant to reflective leadership in teams where clients and health professionals and the relationships between and within them achieve co-produced or co-constructed systems of care and treatment. This is recommended and regarded as delivery of efficient healthcare. Reflective leadership is required to enable formulations to be constructed from complex sources of information and achieve the values above.

A service context

Working in a multi-disciplinary team with clients as co-contributors has been the approach of community services that recognise the value of systemic working. 'Network Training'(Jenkins & Parry, 2006) has been a long-standing systemic intervention in my context, which has been further developed over time. The ideas in Network Training are associated with 'Team Formulation' (Ingham, 2015), where interventions encompass the coming together of a team and client to co-construct a response to a problem or difficulty. These interventions are typically facilitated by a psychologist with skills in reflective practice and the ability to 'hold' competing or complementary perspectives. Schön (2006) refers to the challenges associated with a multiplicity of professional opinion in that:

> Each view of professional practice represents a way of functioning in situations of indeterminacy and value conflict, but the multiplicity of conflicting views poses a predicament for the practitioner who must choose among multiple approaches to practice or devise his way of combining them (p. 17).

Individual context and reflective leadership

Earlier I touched upon the times when I am struggling to make sense of a situation, a project or someone I am working with, I return to my core identity as a counselling psychologist and the philosophy that I hold. This helps me understand my role in a situation as well as the situation itself, to enable me to work with it and others in it. Although my core philosophy of practice was developed through learning, reflection and personal therapy during my core training, learning and on-going reflection mean I am continuously developing and growing an understanding of myself. Whilst in training, I was focused on in-depth understanding of core psychological therapeutic models. It is important to emphasise that I am not constantly engaging in therapy but use this knowledge and philosophy generalising across settings and interventions. In my practice this is fundamental in being able to lead in a reflective way.

Reflective leadership could be described as enabling a 'space' in which the values of understanding and ongoing reflection for the individual and team can be sustained, providing a model of support within the multi-disciplinary team which includes the client as the consultant to and driver of the intervention. The idea of 'holding' is reflective of the work originally of Winnicott (1960, p. 589), who described a holding relationship which facilitates an optimal environment for development (Finlay, 2015). Reflective leadership can provide an environment which enables and facilitates openness and transparency in situations that require 'holding' highly charged emotion, chronic sorrow and sometimes acute physical and psychological difficulty. These situations do not necessarily allow precise pre-planning and measurement of outcomes of exacting targets. Strategy is important as is planning, but health practitioners need the ability to re-consider and re-design to meet the complex needs of their clients.

Outcomes should be measured reflecting the perceived outcome for the client and service development. In relation to reflective leadership, keeping the client at the centre of the intervention requires plans and the practitioners working with them to remain flexible. Essentially if the plan is A to B to C yet B and part way to C is as far as the client wants the journey to progress or can achieve, then this needs to be measured as an outcome achieved for the client and the service not as a failure to meet an outcome. This can be achieved by supporting a client and/or a team to reflect on the progress of the client and to re-formulate around gains and setbacks, understanding that supporting an intervention that is required at the time is a way of being prudent in the delivery of healthcare. In addition, the client is supported to co-produce their own healthcare aims and outcomes.

Key skills for psychologists as reflective leaders

As discussed above a key skill for a psychologist in these often highly complex situations is the ability to psychologically 'hold' the anxiety of the client and the network of support which may include other health professionals. A reflective leader is one that enables discussion of difficult issues and situations and supports clients and teams to manage the discussion. It is helpful to enable the client and the team to reflect on the cycle of change and tolerate the loops, dips and highs.

Fredrickson (2009) cited in West (2012) emphasises the importance of positivity and suggests that it means:

> Being appreciative (particularly of team members contributions), open to ideas, learning and others; curious to learn about difference, new and improved ways of doing things and effective team-working practices; kind in dealing with colleagues; and above all real and genuine interactions with colleagues at work (p. 61).

One of the models that I have assimilated into my thinking and facilitation of the team process is Kolb's reflective cycle of learning (1984) (see Figure 13.1), which rather than being a linear process or pathway regards reflection as a cyclical process as outlined below.

In health and social care systems, protocols are often linear and directive in form and this does not always encourage or enable reflection or a reflexive approach. Protocols are important particularly when relevant to best practice guidelines, but it is often the role of a reflective leader to synthesise protocols and a process such as Kolb's which is a more cyclical and reflective process. It is possible to use Kolb's model along a pathway. At the planning stage of the cycle, it is possible to move to the next stage on a pathway. The relevance of this approach is that it allows teams to carry out interventions either together or independently (experience). Most importantly the value here is that the team can be supported to come together to reflect and be supported to share the experience and outcome of their intervention and synthesise their approaches and interventions. Following reflection, the team will be better able to understand as a team ongoing difficulties, successes and most importantly, where there are overlaps in interventions, how this can be avoided and how information can be shared to build a formulation. This enables a more

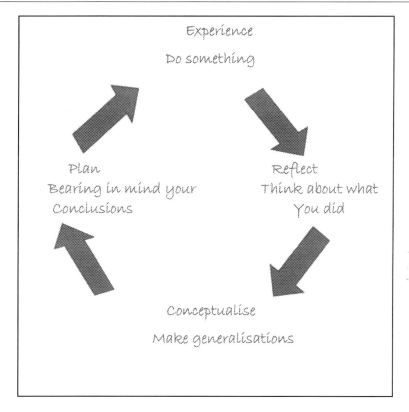

Figure 13.1 Kolb's reflective cycle of learning (1984).

prudent approach to care, which also supports the client in not having to share the same information over and over and experiencing a more tailored intervention. The team is then able to conceptualise the outcomes so far and then formulate the next steps (plan). How might this work in practice?

Case study

Sara is a young woman who has complex support needs. She has a mild intellectual disability and a deteriorating neurological condition. She is supported by her local Community Learning Disability Team. Sara is in her twenties and lives in a residential care home which provides a good level of care to meet her physical support needs. Due to the complexity of her physical presentation and the effects this has on her speech and cognitive, physical and psychological wellbeing, she has a large multi-disciplinary team working with her, advising the support staff in the house where she lives. Sara enjoys seeing her mum and meets with her a couple of times each month. Unfortunately, due to a situation in her family home when she was a child Sara has lived away from her mum since she was seven years old and has missed out on the psychological security that a stable supportive childhood can bring. Sara's mum describes being devastated when Sara was removed to foster care and developed and continues to experience depression which appears to be exacerbated by her fears about Sara's continued deterioration. This means that she often misses her visits because she cannot face the journey to see Sara and this really upsets Sara. Some of Sara's support staff and the health professionals working with her find Sara's mother difficult to understand. The different professions in the multi-disciplinary team and staff team working with Sara are committed to ensuring that Sara gets the best care possible. I noticed however that working relationships in the team appear to be fractious when coming together to review and plan Sara's support. I noticed that allegiances appear to be developed amongst professions that share similar opinions about what is the best course of care for Sara and advocate strongly for their position during meetings. The team thinks that Sara is experiencing confusion and anxiety. One way of approaching this might be one of the clinicians or the lead professional/ care coordinator listens to all the views and then make decisions about the way forward, plans the intervention and then evaluates and measures outcomes when aims are achieved.

A more reflective approach

The questions are: What might be happening in this team? Does the team process and behaviour affect Sara? Could the team adopt a more reflective approach? Can the team be 'held' to develop a more reflective approach and develop a tentative formulation that includes a reflection on their own process?

Tentative formulation

The whole team appears to be split, and a team intervention that enables a co-productive approach is missing. Strong connections are built between Sara and the individuals working with her, and feelings about Sara's mum appear to have resulted in different approaches and allegiances. As a result, the care she receives is split. It is possible that this replicates Sara's feelings of confusion and anxiety, as she is unable to receive consistent and predictable care.

Team formulation

A team formulation session was planned, and I acknowledged that I would need to be in a position whereby I am able support the team to explore and simultaneously 'hold' difficulties in the team whilst also being an active team member. Although Sara was made aware of the team formulation meeting, she decided that she did not want to attend but consented to her mother attending to talk about her early years. The formulation session began with setting out ground rules including the limit of confidentiality and agreeing that each contribution would be valued and agreeing that all members of the team needed to respect the views of others. The team agreed that each individual member should take care of themselves in the session and could leave if they needed to.

Finally, there was a focus on what each wanted to achieve. An initial reflection on the individual interventions and the feelings professionals had about working with Sara revealed that there was an overwhelming sorrow felt by professionals, as Sara's health is unpredictable and her neurologist has indicated that her health will deteriorate further. Reflecting on this led the team to be quieter, 'softer' and reflective within and between them. Sara's mother was surprised to hear these accounts expressed in this way, as she had experienced the professionals and support staff as unfriendly, especially when she was unable to keep to arrangements to see Sara. Sara's mother then felt comfortable to talk about her hopes for Sara when she was born. Sara's mother was a single parent, and this brought challenges, but she told the team how beautiful Sara was when she was a baby. Sara's mother then married Sara's stepfather. This was helpful to Sara' mother because of the support it gave to her, but it was not a successful marriage. Sara's mother experienced post-natal depression when Sara's younger brother was born. This caused resentment in the family about the effect that Sara's support needs had on the family. Sara's social worker became concerned about the safety of Sara and the ability of the family to support her and a decision was made that Sara would live in a care home that would be able to support her more consistently. Sara's mum described the experience of feeling devastated when she was not able to look after Sara and from this time onwards experienced chronic and acute mental health difficulties.

The team and Sara's mother listened to one another and were given the opportunity to sensitively reflect on the accounts they heard within the safety and security of the formulation meeting. A feeling of greater respect for one another's position appeared to be developing. The team also discussed how much they care about Sara and reflected on how she reminds them of members of their own family or wider social group. We further reflected upon the complexity of these feelings. Sara's mother was pleased that she could see how much the health professionals value Sara and the feelings that they manage in their professional roles. The team was supported to reflect on how this could interrupt the delivery of effective care if not managed. They acknowledged that this may be why allegiances and splits had developed in the team. The team reflected that they are caring individuals working in the health and care sector, but this often needs to be balanced alongside an understanding that love and affection come from Sara's mother and good quality team working comes from the health and support staff. This included an acknowledgement by the team of professionals working with Sara that they experience emotions which they attribute to caring about Sara's support needs and that there has been a tendency in the team to allow this to 'spill over' into unconsciously adopting a parental role. The team acknowledged that they need to be careful about boundaries and understanding of the complexity of this situation. Generally, many professional groups do not have training or—crucially—ongoing support to recognise and manage their emotions and feelings. As a result, these emotions can often be responded to in way that is unhelpful. It can create divisions of care (for example, in the case of Sara) and be destructive to the professional who will be increasingly exposed to highly emotional situations.

Further facilitated reflections within the team only and with individuals took place, focussing on how health professionals and support staff can take care of themselves and each other when working with clients that stimulate such strong feelings; that care includes their own plans for support and how they can support one another, which will hopefully address the split that had previously occurred in the team.

Supervision and collegiate support

A reflective leader is likely to observe the difficulties that are experienced by health professionals in their work. It is recognised that Health and Social Care services are experiencing increasingly difficult conditions associated with the delivery of care. The effect of this can be on patients, clients and professionals working in services. Professionals working in these systems may be experiencing conditions in which they are under more pressure and the likelihood of stress is increased. The assumption is also frequently made that the most effective way to achieve an outcome for the client is to work as a team. This is not always the natural way that all professionals perform at their best. This puts me in mind of the work of Cain (2012, p. 4), who questions the overwhelming value placed on working as a team and thinking as a group. She suggests that most value is placed on extroverts whilst introverts are widely overlooked; she argues that 'we live with a value system that I call the Extrovert Ideal—the omnipresent belief that the ideal self is gregarious, alpha and comfortable in the spotlight'. This is relevant to team members and leaders. Cain (2012) proposes that there is a value to practice and leadership from individuals more likely to be identified as introverts. Grant et al. (2011, p. 533), who proposes that 'it makes sense that introverts are uniquely good at leading initiative-takers. Because of their inclination to listen to others and lack of interest in dominating social situations, introverts are more likely to hear and implement suggestions' (cited in Cain, 2012, p. 57).

Conclusion

A reflective leader can offer the conditions in which colleagues are able to reflect on their skills, their relationships within health and social care settings and other relationships that influence the work they do. It is often helpful to think about past experiences and if those experiences influence the contemporary work they are engaged in. 'Sitting' with this and supporting thoughts and reflections of one or more members of the multi-disciplinary team can support the work of the individual and the team. This approach can contribute to the wellbeing of the individual and functioning of the team. This approach can also contribute to the requirement to reduce inappropriate variation in the approach of the team.

References

1000 Lives Improvement. (2014). The Quality Improvement Guide: The Improving Quality Together Edition Cardiff: 1000 Lives Improvement Bevan Commission (2015). Prudent Healthcare Principles. http://www.bevancommission.org/opendoc/268182

British Psychological Society. (2017). *Professional Practice Guidelines Third edition published by British Psychological Society.* Leicester: British Psychological Society. Retrieved from:https://www.bps.org.uk/sites/bps.org.uk/files/Policy%20-%20Files/BPS%20Practice%20Guidelines%20(Third%20Edition).pdf

Cain, Susan. (2012). *Quiet: [the power of introverts* in a world that can't stop talking]. New York: Random House, Inc.

NHS England and Coalition for Collaborative Care. Personalised care and support planning handbook: The journey to person-centred care. Leeds: NHS England and Coalition for Collaborative Care, 2015. Retrieved from: https://www.england.nhs.uk/wp-content/uploads/2016/04/core-info-care-support-planning-1.pdf

Fredrickson, B. L. (2009). *Positivity.* New York, NY: Crown (cited in West, (2012), p. 61, op cit).

Grant, A. M., Gino, F. & Hoffman, D.A. (2011). "Reversing the Extraverted Leadership Advantage: The Role of Employee Proactivity". *Academy of Management Journal, 54*(3), pp. 528–550 (cited in Cain, (2012), p. 57, op cit).

Finlay, L. (2015). Relational Integrative Psychotherapy: Process and Theory in Practice, Chichester, Sussex: Wiley.

Ingham, B. (2015). Team Formulation within a learning disabilities setting. Clinical Psychology Forum, *275,* 33–37.

Jenkins, R., & Parry, R. (2006). Working with the support network: applying systemic practice in learning disabilities services. *British Journal of Learning Disabilities, 34*(2), 77–81.

Kolb, D. A. (1984). *Experiential Learning: Experience as the Source of Learning and Development.* Englewood Cliffs, NJ: Prentice-Hall.

Schön, D. A. (1983). *The reflective practitioner: How professionals think in action.* New York: Basic Books.

West, M. A. (2012). *Effective Teamwork: Practical Lessons from Organizational Research* (3rd ed.). British Psychological Society: John Wiley & Sons Ltd.

Winnicott, D. (1960). *The theory of the parent-child relationship, Int. J. Psychoanal., 41,* 585–595.

Women in senior management: Exploring the dynamics of diversity in attaining senior leadership positions

Roxane L. Gervais

Introduction

> Plus ça change, plus c'est la même chose.
>
> Jean-Baptiste Alphonse Karr 1808–1890

Despite the many advances in promoting and legislating on equality in respect of gender, age, race, ethnicity and sexuality over the past decades, the workplace continues to reflect a lack of diversity and inclusion. This lack of diversity and inclusion is especially pertinent for women, who, despite being half of the world's population, find it challenging still to attain senior leadership positions within organisations. The figures outlining women's representation in senior management highlight a decisive lack of growth despite more women entering the workplace. For example, when the figures from the United States (US) are considered, they show that in 2005, eight (1.6%) Fortune 500 companies had female Chief Executive Officers (CEO); however, this number had not increased significantly from the past ten years (Catalyst, 2007). In 2007, this number had decreased slightly with just one per cent of *Fortune* magazine's Global 500 companies having women as CEOs (Eagly & Carli, 2007). These figures are lower for women of colour, who represented 3.1 per cent of Fortune 500 corporate board positions, when compared with all women who held 14.6 per cent of such board positions (Catalyst, 2007). Black men are much more likely than black women to hold senior leadership positions, even though black women attain higher levels of education than black men (Zweigenhaft, 2013). Further, black women, when compared to other women of colour, are the ones most likely to see their opportunities to advance to senior leadership positions decline over time, even when diversity policies and practices are in place within organisations (Catalyst, 2004).

Figures from 2015 show that women's representation on global corporate boards is increasing, averaging 12 per cent to 15 per cent (Catalyst, 2017). However, the percentage of women who are CEOs of Fortune 500 companies has not increased substantially. In 2017, there were 32 female CEOs in these companies, which translated to 6.4 per cent of the US's biggest companies (by revenue) being run by women. These figures reflect the highest proportion of female CEOs in the 63-year history of the Fortune 500 (Fortune, 2017). Further, of these, only seven women were in the top one hundred companies as ranked by Fortune 500, and of these three in the top fifty, and one was in the top ten. Research shows that larger boards that have more non-executive directorships tend to be more diverse; moreover, although the proportion of female directors on a board is positively related to both board size and composition, there is not a corresponding significant relationship for the proportion of non-white directors (Brammer, Millington & Pavelin, 2007).

Within Europe in 2016, while the numbers are higher than in the US, these could be improved also. Italy had close to one third (29%) of women in senior roles, while Ireland (19%), the Netherlands (18%) and Germany (15%) performed lower than the global average (24%; Grant Thornton, 2016). The figures were similar for the United Kingdom (UK) at 21%, but over one third (36%) of UK businesses did not have women in senior roles (Grant Thornton, 2016). Within the European Union (EU-28) generally in 2016, among the largest publicly listed companies only 15% of executives and 5% of CEOs were women (EC, 2016). So, while there has been progress, the figures reveal the continuing dominance of men in senior leadership positions. The reasons for this are varied and will be explored as the chapter progresses.

A concerted effort in the UK to increase the number of women on the Financial Times Stock Exchange (FTSE) boards was fruitful, with numbers rising from 12.5 per cent ($n = 135$) in 2010 to 26.1 per cent ($n = 286$) in 2015 on FTSE 100 boards (Davies, 2015). In terms of the existence of all-male boards in the FTSE 250, these decreased from 152 in 2011 to 15 in 2015; with a positive outcome reflecting that within the FTSE 100 there were no all-male boards in 2015. Unfortunately, these data do not provide the race or ethnicity of the women, which limits an understanding of the diverse breakdown of the women on said boards.

The data that are available on ethnicity on FTSE boards do not differentiate between the genders. The figures from July 2017 show that 85 of the 1,050 director positions in the FTSE 100 were held by individuals from ethnic minorities. Further, only two per cent of director positions were held by people from ethnic minorities who are UK citizens, despite ethnic minorities consisting of 14 per cent of the total UK population (up from 2% in 1971). Fifty-one companies of the FTSE 100 did not have any ethnic minorities on their boards, while six people of colour held the position of Chair or CEO (Parker, 2017). The available figures illustrate that there is inconsistency in knowing the representation of women of colour in senior leadership positions. This knowledge gap has to be closed for there to be a better acknowledgement of the lack of representation of black and other minority ethnic groups within the echelons of organisations.

Interestingly, McDonald (2004) discusses that this new reality of women's positions within the workplace has not been the 'norm' for women in business. She notes that in pre-industrial times, women held managerial roles and ran their own or their families' businesses. Nevertheless, within the 21st century workplace an 'unconscious' or 'conscious' policy of reducing women's abilities to lead seems to have become the norm. This policy extends to black women's abilities also, even when within a community setting, women are twice as likely as black women to run schools boards, lead youth initiatives and head up a charity or communication organisation (Hewlett & Wingfield, 2015). As Hewlett and Wingfield (2015) highlight, these achievements and experiences tend not to be acknowledged within a work setting.

The challenges for women overall in gaining senior management positions is even more testing for women of colour. LeanIn.Org and McKinsey & Company (2016) noted that although women of colour are more likely to want to be a top executive, they are less likely to be offered opportunities, such as promotion and being developed or trained, that would improve their career development. See Table 14.1. This lack of opportunity, as Acker (2009) highlighted, extends to men being more likely to be given line management opportunities more than women and, it could be conjectured, inclusive of black women. Line management opportunities are seen as one of those 'visible' tasks that supports individuals in being noticed as potential senior leaders (Acker, 2009).

Further, women of colour are even less likely to be appointed to positions within the C-Suite[1]. Figure 14.1 reflects that while 20 per cent of women were part of the C-Suite, only three per cent of these were women of colour. These figures from the US illustrate the stark disparity of women's representation at very senior levels within organisations.

Table 14.1 Women's career advancement and opportunities offered by ethnicity (%)

	White	Black	Asian	Hispanic
Interest in senior executive positions	37	39	53	53
Got a promotion	29	22	28	31
Got a better job title	29	22	27	31
Got a challenging assignment/project	64	51	65	56
Participated in an important development/ training opportunity	49	43	44	44

$N = 34,000$ (employees: men and women), Piazza, 2016

1 The C-Suite refers to those top senior executives' roles with titles that tend to start with the letter C (e.g., chief executive officer, chief operating officer, chief information officer, chief financial officer, and chief technology officer).

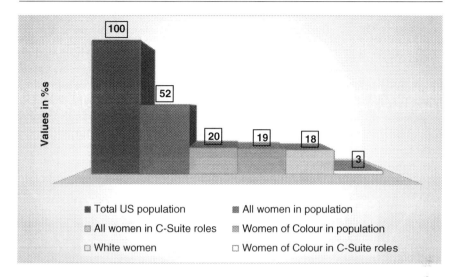

Figure 14.1 Percentage of women and women of colour in C-Suite roles relative to the proportion of the population.

McKinsey & Company & LeanIn.Org. (2017, pp. 4–5)

Some of the reasons for the few women who make it to C-Suite roles could be due to the lack of support that women of colour receive within organisations. As Figure 14.2 shows, black women especially are less likely to get the support and opportunities they need to advance through their respective

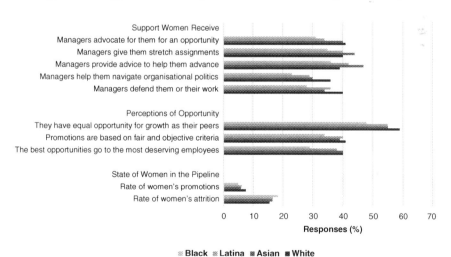

Figure 14.2 Women's perceptions of support and opportunities in their organisations.

McKinsey & Company & LeanIn.Org. (2017, p. 12)

organisations. This is especially in respect of social capital, with black women less likely than white, Asian or Latina women to have managers who assist them with organisational politics or defend them or their work if required. The lower levels of support and the fewer opportunities that are available to black women could explain why they are less likely to be promoted and more likely to leave organisations as shown in Figure 14.2.

In terms of senior leadership positions within the UK, the proportion of BME employees at senior management level within the civil service remained stable at 7% from 2016 to 2017, despite close to 12% (11.6%) of civil servant employees identifying as being from an ethnic minority group (Office of National Statistics [ONS], 2017). Wyatt and Silvester's (2015) research showed that BME civil servant managers have to rely on their explicit knowledge about the formal paths that are required to attain senior leadership positions. Further, they do not gain information through informal sources (i.e., networks, mentors and informal relations with senior managers) that could assist them in promotional opportunities; their white colleagues tend to have access to these informal channels that assist them in progressing more quickly to leadership roles. For those BME workers with access to informal networks, these tended to be with BME colleagues with an interest in advancing within the organisation (Johnson & Campbell-Stephens, 2013).

Within Europe, a 2010 report showed the disparity between women and men in senior leadership positions within the European Commission Civil Service. This disparity is evident with men taking up 81% of the top two administrative grades and 76% of the top two assistant grades (European Commission [EC], 2010). This is despite men and women having equal employment levels within the civil service. This disproportion is even more distinct on the Council of the EU, the smallest of the three services, with 84 per cent men and just 16 per cent women in the top two levels of the service. Within the judiciary, the judges of the supreme courts in all of the EU countries consist of 31% women and 69% men, while the European Court of Justice has only four women within the twenty-seven judges nominated by Member States. The only service with less stark numbers is the European Parliament, in which women hold 41% of the most senior positions (EC, 2010). Another aspect of women's leadership positions is that they are disposed to be placed in peripheral positions across types of organisations, for example, in ministries with 'soft' portfolios rather than those that focus on key economic functions (EC, 2010).

Women's contribution to the workplace

As noted, while women's representation in senior leadership positions has increased over the past few years, this fails still to reflect adequately the contribution that women make to the economy. Women's labour is required to sustain economies worldwide (World Bank, 2011), inclusive of the growing and elderly populations (Korczyc, Matia, Vincelette, Cuaresma & Loichinger, 2013). In terms of leadership, the benefits to women in the workplace in general, when women are in influential positions are: lower wage gaps (Cohen & Huffman, 2007; Hultin & Szulkin, 2003), as well as a reduction in gender discrimination (Cohen & Huffman, 2007; ILO, 2015). Additionally, when women are in senior positions within government, this could allow them to promote more effectively equality legislation and policies that support more women at work and thereby assist them in becoming on an equal basis with men (EC, 2010). Further, women in organisations can support women and those who wish to be leaders in the future in their personal and professional development by acting as role models and mentors (EC, 2010).

Moreover, some individual studies have shown that companies that consistently promote women tend to be more profitable that those that do not (e.g., Johns, 2013; Lückerath-Rovers, 2013). However, this is not sustained when analysing aggregated data. More recent research that used meta-analyses to assess the business impact of women on boards (Pletzer, Nikolova, Kedzior & Voelpel, 2015; Post & Byron, 2015) did not find that having women on boards led to a change in company performance. Despite this, those countries with greater gender parity tended to show a positive relationship between female board representation and market performance, while those countries with lower gender parity tended to show a more negative relationship between female board representation and market performance (Post & Byron, 2015). In addition, organisations with a more diverse workforce are more likely to report a growth in market share or gain access to new markets (Hewlett & Wingfield, 2015); more diverse boards support a positive impact on firm value (Campbell & Mínguez-Vera, 2008). Women's presence on boards tends to reflect a positive relationship with accounting returns (i.e., the profitability of firms), with this relationship showing even more positive impact in those countries with stronger shareholder protections; this was in respect of when boards are encouraged to use each member's knowledge, experience, and values (Post & Byron, 2015). Post and Byron (2015) found also that female board representation is positively related to two of the primary responsibilities of boards, monitoring and strategy involvement. Other research has established the link between women and monitoring (see Adams & Ferreira, 2009; Campbell & Mínguez-Vera, 2008), especially in the context of its importance as a corporate governance control mechanism. Monitoring has gained prominence in the light of the continuing failure of companies' board effectiveness (Campbell & Mínguez-Vera, 2008). As such, a more diverse board could provide a more robust check and balance system within organisations.

So although there may be an aspect of tokenism in appointing women to board directorships (Burgess & Tharenou, 2002), with this token approach perhaps extending to women of colour, there are various positive effects that occur when organisations increase the number of women, inclusive of women of colour on boards. This could include gaining a female perspective on decisions due to women's strong influence on consumer purchases and on the workforce (Burgess & Tharenou, 2002). This influence would extend to BMEs as well, as BMEs could provide insight into non-white consumer preferences. Estimations on buying power in the US highlighted that African Americans were expected to control US$1.1 trillion by 2015 (Nielsen, 2012), while lesbian, gay, bisexual and transgender (LGBT) individuals controlled US$790 billion in 2012 (Hewlett, Sears, Sumberg & Fargnoli, 2013). Access to these markets could be reduced or lost without an understanding of them, which can be gained by the expert knowledge of those who come from those groups and who can influence direction (i.e., leaders) (Hunt, Layton, & Prince, 2015; U.S. Glass Ceiling Commission, 1995). In light of the benefits that women of colour can bring, organisations may wish to focus more on ensuring inclusivity at senior levels.

The continuing perceptions of what is effective leadership

Effective leadership continues to perpetuate its links to 'male' traits. In describing those organisations and leaders that are deemed to be successful, these tend to be portrayed as having stereotypically masculine characteristics such as strength, aggressiveness and competitiveness (Kanter, 1977; Wajcman, 1998). These stereotypical views have been recorded for over thirty years and continue into the 21st century; they constitute a major barrier to women's entry into top level management, particularly in the private sector (Ridgeway, 2001), but also in academia and in the public sector. As a whole, the fallacy persists that women do not fit the image of the (masculine or male) leader. The 'think manager–think male' stereotype as proposed over forty years ago (Schein, 1973, 2001) seems still to be prominent in what is acceptable in terms of leadership within organisations. Interestingly, this phenomenon that male and manager are synonymous seems to be one that persists also at a global level (Schein, 2001; Schein & Davidson, 1993; Schein & Mueller, 1992). More recent studies (e.g., Cuadrado, García-Ael & Molero, 2015) continue to support the gender-bias perception that male equates to manager. These stereotypes in favour of men are seen as contributing more to the glass cliff effect than those stereotypes held about women and their leadership abilities (Bruckmüller & Branscombe, 2010).

Women who aspire to be leaders tend to be judged across two spheres, neither of which supports conclusively their ability to lead. They are seen as too masculine and too assertive, or conversely, as too feminine and soft (Kanter, 1977), neither of which works in their favour in supporting their leadership capabilities. Therefore, when women's behaviour appears too assertive and too masculine, this could lead to them being categorised as competent but not likeable; but if their behaviour is too feminine, they could be considered as likeable but incompetent (Eagly & Carli, 2007). In addition, as Acker (2009) noted, women who do not confirm to expected conventions, inclusive of accepting their subordination to men, could be branded as either 'witches' or 'bitches'. These underlying stereotypical perceptions of women's leadership behaviours could result in two forms of prejudice, at least, according to Eagly and Karau (2002). These would include women receiving a less favourable evaluation of the potential for them to take on leadership roles, when compared with men and secondly, and female leaders receiving less favourable evaluations of their actual behaviour. These perceptions seem to lead to a 'lose-lose' situation for women, and perhaps for women of colour also. For example, the 'angry' black woman or man (Holder, Jackson & Ponterotto, 2015; Sue, Capodilupo, Torino, et al., 2007) tends to be seen as aggressive, rather than assertive, and therefore not suitable for leadership roles.

This shows that there are various standards that are contradictory on how women should act within the workplace. This includes a double standard of how they should behave and interact, and which continues to adversely affect them while at work. For example, while men are encouraged to self-promote their achievements and accomplishments to highlight their competence, the same allowance is not afforded to women, even those with comparable or higher competences (Eagly & Carli, 2007; Isaac, Kaatz & Carnes, 2012). Remarkably, men benefit more than women even when they engage in so called 'feminine' traits, such as warmth, altruism and being considerate (Eagly & Carli, 2007).

Eagly and colleagues (Eagly & Karau, 2002; Eagly & Carli, 2003) have advanced another theory for the non-recognition of women's leadership ability. This states that women's less favourable perception as leaders stems from the incongruity between how people view women's characteristics and what is required as a leader. For example, women may be seen as sensitive, strong, nurturing and helpful, while leaders are meant to be aggressive, dominant, forceful and ambitious. This incongruity may lead to a prejudicial perception that women may not be suitable to be leaders (Eagly & Karau, 2002). Notwithstanding this limited concept of what leadership entails, Eagly and Carli (2003) proposed that traits such as cooperation, mentoring and collaboration are essential to leadership as well. Interestingly, Livingston, Rosette and Washington's (2012) research found that black women and white men who expressed dominance were accepted as leaders, whereas black men and white women who expressed dominance rather than communality were perceived less favourably as leaders.

Diversity, competence and leadership abilities

While evidence exists on the lack of differences between the sexes (Hyde, 2005), especially in the context of cognitive abilities, verbal and nonverbal communication, aggression and leadership (APA, 2005; 2014), the myth that there are distinct differences continues. This misconception continues to ignore the research showing that women's leadership styles tend to be more effective than those of men (Eagly & Carli, 2007). They are more likely to use a transformational approach, thereby supporting and rewarding their subordinates to a greater extent than men. This research showed also that men tended to be more transactional in their styles, with less regard for managing than women who focus on a more collaborative and participatory approach. However, transformational leadership does not necessarily work to women's advantage. Hentschel, Braun, Peus and Frey (2018) found that men who used a transformational leadership approach were perceived to be more effective as leaders than were women. They were also more likely to be seen as more promotable than women.

Even with the evidence that supports a more diverse workforce, the lack of diversity across organisations and especially at more senior levels remains the norm. While this may be remiss, it cannot be due to ability and competence. The educational qualifications, skills and competencies of women when compared to men are not in question, and while there has been some advancement of women, this advancement does not seem to have had a major influence on their progression onto boards and senior leadership positions (Campbell & Mínguez-Vera, 2008). Interestingly, while black women tend to have more graduate qualifications than white women, it is the white women who are more likely to advance more quickly within organisation (Hewlett & Wingfield, 2015). It would reason therefore that graduate qualifications as a criterion does not seem to assist black women in their career. This tendency not to 'see' black women in terms of their qualifications, contributions and abilities could link to their 'invisibility' in the workplace (Sesko & Biernat, 2010). This invisibility has been described as another form of discrimination that does not recognise black women's contribution or credit them accurately for said contributions (Sesko & Biernat, 2010). In this respect, it is easier therefore to not 'see' black women and their achievements when assessing those individuals who could be promoted to senior leadership positions.

The diverse barriers to advancement

So, taking account of the gains listed above, why do challenges remain for women, and especially women of colour, who wish to advance through the organisation and eventually lead it? Research has shown that there are various metaphorical elements that contribute to women's inability to gain leadership positions. These include for example, the 'glass escalator', the 'glass ceiling' and the 'concrete ceiling'. A discussion on these elements follows and illustrates that they are relevant still in limiting women's, and especially diverse women's, promotional opportunities and other ways to advance within organisations.

The glass escalator

The 'glass escalator' effect proposes that the pattern of male advancement to more senior positions exists even within women predominated fields, such as nursing or elementary school teaching; men move more quickly than women into senior leadership positions (Budig, 2002; Williams, 1992). Further, men who work in women dominated professions are discouraged from focusing their careers on the perceived 'feminine' aspect of their professions, such as paediatric nursing or children's librarianship; rather, they are supported and encouraged into more leadership roles (Williams, 1995). These invisible pressures work to the advantage of men, even within feminine professions, but to the disadvantage of women who constitute the majority in these professions, for example nursing or teaching, or other care roles. These practices could be based in how societies perceive traditional roles between men and women, which continues to manifest across all spheres of society.

However, Williams (2013) acknowledged that the glass escalator concept is limited in understanding all those factors that perpetuate gender inequality in the 21st century. She recognised that intersectionality has to be added to any assessment of gender inequality and thereby has to take account also of other factors, such as race/ethnicity, class and sexuality. Other studies support the use of intersectionality in gender focused research to take account of any biases that could impact on the outcome (see Acker, 2009; Biron & Hanuka 2018; Crenshaw, 1989; Davis, 2008; Shore et al., 2011). The importance of intersectionality to this debate cannot be understated. It acknowledges the interactions among gender, age, race and other categories that show the differences in individual lives, that is, overlapping and intersecting identities and the outcomes of these interactions in terms of power, especially in creating overlapping and interdependent systems of discrimination or disadvantage and inequality (Crenshaw, 1989; Davis, 2008).

As Crenshaw (1989) proposed, intersectionality challenges the conceptual limitations of the single-issue analyses of discrimination based solely on race. In this respect, although black women can experience discrimination in various ways, this discrimination has generally been seen to occur based on race only, rather than all the other factors that impact on why the discrimination is occurring (Crenshaw, 1989). Sanchez-Hucles and Davis (2010) add to the discussion in proposing that intersectionality allows a focus on those distinctive challenges that women face, especially women of colour, when they pursue leadership positions. In this respect, by intersecting race with leadership it highlights the challenges to which, for example, black women are subjected when they seek leadership positions; these include racial and sexual stereotyping, being given token status, having their work productivity inaccurate assessed, and being given unrealistic expectations that reduces their attainment of higher level positions (Madden, 2005).

The glass ceiling

One phenomenon that is used to describe the lack of progression in women's advancement to senior leadership positions is the glass ceiling effect. This invisible barrier, acknowledged since the 1980s (Hymowitz & Schelhardt, 1986; Morrison, White, Van Velsor & CLC, 1987), proposes that although women advance to leadership positions in organisations, only a very few are able to attain very senior and prominent leadership positions. This is despite their qualifications and achievements (U.S. Glass Ceiling Commission, 1995). Acker (2009) notes that due to the fewer number of women in prominent positions this makes it more challenging for those women who do not hold leadership positions. The glass ceiling effect emphasised moreover that women are assessed to different standards than men, inclusive of needing to perform to a higher standard; however, they are not compensated to the same standard as men when doing the same role (Morrison et al., 1987). Compensation is a key element in determining the glass ceiling effect, as the earnings of both white and black women never attain those of men over their working lives, which sustains their unequal status (Acker, 2009; Cotter, Hermsen, Ovadia, & Vanneman, 2001), and thereby limits their advancement within an organisation.

Research shows the glass ceiling effect occurs in academia, across industries (Harlander, 1996), and adversely affects minority groups (Acker, 2009; Cotter et al., 2001; Wilson, 2014). The adverse effect on minority groups is driven by those specific practices that exist within the organisational structure. These include how work is organised to reflect the needs of an unencumbered worker, the selective hiring and promotion practices, the gender and race segregation of jobs in which 'women's jobs' do not have support systems to allow mobility or for them to gain the experience necessary for senior management positions, and the discrimination against women when they begin to take time away from the workplace when having children (Acker, 2009).

It has been acknowledged that the glass ceiling is not sustainable and has to be broken, especially in terms of its economic implications that are driven by three main occurrences: '*1) changes in the demographics of the labour force; 2) changes in the demographics of national consumer markets; and 3) the rapid globalisation of the marketplace*' (U.S. Glass Ceiling Commission, 1995, p. 18).

The glass cliff

The glass cliff effect, which advocates that women are more likely to be appointed to leadership positions during time of crisis, while men are appointed to a greater extent during prosperous times (Bruckmuller & Branscombe, 2010), has generated considerable support and research in further understanding women's leadership journey. Ryan, Haslam and their colleagues (e.g., 2005; 2007; 2011) have written extensively on the topic. Their research shows that women in senior leadership positions could find themselves on a glass cliff, as their positions tend to be associated with a greater risk of failure (Ryan & Haslam, 2005). Specifically, Ryan, Haslam and colleagues proposed that when crisis situations occur that rather than thinking 'think manager–think male' (Schein, 1973), those needing to appoint leaders are more likely to 'think crisis–think female' (Ryan, Haslam, Hersby, & Bongiorno, 2011). This is due to perceiving that women are more suitable than men for senior positions and have more leadership ability when an organisation's performance is on the decline (Haslam & Ryan, 2008). Conversely, the perceptions switch when an organisation's performance is positive. This perception of women's suitability under certain conditions is most likely based on accepting that women possess certain traits (e.g., being understanding, intuitive and creative), which are alleged as relevant during times of crisis (Ryan & Haslam, 2007). Bruckmuller and Branscombe (2010) propose also that while women are seen as having those attributes, men are seen as lacking in those attributes, making them less suitable as leaders during times of crisis. There is a perception also that women have people management skills and can take the blame for organisational failure (Ryan et al., 2011). As such, gender per se, has a causal role to play in the perceived suitability of women for glass cliff positions (Ryan & Haslam, 2007).

Ryan et al. (2016) highlight that many elements need to be in place for glass cliffs to occur and that they are context dependent. They clarify further that the glass cliff effect is driven by four conditions. These are: *selection bias*—in favour of women when an organisation's performance is declining; *gender and leadership stereotypes*—in favour of women and their perceived communality during times of crisis; *organizational need for change*—to show a departure from the norm during crises; and *the structure of women's preferences and opportunities*—women wish to have a challenge and will accept the opportunity to lead as these rarely occur for them.

These perceptions of women's suitability for senior leadership positions, only under specific conditions, highlights the continuing sexism that women have to overcome. Ryan, Haslam and Postmes (2007) note that it is a new form of subtle sexism that exists in the workplace, which requires having practical interventions in place to help eradicate these discriminatory appointment practices. The discriminatory practices outlined by the glass cliff effect extend also to other minority groups. One study of the US public sector found that when people of colour were promoted to administrative positions in the system, they were overrepresented in the poor and struggling school districts (Kozol, 1991). In other research, and in acknowledging that women and BME employees tend to be promoted as CEOs of poorly performing firms, Cook and Glass's (2014) research showed moreover that when performance declined within firms with an occupational minority individual as the CEO, this person was more likely to be replaced by a white man.

Cook and Glass termed this the 'saviour effect'. This research adds to the glass cliff effect and illustrates the precarity of BME groups when they are appointed to a leadership position.

The concrete ceiling

As research by McKinsey & Company and LeanIn.Org. (2017) shows, black women are less likely than their white colleagues to gain senior leadership positions. While this lack of progression could be attributed to the glass ceiling effect, Davidson (1997) proposed that in addition to the glass ceiling effect, another barrier to women who are black and from other BME groups, and who wish to gain leadership positions, is the concrete ceiling.

The concept of the concrete ceiling effect was introduced to account for the lack of progression of black and other minority ethnic groups of women in the workplace. This is especially noticeable when these opportunities to progress are significantly reduced or are non-existent (Catalyst, 2002; Piazza, 2016). The concrete ceiling, unlike the glass ceiling that is transparent and can be shattered, is opaque and therefore more challenging to penetrate as one cannot see through it, and it is not as easily shattered (Catalyst, 2004; Piazza, 2016). In acknowledging the concrete ceiling effect, this discussion has to take into account that women of colour continue to experience the double negative effects of racism and sexism (Davidson, 1997; Holder, Jackson & Ponterotto, 2015). This again raises the issue of intersectionality to add to the understanding of the lack of BME women's career progression through an organisation. So, while both white and non-white women have reported that the glass ceiling is a significant factor that adversely affects their advancement within organisations (Key et al., 2012), non-white women have been subjected to racial discrimination during their employment, their advancement, and in the perceptions of their leadership abilities (Key et al., 2012). The experience of racial discrimination could perhaps account for the perception held by women of colour that organisations are not inclusive and do not support openness and diversity (Catalyst, 2002, Piazza, 2016).

There is considerable anecdotal and grey literature on the concrete ceiling concept. However, a greater understanding of the many and varied challenges that women of colour have to navigate within an organisation to attain senior leadership positions is required and much more research is needed on this topic.

Moving beyond ceilings and cliffs

While acknowledging that there are processes and procedures that hinder women's progression within organisations, some researchers propose a more holistic interpretation of what affects women's career equality. This means that it does not rest solely at the organisational level, as detailed in the focus on the ceilings and cliffs metaphors, but rather covers a wider sphere inclusive of societal influences. Acker (2009) proposed that instead of the glass ceiling, a more appropriate description is 'Inequality Regimes', as this reflects the consistent inequalities to which women are subjected at every layer of the organisation. According to Acker, there has to be a focus on race/ethnic and class processes also, as gender is not an inequality that exists on its own; she acknowledges therefore a more holistic understanding of women's struggle within the workplace. It is important to note that all organisations have inequality regimes, which are defined as those loosely interrelated practices, processes, actions and meanings that result in and support the class, gender and racial inequalities that are present within some organisations. So while, the total exclusion of racial and ethnic minorities from senior positions is no longer a reality, the inclusion of individuals who 'differ' is still sporadic (Smith, 2002). Acker (2009) notes that those informal interactions and practices which create the constructs of class, race and gender inequalities in mutually reinforcing processes have not often been documented, but class processes are usually inherent within studies of gendered or racialized inequalities.

In recognising that challenges exist along every stage of the managerial progression route and are beyond one specific barrier, Eagly and Carli (2007) offer the concept of the labyrinth to explain women's restricted progression within organisations. They outline that a labyrinth conveys the complexity and variety of challenges that can appear along the way, as to navigate it requires persistence, awareness of one's progress and a careful analysis of the puzzles that lie ahead. So while the routes to the centre are there, they are not direct, but rather consist of the expected and the unexpected, varied twists and turns (i.e., those prejudices against women seeking leadership positions).

Women and social capital

As outlined thus far, women continue to trail men in terms of career advancement, in the levels of compensation attained, and in gaining higher status. One of the factors that has been proposed to explain why women are hindered in their efforts to achieve career advancement and its associated benefits is their inability to invest adequately in building social capital within organisations (Eagly & Carli, 2007). As various researchers have highlighted (e.g., Sanchez-Hucles & Davis, 2010), social capital is essential to ensure that leaders have the required support and commitment to succeed in their roles. Informal networks, such as those developed when taking part in after work activities, tend to be male formed and dominated by men, with women less likely to have access to or able to become part of such clubs (Eagly & Carli, 2007; Timberlake, 2005). Men seem to be more successful than women in navigating informal networks, which allows them an understanding of organisational norms, values and aims, and how to adopt these, in order to strengthen their ability to gain organisational power (Timberlake, 2005). This success occurs even though women and men enter organisations with the same amount of human capital, defined as intelligence, education, skills and experience (Timberlake, 2005).

Women of colour are even less likely to be able to increase their social capital, which hinders greatly their advancement, as it is a valuable organisational commodity and source of the knowledge, resources and networks that are essential for career development and maturation. However, black women, rather than other women of colour, are more likely to have a mentor at work (Catalyst, 2004), and through having a mentor to increase their social capital (Sanchez-Hucles & Davis, 2010). All potential leaders, inclusive of women, need networks, mentoring and opportunities to lead, but for BME women within the education industry, this was found to be adversely affected by subtle and obvious discrimination from teachers, parents and administrators (Johnson & Campbell-Stephens, 2013).

Another explanation, somewhat less frequently generated but nevertheless visible, is women's lack of support within organisations, which is linked also to their ability to generate social capital. The factor of support has been described as a social support framework that is not fit for purpose and does not assist women in advancing within an organisation (Johns, 2013). Specifically, Ryan et al. (2007) described the support required by women to be multifaceted and cutting across three areas: material support (e.g., having adequate resources and the appropriate infrastructure in place); intellectual support (e.g., having their endeavours and decisions reinforced by others within the organisation); and emotional support (e.g., this could involve looking out for colleagues). Complementary to Ryan et al.'s (2007) support criteria, Kossek, Su and Wu (2017), in recognising the social elements within which an individual's career functions, proposed three organisational dimensions that are needed to ensure gender inclusion: fairness, leveraging talent and workplace support. Women benefit when the work environment is more democratic and equal (Timberlake, 2005).

Diversity bias within a micro effect context

One of the continuing aspects of diversity that rarely gets cited as a source that influences advancing to senior leadership are those micro-aggressions that exist within the work environment. Pierce (1970) highlighted these as offensive mechanisms that adversely impact on interpersonal relationships. They include ignoring those individuals who are 'different' to you, as well as minimising their value and worth. He noted that such actions are not necessarily overt, but rather subtle, and ongoing; most interestingly these accumulate over time through micro-offenses. He proposed also that these offensive mechanisms are in fact micro-aggressions that serve to alienate, make subservient and minimise the worth of the individual to which they are targeted.

These micro-aggressions may reflect that although many researchers do not accept that race has any biological validity, it still maintains its social meaning (Catalyst, 2004).

Sue et al. (2007) built on Pierce's research by defining micro-aggressions as consisting of three main practices:

Microassaults: Those conscious and intentional actions or slurs that involve name calling, or deliberate discriminatory actions, such as showing preferential treatment to a white person before a person of colour in stores.

Microinsults: These involve unconscious verbal and nonverbal communications that are subtle, but nonetheless rude and insensitive and result in demeaning a person's racial heritage or identity. Sue and colleagues (2007) cite as an example an employee who implies that a colleague of colour obtained her job through a quota system.

Microinvalidations: These focus on the unconscious communications that subtly exclude, negate or nullify the thoughts, feelings or experiential reality of a person of colour. Examples of these would include asking people of colour where they were born, or stating that they speak 'good' English, if living in an English speaking country, and thereby inferring that they do not belong to the country in which they were born.

Sue focuses on microinsults and microinvalidiations because of their less obvious nature, which put people of colour in a psychological bind. When such behaviours occur, it may result in the individual feeling insulted, but not exactly sure of this reaction, and while the person may feel insulted, she is not sure exactly why, and the perpetrator is unaware also that the behaviour has been offensive. These microaggressions are especially pertinent to those women of colour who wish to advance to senior management positions. Holder et al.'s (2015) research showed that black women in senior leadership positions had to validate constantly their decisions, experience and expertise in order to realise any standing with their clients and colleagues.

Previous research found also that black women were queried more frequently about their credibility and authority (Catalyst, 2004). This subtle double standard works to diminish the competencies and abilities of black women, and it could be hypothesised supports their lack of progression to senior leadership roles. This is reinforced, as research shows that some women who experience continued subtle and consistent incidents of exclusion, denigration and indifference may choose not to want to lead within organisations (Krefting, 2003).

Basford, Offermann and Behrend (2014) highlight that discrimination is not on the decline but has adjusted to a more subtle and ambiguous form, which is reflected in those microaggressions that occur within the workplace. Other research supports this increase in these more subtle forms of discrimination that manifest within the work environment, but as they are harder to identify and address, their adverse impact on employee well-being and organisational functioning remains (Jones, Arena, Nittrouer, Alonso, & Lindsey 2017). Research has shown that subtle forms of bias are just as harmful to workers as less subtle forms, as well as hindering their advancement in the workplace (Hewlett & Wingfield, 2015; Johnson & Campbell-Stephens, 2013; King & Jones, 2016; Wyatt & Silvester, 2015). However, it is the overt and intentional forms of bias (not subtle and unintentional ones) that favour plaintiffs in respect of legal discrimination claims (King & Jones, 2016).

Despite the acknowledgement of the microaggressions concept, there is a need to be cautious of it due to the lack of substantial research to support it fully (Lilienfeld, 2017). Further, there are challenges in developing instruments that explicitly measure unconscious racism (Blanton & Jaccard, 2008), and it can be hypothesised, unconscious bias in general. However, as noted by Blanton and Jaccard (2008) and Blanton et al. (2009), implicit measures are the only hope of gaining access to unconscious attitudes. Therefore, although racism appears to be on the decline when assessed with explicit measures, it seems to remain strong and prevalent when assessed with implicit measures (see Dovidio & Gaertner, 2004; Nosek et al. 2007).

Women and family commitments

Women continue to retain most of the child care responsibilities, even when working full-time, whilst working part-time is more likely to disadvantage women in being put forward for or gaining senior leadership positions. This 'double shift' pattern of work combined with child care continues to put women at a disadvantage for promotional opportunities. This disproportionate split extends to professional couples, and even when both work full-time, women undertake 41% more of the child care, and complete 30% more of the chores (McKinsey and Company, & Lean In, 2015). In addition to child care, women spend more time also on elder care than do men (Bianchi & Milkie, 2010). Moreover, the lack of a connection between work patterns, child care and school times, and thereby provide support to women who choose to work, has been noted (see Gervais, 2015). This extends to finding suitable and affordable after school care and supervision, which is known to be challenging (Kossek et al., 2017).

While more men are assuming more active parenting roles, women are still viewed as primary caretakers (Harlander, 1996). Further, when both paid and unpaid work (domestic tasks, caring for children and/or elder care) are considered, women have the longest total working week, especially if they work full-time (Forastieri, 2000; European Foundation for the Improvement of Living and Working Conditions [Eurofound], 2007). The availability of flex-time is useful in supporting women with child care responsibilities (Eurofound, 2012; Gervais, 2015).

These challenges for women who wish to advance within organisations are compounded further as the structure of jobs and of organisations tend to benefit men more (Acker, 1990; Williams, 1992, 1995). This is due to women's earnings reducing when they marry and have children, while that of men's increases. Further, as women retain most of the care and housework duties, they are assessed as being less of an ideal worker, as such a male worker is seen as one with few non-work obligations (Budig, 2002).

With respect to women of colour, one of the greatest challenges that they face in their private sphere is simultaneously balancing child care and elder care. (Pompper, 2011). BME women, due to cultural expectations, are more likely than their white counterparts to have double caring responsibilities, to become part of the 'sandwich' generation and to undertake these with limited to no support from their employers (Pomper, 2011).

What next?

> Sure he (Fred Astaire) was great, but don't forget that Ginger Rogers did everything he did, …backwards and in high heels.
>
> Bob Thaves, 1982

The evidence on why women, and those women in ethnic groups, specifically black women, find it challenging to advance to senior management positions has been available for more than a few decades. Despite this compelling evidence, black women and women from other minority ethnic groups do not seem to be able to break through to a great extent the many ceilings or cliffs that exist metaphorically within organisations. This present chapter outlined why the challenges remain. It will offer in this section various options that organisations could pursue to enhance the diversity of its workforce, thereby making it more inclusive. These policies and practices are not new and should be promoted at every opportunity.

Most of the research discussed in this chapter focuses on 'women' as one holistic group. The evidence on BMEs does not seem to be assessed to a great extent. One recommendation for understanding the concerns of BME women, particularly black women, is more research on women of colour.

There remains a pervasive need within societies to not accept the full competencies and skills of women, especially those of colour. Organisations have to start accepting that diversity and inclusion will benefit definitively their bottom line, return on investment, innovation and creativity. They cannot afford to only give it lip service and continue to use the line that they promote on merit, in which merit is white, male and middle class; otherwise, women are never likely to receive fair treatment within organisations and their contributions will never be realised. The emphasis on diversity is gaining traction as millennials have grown up expecting diversity, a gig economy and work-life balance as part of working life. This should translate to changes within the workplace, but it is not expected that these would occur over the short term.

Most of the research is US driven and assessed from a Western perspective, which limits a fuller understanding from a global perspective. More research is required from non-Western countries that focus on the issues that stop women's careers from advancing at a global level.

As various researchers have proposed (see Eagly & Carli, 2007; Equality and Human Rights Commission, 2016); LeanIn.Org and McKinsey & Company, 2016), there are actions that could be put in place, but as these do not seem to be progressing as quickly as they should, it is essential that the following remain on the agenda of organisations.

Organisations have to continue to raise workers' awareness of the **psychological drivers of prejudice toward female leaders, especially towards women of colour** and to eliminate those unjust perceptions. Use unconscious bias training to show that 'the angry black woman' does not pertain to all women of colour. Any training should be supported and sustained within the organisational culture once individuals return to the workplace.

The 24/7 and gig economy seems to have increased, rather than decreased **the long hours culture** that works to men's benefit. Research has shown that presenteeism (being seen) in the context of increased productivity is not a valid measure of productivity. While work is good for individuals, workers with enhanced well-being (i.e. having the capacity to rest, understand their role and have support to complete their tasks) should be more productive.

Continue to improve on **performance evaluation** to reduce the subjectivity of how this is assessed within organisations. The performance management system is linked to unfair work practices that remain in how women and especially those of colour are hired and promoted within organisations. Eagly and Carli (2007) process that all criteria have to be explicit to reduce those conscious and unconscious biases that continue to influence workers' ratings. Pulakos and O'Leary (2011) stipulate further that performance management has evolved into a prescriptive and formulaic practice that does not reflect what the organisation actually wants the individual to achieve. They propose that improved communication in terms of what is expected as a work outcome, as well as setting short-term guidelines and expectations and providing continuous guidance, realises much better end results.

Overall, the entire **selection and hiring process has to be as objective** as can be attained to ensure that it is a fair and unbiased process. Eagly and Carli (2007) recommend using external advertising and employment agencies to recruit staff, rather than relying on internal referrals and recommendations. In addition, any internal development and promotional opportunities have to be transparent and advertised widely to ensure that women are aware of these and can apply for them.

The presence of more women in senior management positions, especially women of colour, would signify that these women are not symbolic of inclusivity, but are rather providing a valid input into organisations' effectiveness, competitiveness and saliency. Conversely, fewer women in such positions could be categorised into stereotypical roles, thereby hindering the most effective use of their competencies and abilities (Eagly & Carli, 2007).

Support women in enhancing their social capital. Women's progression to the C-suite is more likely when they have strong and supportive mentoring relationships and are part of influential networks (Eagly & Carli, 2007; Harlander, 1996; Johns, 2013). Organisations should ensure that there are opportunities for women to be mentored and to network and thereby gain more social capital (i.e. having individuals who support them in their development and progression through the organisation). Social capital is even more important for women of colour who may be stereotyped as individuals who cannot network in those activities. Black women who had sponsors and mentors at their workplace felt empowered and that their presence was validated in the workplace (Holder et al., 2015). Holder et al.'s research showed also that this support system helped them to cope better with the microaggressions that they experienced at work.

Design effective leadership development programmes to support women in gaining critical leadership skills, as well as identifying and using effectively their strengths (McKinsey & Company, 2010; 2012). Women should be encouraged to become comfortable in taking risks, as they tend to be risk averse (Institute of Leadership and Management, 2011). These steps could increase their confidence, and provide them with those tools and techniques they need to better address any barriers they come across. Women, especially women of colour, need also to promote themselves more and raise the value that they bring to the organisation (McKinsey & Company, 2010).

Conclusion

This chapter presented an overview of the challenges that continue to exist for women, and especially women of colour, in their quest to attain senior leadership positions. Despite the developments in laws, quotas and programmes to increase the ratio of women on boards and in the C-Suite, the progression of women into these roles could be much faster. The chapter outlined some of the benefits for having women of colour in senior management positions. This is not only around improved corporate responsibility, but also covers the financial gains from having a more diverse and inclusive senior management structure.

The lack of research on BME in leadership positions and especially BME women is a major challenge in finding the specific number of women in leadership roles. The research tends to focus generally on women or on BMEs as one group, inclusive of men. This is not a useful way to understand the specific challenges of these women. Women of colour are not a holistic group and in order to support them in managing their challenges, the research in this area has to delineate between the various groups.

Overall, while advances have been made in promoting women, less so with women of colour, as senior leaders. The pace of this has to increase, even if only to represent the wider diverse workforce.

References

Acker, J. (1990). Hierarchies, occupations, bodies: A theory of gendered organizations. *Gender and Society, 4*(2), 139–158. https://doi.org/10.1177/089124390004002002

Acker, J. (2009). From glass ceiling to inequality regimes. *Sociologie du Travail, 51*(3), 199–217. doi:10.1016/j.soctra.2009.03.004

Adams, R. B. & Ferreira, D. (2009). Women in the boardroom and their impact on governance and performance. *Journal of Financial Economics, 94*(2), 291–309. doi: 10.2139/ssrn.1107721

American Psychological Association. (2005, October 20). Men and women: No big difference. *Psychological Science: Research in Action.* Retrieved from http://www.apa.org/research/action/difference.aspx

American Psychological Association. (2014, August). Think again: Men and women share cognitive skills. *Psychological Science: Research in Action.* Retrieved from http://www.apa.org/research/action/share.aspx

Basford, T. E., Offermann, L. R., & Behrend, T. S. (2014). Do you see what I see? Perceptions of gender microaggressions in the workplace. *Psychology of Women Quarterly, 38*(3), 340–349. doi:10.1177/0361684313511420

Bianchi, S. & Milkie, M. (2010). Work and family research in the first decade of the 21st century. *Journal of Marriage and Family, 72*(3), 705–725. doi:10.1111/j.1741-3737.2010.00726.x

Biron, M. & Hanuka, H. (2018). Non-cognitive antecedents of pay and pay expectations: gender-based differences in a masculine work setting, *European Journal of Work and Organizational Psychology, 27*(1), 100–111. doi: 10.1080/1359432X.2017.1400967

Blanton, H. & Jaccard, J. (2008). Unconscious racism: A concept in pursuit of a measure. *Annual Review of Sociology, 34*(1), 277–297. https://doi.org/10.1146/annurev.soc.33.040406.131632

Blanton, H., Jaccard, J., Klick, J., Mellers, B., Mitchell, G., & Tetlock, P. E. (2009). Strong claims and weak evidence. Reassessing the predictive validity of the IAT. *Journal of Applied Psychology, 94*(3), 567–582. doi: 10.1037/a0014665

Brammer, S., Millington, A., & Pavelin, S. (2007). Gender and ethnic diversity among UK corporate boards. *Corporate Governance, 15*(2), 393–403. doi: 10.1111/j.1467-8683.2007.00569.x

Bruckmüller, S. & Branscombe, N. R. (2010). The glass cliff: When and why women are selected as leaders in crisis contexts. *British Journal of Social Psychology, 49*(3), 433–451. doi: 10.1348/014466609X466594

Budig, M. J. (2002). Male advantage and the gender composition of jobs: Who rides the glass escalator? *Social Problems, 49*(2), 258–277. https://doi.org/10.1525/sp.2002.49.2.258

Burgess, Z. & Tharenou, P. (2002). Women board directors: Characteristics of the few. *Journal of Business Ethics, 37*(1), 39–49. https://doi.org/10.1023/A:101472600

Campbell, K. & Mínguez-Vera, A. (2008). Gender diversity in the boardroom and firm financial performance, *Journal of Business Ethics, 83*(3), 435–451. doi: 10.1007/s10551-007-9630-y

Catalyst. (2002). *Women of color in corporate management: Three years later.* Retrieved from http://www.catalyst.org/system/files/women_of_color_in_corporate_management.pdf

Catalyst. (2004). *Advancing African American women in the workplace. What managers need to know.* New York, NY. Catalyst. Retrieved from http://www.catalyst.org/system/files/Advancing_African_American_Women_in_the_Workplace_What_Managers_Need_to_Know.pdf

Catalyst. (2017). *Quick Take: Women on Corporate Boards Globally.* New York: Catalyst, January 4, 2017. Retrieved from http://www.catalyst.org/knowledge/women-corporate-boards-globally

Cohen, P. N. & Huffman, M. L. (2007). Working for the woman? Female managers and the gender wage gap. *American Sociological Review, 72*(5), 681–704.

Cook, A. & Glass, C. (2014). Above the glass ceiling: When are women and racial/ethnic minorities promoted to CEO? *Strategic Management Journal, 35*(7), 1080–1089. doi: 10.1002/smj.2161

Cotter, D. A., Hermsen, J. M., Ovadia, S., & Vanneman, R. (2001). The glass ceiling effect. *Social Forces, 80*(2), 655–681. doi:10.1353/sof.2001.0091

Crenshaw, K. (1989). Demarginalizing the intersection of race and sex: A black feminist critique of antidiscrimination doctrine, feminist theory and antiracist politics. *University of Chicago Legal Forum, 1989*(1), Article 8. Retrieved from http://chicagounbound.uchicago.edu/uclf/vol1989/iss1/8

Cuadrado, I., García-Ael, C., & Molero F. (2015). Gender-typing of leadership: Evaluations of real and ideal managers. *Scandinavian Journal of Psychology, 56*(2), 236–244. doi: 10.1111/sjop.12187

Davidson, M. J. (1997). *The Black and Ethnic Minority Woman Manager: Cracking the Concrete Ceiling.* Sage Publications UK.

Davies, E. M., Lord. (2015). *Improving the Gender Balance on British Boards.* Women on Boards Davies Review Five Year Summary October 2015. London: Department for Business, Innovation & Skills. Retrieved from https://www.gov.uk/government/uploads/system/uploads/attachment_data/file/482059/BIS-15-585-women-on-boards-davies-review-5-year-summary-october-2015.pdf

Davis, K. (2008). Intersectionality as buzzword: A sociology of science perspective on what makes a feminist theory successful. *Feminist Theory, 9*(1), 67–85. doi:10.1177/1464700108086364

Dovidio, J. F. & Gaertner, S. L. (2004). Aversive racism. In M. Zanna (Ed.) *Advances in experimental social psychology* (Vol. 36, pp. 1–52). San Diego, CA: Academic Press.

Eagly, A. H. & Carli, L. L. (2003). The female leadership advantage: An evaluation of the evidence. *The Leadership Quarterly, 14*(6), 807–834. https://doi.org/10.1016/j.leaqua.2003.09.004

Eagly, A. H. & Carli, L. L. (2007). Women and the labyrinth of leadership. *Harvard Business Review, 85*(9), 63–71. doi: 10.1037/e664062007-001

Eagly, A. H. & Karau, S. J. (2002). Role congruity theory of prejudice toward female leaders. *Psychological Review, 109*(3), 573–598. doi: 10.1037//0033-295X.109.3.573

Equality and Human Rights Commission. (2016). How to improve board diversity: a six-step guide to good practice. Retrieved from https://www.equalityhumanrights.com/sites/default/files/how_to_improve_board_diversity_web.pdf

Eurofound (European Foundation for the Improvement of Living and Working Conditions). (2007). Parent-Thirion, A., Fernández Macías, E., Hurley, J. & Vermeylen, G., Fourth European working conditions survey, European Foundation for the Improvement of Living and Working Conditions, Office for Official Publications of the European Communities, Luxembourg. Retrieved from http://www.eurofound.europa.eu/pubdocs/2006/98/en/2/ef0698en.pdf

Eurofound (European Foundation for the Improvement of Living and Working Conditions). (2012). Fifth European Working Conditions Survey. Luxembourg: Publications Office of the European Union. doi:10.2806/34660. Retrieved from http://www.eurofound.europa.eu/pubdocs/2011/82/en/1/EF1182EN.pdf

European Commission, Executives and Non-Executives, Women and Men in Decision-Making Database (2016). Retrieved from http://www.catalyst.org/knowledge/women-management

European Commission, Directorate-General for Employment, Social Affairs and Equal Opportunities Unit. 2010. *More women in senior positions. Key to economic stability and growth.* Brussels: European Community. Luxembourg: Publications Office of the European Union, 2010. doi:10.2767/92882 Retrieved from http://ec.europa.eu/social/BlobServlet?docId=4746&langId=en

Forastieri, V. (2000). 'Information note on women workers and gender issues on occupational safety and health', Safe Work. Geneva: International Labour Office. Retrieved from http://www.ilo.org/wcmsp5/groups/public/---ed_protect/---protrav/---safework/documents/briefingnote/wcms_146255.pdf

Fortune. (2017, June 07). These Are the Women CEOs Leading Fortune 500 Companies. Retrieved from http://fortune.com/2011/10/26/fortune-500-women-ceos/

Gervais, R. L. (2015). Work patterns, child care and school times: In or out of sync? *Division of Occupational Psychology - Work-Life Balance Working Group Newsletter, 8,* 7–9.

Grant Thornton, Women in Business: Turning Promise Into Practice (2016): p. 5, 8.

Harlander, S. K. (1996). Breaking through the glass ceiling: an industrial perspective. *Journal of Animal Science, 74*(11), 2849–2854. doi: 10.2527/1996.74112849x

Haslam, S. A. & Ryan, M. K. (2008). The road to the glass cliff: Differences in the perceived suitability of men and women for leadership positions in succeeding and failing organizations. *The Leadership Quarterly, 19*(5), 530–546. doi: 10.1016/j.leaqua.2008.07.011

Hentschel, T., Braun, S., Peus, C., & Frey, D. (2018). The communality-bonus effect for male transformational leaders - leadership style, gender, and promotability. *European Journal of Work and Organizational Psychology, 27*(1), 112–125, doi: 10.1080/1359432X.2017.1402759

Hewlett, S. A., Sears, T., Sumberg, K., & Fargnoli, C. (2013). The Power of "Out" 2.0: LGBT in the Workplace. Center for Talent Innovation. Retrieved from http://www.talentinnovation.org/_private/assets/PowerOfOut-2-ExecSumm-CTI.pdf

Hewlett, S. A., & Wingfield, T. (2015, June 11). Qualified Black women are being held back from management. *Harvard Business Review.* Retrieved from https://hbr.org/2015/06/qualified-black-women-are-being-held-back-from-management?referral=03758&cm_vc=rr_item_page.top_right

Holder, A. M. B., Jackson, M. A., & Ponterotto, J. G. (2015). Racial Microaggression experiences and coping strategies of Black women in corporate leadership. *Qualitative Psychology, 2*(2), 164–180. http://dx.doi.org/10.1037/qup0000024

Hyde, J. S. (2005). The gender similarities hypothesis. *American Psychologist, 60*(6), 581–592. doi:10.1037/0003-066X.60.6.581

Hymowitz, C. & Schelhardt, T. D. (1986). The glass-ceiling why women can't seem to break the invisible barrier that blocks them from top jobs. *The Wall Street Journal, 57,* D1, D4–D5.

Hultin, M. & Szulkin, R. (2003). Mechanisms of inequality: Unequal access to organizational power and the gender wage gap. *European Sociological Review, 19*(2), 143–159. https://doi.org/10.1093/esr/19.2.143

Hunt, V., Layton, D., & Prince, S. (2015). *Diversity Matters.* McKinsey & Company. Retrieved from https://www.mckinsey.com/~/media/mckinsey/business functions/organization/our insights/why diversity matters/diversity matters.ashx

International Labour Organization, Women in Business Management: Gaining Momentum: Global Report (2015). http://www.ilo.org/wcmsp5/groups/public/---dgreports/---dcomm/---publ/documents/publication/wcms_316450.pdf

Institute of Leadership and Management. 2011. Ambition and Gender at Work. Retrieved from https://www.institutelm.com/asset/89DEB7DA%2DB479%2D410D%2DACA5F141D56901E3/

Isaac, C., Kaatz, A., & Carnes, M. (2012). Deconstructing the Glass Ceiling. *Sociology Mind, 2*(1), 80–86. doi: 10.4236/sm.2012.21011.

Johns, M. L. (2013). Breaking the Glass Ceiling: Structural, Cultural, and Organizational Barriers Preventing Women from Achieving Senior and Executive Positions. *Perspectives in Health Information Management/AHIMA, American Health Information Management Association,* 10(Winter), 1e.

Johnson, L. & Campbell-Stephens, R. (2013). Developing the next generation of black and global majority leaders for London schools. *Journal of Educational Administration, 51*(1), 24–39. doi: 10.1108/09578231311291413

Jones, K. P., Arena, D. F., Nittrouer, C. L., Alonso, N. M., & Lindsey, A. P. (2017). Subtle discrimination in the workplace: A vicious cycle. *Industrial and Organizational Psychology, 10*(1), 51–76. https://doi.org/10.1017/iop.2016.91

Kanter, R. M. (1977). *Men and Women of the Corporation.* New York: Basic Books.

Key, S., Popkin, S., Munchus, G., Wech, B., Hill, V., & Tanner, J. (2012). An exploration of leadership experiences among white women and women of color. *Journal of Organizational Change Management, 25*(3), 392–404. doi: 10.1108/09534811211228111

King, E. & Jones, K. (2016, July 13). Why subtle bias is so often worse than blatant discrimination. *Harvard Business Review.* Retrieved from https://hbr.org/2016/07/why-subtle-bias-is-so-often-worse-than-blatant-discrimination?referral=03759&cm_vc=rr_item_page.bottom

Korczyc, E., Matia, L., Vincelette, G. A. et al. (2013). *EU11 regular economic report – Macroeconomic report: Faltering recovery – special topic: The economic growth implications of an aging European Union.* Washington, DC: The World Bank. Retrieved from http://documents.worldbank.org/curated/en/2013/01/17183435/eu11-regular-economic-reportmacroeconomic-report-faltering-recovery-special-topic-economic-growth-implications-aging-european-union.

Kossek, E. E., Su, R., & Wu, L. (2017). "Opting out" or "pushed out"? Integrating perspectives on women's career equality for gender inclusion and interventions. *Journal of Management, 43*(1), 228–254. doi: 10.1177/0149206316671582

Kozol, J. 1991. *Savage inequalities: Children in America's public schools.* New York: Harper Collins.

Krefting, L. A. (2003). Intertwined discourses of merit and gender: Evidence from academic employment in the USA. *Gender, Work & Organization, 10*(2), 260–278. doi: 10.1111/1468-0432.t01-1-00014

LeanIn.Org & McKinsey & Company. Women in the Workplace 2016. Retrieved from https://womenintheworkplace.com/2016

Lilienfeld, S. O. (2017). Microaggressions: Strong claims, inadequate evidence. *Perspectives on Psychological Science*, *12*(1), 138–169. https://doi.org/10.1177/1745691616659391

Livingston, R. W., Rosette, A. S. & Washington, E. F. (2012). Can an agentic Black woman get ahead? The impact of race and interpersonal dominance on perceptions of female leaders. *Psychological Science*, *23*(4), pp. 354–8. doi: 10.1177/0956797611428079.

Lückerath-Rovers, M. (2013). Women on boards and firm performance. *Journal of Management & Governance*, *17*(2), 491–509. doi: 10.1007/s10997-011-9186-1

Madden, M. (2005). 2004 Division 35 presidential address: Gender and leadership in higher education. *Psychology of Women Quarterly*, *29*, 3–14. doi:10.1111/j.1471-6402.2005.00162.x

McDonald, I. (2004). Women in management: An historical perspective, *Employee Relations*, *26*(3), 307–319. doi 10.1108/01425450410530673

McKinsey and Company, & Lean In. (2015). Women in the workplace. Retrieved from https://womenintheworkplace.com/Women_in_the_Workplace_2015.pdf

McKinsey & Company & LeanIn.Org. Women in the Workplace 2017. Retrieved from https://womenintheworkplace.com/Women_in_the_Workplace_2017.pdf

McKinsey & Company. Women Matter 2010. Retrieved from http://www.mckinsey.com/locations/swiss/news_publications/pdf/women_matter_2010_4.pdf

McKinsey & Company. (2012). https://www.mckinsey.com/~/media/McKinsey/Business%20Functions/Organization/Our%20Insights/Women%20matter/Women_matter_mar2012_english%20(1).ashx

Morrison, A. M., White, R. P., & Van Velsor, E. Center for Creative Leadership (CCL) (1987). *Breaking the glass ceiling: Can women reach the top of America's largest corporations?* Reading, MA: Addison-Wesley Publishing Co.

Nielsen (2012). *African-American consumers: Still vital, still growing.* The Nielsen Company. Retrieved from http://www.nielsen.com/content/dam/corporate/us/en/reports-downloads/2012-Reports/African-American-Consumers-Still-Vital-Still-Growing-2012-Report.pdf

Nosek, B. A., Smyth, F. L., Hansen, J. J., Devos, T., Lindner, N. M., Ranganath, K. A., Smith, C. T., Olson, K. R., Chugh, D., Greenwald, A. G., & Banaji, M. R. (2007). Pervasiveness and correlates of implicit attitudes and stereotypes. *European Review of Social Psychology*, *18*, 36–88.

Office for National Statistics (ONS, 2017). Civil Service statistics, UK: 2017. Retrieved from https://www.ons.gov.uk/employmentandlabourmarket/peopleinwork/publicsectorpersonnel/bulletins/civilservicestatistics/2017/pdf

Parker, Sir John, (2017). A Report into the Ethnic Diversity of UK Boards. The Parker Review Committee. Department for Business, Energy & Industrial Strategy. Retrieved from http://www.ey.com/Publication/vwLUAssets/The_Parker_Review/$FILE/EY-Parker-Review-2017-FINAL%20REPORT.pdf

Piazza, J. (2016). Women of Color Hit a 'Concrete Ceiling' in Business. Retrieved from ttps://www.wsj.com/articles/women-of-color-hit-a-concrete-ceiling-in-business-1474963440

Pierce, C. (1970). Offensive Mechanisms. In F. B. Barbour (Ed.). *The Black Seventies* (pp. 265–282). Boston, MA: Porter Sargent.

Pletzer, J. L., Nikolova, R., Kedzior, K. K., & Voelpel, S. C. (2015). Does gender matter? Female representation on corporate boards and firm financial performance - A meta-analysis. *PLoS ONE 10*(6): e0130005. doi:10.1371/journal.pone.0130005

Pompper, D. (2011). Fifty years later: Mid-career women of color against the glass ceiling in communications organizations. *Journal of Organizational Change Management*, *24*(4), 464–486. doi: 10.1108/09534811111144629

Post, C., & Byron, K. (2015). Women on boards and firm financial performance: A meta-analysis. *Academy of Management Journal*, *58*(5), 1546–1571. https://doi.org/10.5465/amj.2013.0319

Pulakos, E. D. & O'Leary, R. S. (2011). Why is performance management broken? *Industrial and Organizational Psychology*, *4*(2), 146–164. doi: 10.1111/j.1754-9434.2011.01315.x

Ridgeway, C. L. (2001). Gender, status, and leadership. *Journal of Social Issues*, *57*(4), 637–656. https://doi.org/10.1111/0022-4537.00233

Ryan, M. K., & Haslam, S. A. (2005). The glass cliff: Evidence that women are over-represented in precarious leadership positions. *British Journal of Management*, *16*(2), 81–90. doi: 10.1111/j.1467-8551.2005.00433.x

Ryan, M. K. & Haslam, S. A. (2007). The glass cliff: Exploring the dynamics surrounding the appointment of women to precarious leadership positions. *The Academy of Management Review*, *32*(2), 549–572. doi: 10.5465/AMR.2007.24351856

Ryan, M. K., Haslam, S. A., Hersby, M. D., & Bongiorno, R. (2011). Think crisis–think female: The glass cliff and contextual variation in the think manager–think male stereotype. *Journal of Applied Psychology*, *96*(3), 470–484. doi: 10.1037/a0022133

Ryan, M. K., Haslam, S. A., Morgenroth, T., Rink, F., Stoker, J., & Peters, K. (2016). Getting on top of the glass cliff: Reviewing a decade of evidence, explanations, and impact. *The Leadership Quarterly*, *27*(3), 446–455. https://doi.org/10.1016/j.leaqua.2015.10.008

Ryan, M. K., Haslam, S. A., & Postmes, T. (2007). Reactions to the glass cliff: Gender differences in the explanations for the precariousness of women's leadership positions. *Journal of Organizational Change Management*, *20*(2), 182–197. doi: 10.1108/09534810710724748

Sanchez-Hucles J. V. & Davis, D. D. (2010). Women and women of color in leadership. Complexity, identity, and intersectionality. *American Psychologist*, *65*(3), 171–181. doi: 10.1037/a0017459

Schein, V. E. (1973). The relationship between sex role stereotypes and requisite management characteristics. *Journal of Applied Psychology*, *57*(2), 95–100. doi: 10.1037/h0037128

Schein, V. E. (2001). A global look at psychological barriers to women's progress in management. *Journal of Social Issues*, *57*(4), 675–688.

Schein, V. E. & Davidson, M. J. (1993). Think manager, think male. *Management Development Review*, *6*(3), doi: 10.1108/EUM0000000000738

Schein, V. & Mueller, R. (1992). Sex role stereotyping and requisite management characteristics: A cross cultural look. *Journal of Organizational Behavior*, *13*(5), 439–447. doi: 10.1002/job.4030130502

Sesko, A. K. & Biernat, M. (2010). Prototypes of race and gender: The invisibility of Black women. *Journal of Experimental Social Psychology*, *46*,(2), 356–360. https://doi.org/10.1016/j.jesp.2009.10.016

Shore, L. M., Randel, A. E., Chung, B. G., Dean, M. A., Holcombe Ehrhart, K., & Singh, G. (2011). Inclusion and diversity in work groups: A review and model for future research. *Journal of Management*, *37*(4), 1262–1289. doi: 10.1177/0149206310385943

Smith, R. A., 2002. Race, gender, and authority in the workplace: Theory and research. *Annual Review of Sociology*, *28*, 509–542. doi: 10.1146/annurev.soc.28.110601.141048

Sue, D. W., Capodilupo, C. M., Torino, G. C., Bucceri, J. M., Holder, A. M. B., Nadal, K. L., & Esquilin, M. (2007). Racial microaggressions in everyday life: Implications for clinical practice. *American Psychologist*, *62*(4), 271–286. doi: 10.1037/0003-066X.62.4.271

Timberlake, S. (2005). Social capital and gender in the workplace. *Journal of Management Development*, *24*(1), pp. 34–44. doi: 10.1108/02621710510572335

U.S. Glass Ceiling Commission (1995). *A Solid Investment: Making Full Use of the Nation's Human Capital (Final Report of the Commission)*. Washington, DC: U.S. Government Printing Office. Retrieved from http://digitalcommons.ilr.cornell.edu/key_workplace/120/

Wacjman, J. (1998). *Managing Like a Man*. Cambridge: Polity Press.

Williams, C. L. (2013). The glass escalator, revisited: Gender inequality in neoliberal times, SWS feminist lecturer. *Gender and Society, 27*(5), 609–629. doi: 10.1177/0891243213490232

Williams, C. L. (1992). The glass escalator: hidden advantages for men in the "female" professions. *Social Problems, 39*(3), 253–267. https://doi.org/10.2307/3096961

Williams, C. L. (1995). *Still a Man's World: Men Who Do "Women's Work"*. Berkeley, CA: University of California Press.

Wilson, E. (2014). Diversity, Culture and the Glass Ceiling. *Journal of Cultural Diversity, 21*(3), 83–89.

World Bank. (2011). *World development report 2012. Gender equality and development.* Washington, DC: The International Bank for Reconstruction and Development/The WorldBank. Retrieved from http://siteresources.worldbank.org/INTWDR2012/Resources/7778105-1299699968583/7786210-1315936222006/Complete-Report.pdf.

Wyatt, M. & Silvester, J. (2015). Reflections on the labyrinth: Investigating Black and Minority Ethnic leaders' career experiences. *Human Relations, 68*(8), 1243–1269. doi: 10.1177/0018726714550890

Zweigenhaft, R. L. (2013, August 12). Diversity Among CEOs and Corporate Directors: Has the Heyday Come and Gone? Guilford College. Based on a presentation at the annual meeting of the American Sociological Association, New York City. Retrieved from http://www2.ucsc.edu/whorulesamerica/power/diversity_among_ceos.html

Chapter 15

Diversity from an organisational perspective: Past, present and future directions

Misha Jechand

In the last couple of years, the concept of diversity and inclusion has created a storm for organisations. On one hand organisations are promoting diversity and striving towards a vision of a more balanced workforce which avoids discrimination; however, in practice this isn't the easiest to implement, and some stereotypes just can't seem to be shaken off. Overall, it is important for organisations to consider embedding valuing diversity in their long-term strategy, as having a diverse workforce is linked to a more successful organisation, as well as being a more attractive proposition for future talent.

What is diversity?

Diversity involves people looking at themselves and others, and acknowledging the differences. One aspect is surface level diversity, which categorises gender, race, religion, culture and other protected characteristics; deep level diversity focuses on skill sets, personal experiences and beliefs. Once these differences have been identified, it is then important to understand and recognise these differences to value each other's strengths.

The past

> Seven months into my first job the manager of my department was let go on several charges of discrimination. I personally witnessed her make racist, anti-gay, anti-Semitic nationalist comments. This was an uncomfortable experience and made me feel inferior.
>
> Anonymous, 2017

Several individuals who I interviewed reported that their past involved many stereotypes and managers being able to get away with unfair practices which would now be described as workplace bullying (Lee, 2000). Leadership which lacks ethical conduct can be dangerous, destructive and even toxic (Toor & Ofori, 2009). This is reflective of the characteristics of a toxic organisation where employees exhibit emotions such as low self-efficacy, low morale, lack of belongingness and no support network (Härtel, 2008).

Individuals also reported they thought white people had a natural advantage in life (Lipsitz, 2006) and that males got paid more. For the UK as a whole, the gender pay gap has reduced in the last 10 years but is still in favour of men (Office for National Statistics, 2008). During my career so far, I have witnessed several diversity and inclusion practices. However, being from an ethnic minority myself, there is a lack of understanding over what diversity and inclusion practices exist in organisations amongst my parents' and grandparents' generations.

Their lived experience was impacted by the degree of acceptance, understanding, prejudicial attitudes, stereotyping and ignorance that existed within their culture and surroundings (McIntosh, 2017). Everyone seemed to have a place; I could never have imagined a male secretary, a female engineer or a black CEO whilst growing up. When exploring this further I realised individuals were encouraged and tended to follow the path of least resistance and only pursue the opportunities recommended to them.

Evidence suggests that while women typically experienced an invisible barrier preventing their rise into leadership ranks in organisations, a 'glass ceiling' (Kanter, 2008; Morrison, White & Van Velsor, 1987), men (particularly those in female-dominated professions) were more likely to be conveyed into management positions by means of a 'glass escalator'.

The notion of a glass ceiling made it difficult for females, especially females from ethnic minority groups, to progress and get promotions and pay rises and be presented with further opportunities for development. Furthermore, to this day they are still underrepresented in the upper echelons of organisations (Barretto, Ryan & Schmitt, 2009). Individuals who I interviewed indicated that success in large prestigious organisations only seemed available for a few, and people naturally got ahead due to perceptions, rather than competence, ability and drive.

> Truly committing to a diverse workforce calls for deep evaluation of practices and biases.
>
> Anonymous, 2017

Within my current role as an Assessment Design Specialist at British Airways, I often speak to recruiters who ask for advice and recommendations on assessment strategies and interviewing. Common phrases include, 'I just adapted the interview as I went along'; 'They didn't seem right for the job'; 'They didn't look like a hard worker'. This highlights the bias which exists in selection processes and that many individuals make assumptions without even realising that they are adopting unfair practices (O'Neill-Busidate, 2016; Biernat, 2012; Burton et al., 2015).

Typically, this is more manageable with recruitment campaigns which have fewer candidates (e.g., senior hires). However, there is a higher risk associated with high volume campaigns. Examples of high volume campaigns in my current role are Cabin Crew and Pilots, where it is extremely important to ensure the assessors have a fair and objective mindset, as hundreds of candidates are being interviewed in a campaign. Common biases which still occur every day include:

- **Unconscious bias**—This happens when our brains make incredibly quick judgments and assessments about a candidate without realising. Biases are influenced by our background, cultural environment and personal experiences.
- **Stereotyping**—Forming an opinion about how someone of a given gender, religion, race, appearance or other characteristic thinks, acts, responds or would perform a job without having any evidence that this is the case.
- **First impressions**—Making a judgement about someone based on when you first meet them; positive or negative impressions can then cloud the rest of the assessment process. Another example is if a candidate has a characteristic which you notice straight away (i.e., eccentric clothing, a strong regional accent).
- **Non-verbal bias**—Emphasis may be placed on non-verbal cues which are irrelevant to the job itself (i.e., if the candidate is nervous, type of handshake given).
- **Halo/horns effect**—The halo effect occurs when an assessor allows one strong point about the candidate to overshadow or affect their decision on whether they have passed the selection process (i.e., knowing someone went to a particular university). Alternatively, the horns effect is when one weak point negatively influences the assessor's decision making process.
- **Contrast effect**—Stronger candidates who interview after weaker ones may appear more qualified and this is due to the contrast between the two.
- **Inconsistency in questions**—If you ask each candidate different questions this can lead to a skewed assessment of who would best perform the job. This makes it critical to ensure all candidates are asked the same questions.

When designing a selection process every job role requires a thorough analysis of what makes an individual a high performer. For leadership or specialist roles, individual differences such as having an accent may not impact the selection decision as individuality is valued. However, for customer facing roles, being able to communicate effectively is key, so the selection criteria should assess whether communication is clear, concise and easily understood. Guidance for assessors can be in the form of e-learning modules, practical classroom sessions or being briefed by an occupational psychologist.

Table 15.1 The ORCE approach

Observe	Assessor observes the candidate during the assessment.
Record	The assessor records what the candidate is saying or doing.
Classify	What has been observed is classified against behavioural or competency indicators.
Evaluate	The assessor summarises the candidate's performance and allocates an overall score.

Within my current role, I regularly quality assure new assessors to ensure they are assessing objectively. Organisations can mitigate these biases by promoting the ORCE approach to assessment. See Table 15.1.

The present

> Taking steps to create a more diverse and inclusive workplace is in the interest of all organisations, whether they have 10 employees or 10,000.
>
> Anonymous, 2017

I had a great experience working for Network Rail and really valued their commitment to diversity and inclusion. There was a robust diversity and inclusion strategy in place with a Head of Diversity and Inclusion and a dedicated team. In addition, it was clear that the leadership team was committed and there were lots of talks and initiatives around the head office. For example, 'Everyone Week' was hosted every year where all employees were invited to workshops to share their views and experiences. In addition, there were lots of organisational groups (e.g., Lesbian Gay Bisexual Transsexual (LGBT)), which you could join if you wanted to connect with like minded people.

When you walked around the office building, you met all sorts of people and felt like you were experiencing a knowledge hub, and it was recognisable that individuals in leadership roles were varied in terms of age, gender and ethnicity. However, when you visited operational divisions it was apparent that white middle-aged males dominated. This was due to the nature of roles being historically more male dominated. This example is similar to many organisations which, although they are striving towards implementing diversity, are still experiencing several challenges, demonstrating that change cannot be implemented overnight. Examples of challenges include developing a vision of inclusion, integrative leadership, employees demonstrating competencies of inclusion and implementing objective and fair recruitment practices (Pless & Maak, 2004).

There have been some positive examples of advancements in diversity. For example, in South Africa the Skills Development Levy was introduced through affirmative action in 1994. This provided emphasis on black employees being prioritised to go on training programmes. In addition, last year saw the introduction of the British Diversity Standard (BS 76005 – Valuing people through diversity and inclusion). This code of practice provides recommendations for reviewing, assessing and undertaking a competent and principled approach to diversity and inclusion in the workplace.

Advancements also include 'return to work' programmes for experienced women wanting to work after a career break, as well as diversity workshops which are rolled out throughout the organisation and which give individuals the opportunity to have open discussions with their colleagues. In addition, there is a drive for social development, and many large organisations have programmes which focus on developing the communities they are surrounded by (i.e., by hosting events on site or at local schools).

Over the last two years I have been involved in several projects which promote diversity and inclusion which has fuelled my interest in the subject area. One of my favourite projects was the design of behavioural change sessions for a professional services organisation. The organisation revealed that females and black minority groups were underperforming in two main behavioural areas and required up-skilling sessions designed for these core groups. The aim of these sessions was to provide potential applicants with an opportunity to practice their skills, improve their confidence and have an increased chance of passing the assessment and selection process, contributing to the organisation's global diversity and inclusion framework.

In addition, I completed some analysis in an international call centre where I spent two weeks on site interviewing and job shadowing incumbents. The purpose was to understand what qualities and behaviours a high performer needed to demonstrate and then to compose an insight report and behavioural framework for the organisation. Being on site and experiencing the culture of the organisation made me quickly realise that diversity was important to every single employee, and feeling the buzz when walking around the office showed the direct effect this had on energy levels.

I also regularly run adverse impact analyses to ensure that certain groups are not disadvantaged during a selection process. The analysis ensures that organisations sustain a diverse applicant pool and that there is no discrimination against gender, ethnicity or disability. This is especially important during the psychometric testing phase, as some validation studies of ability tests indicate that ethnic minority groups are naturally likely to be disadvantaged (Roth et al., 2001).

> The world has started to recognise the art of thinking together independently.
>
> Anonymous, 2017

The world has started to recognise the value and impact of diverse teams. In particular, some of the most striking and beautiful structures would not have been possible without the people behind them. Last year I visited the hub of the United Arab Emirates, Dubai, which is a country that shows what people can create. One prime example of this is the Burj Khalifa, which required a combination of visionary ideals and solid science to build, and holds a number of records. It is the tallest building and freestanding structure in the world, has the highest number of storeys, the highest occupied floor, the highest outdoor observation deck and the elevator with the longest travel distance.

Whilst it is superlative in every respect, it is the unique design of this structure that truly sets it apart, and this would not have been possible without the talented minds behind it. You would assume this would be down to architects; however, thousands of engineers, doctors, workers and consultants from across the world were involved. It has created an exceptional standard for future developments.

In contrast, on a trip to Singapore it became apparent that the concept of diversity and inclusion was not heavily promoted, and many people were unaware of the activities to advance diversity and inclusion that are happening in Western countries. This highlighted the lack of knowledge around diversity and inclusion in the East and the need to communicate learning across the world, in particular to organisations that operate on a global basis.

Future directions

> It is time for parents to teach young people early on that in diversity there is beauty and there is strength.
>
> Anonymous, 2017

It is important to teach diversity to children at a young age to prepare them for their working lives. The more open-minded and self-assured individuals are at the start of their working lives, the higher the likelihood they will take on challenges and be successful in their corporate lives. Therefore, it is important for parents to promote a 'growth mindset' (Dweck, 2009) to encourage children to believe that failure is not a proof of unintelligence but an encouraging springboard for growth and development. This is linked to two decades of research which found that the view you choose to embrace for yourself deeply affects how you live your life, determining whether you become who you want to be and whether you achieve your full potential.

As a result of diversity and inclusion initiatives (e.g., encouraging females to study science, technology, engineering and maths (STEM) subjects), young people are now presented with more opportunities. They are presented with a number of options when they leave school and they can choose whether they go to college, apply for an apprenticeship or go to university and study a particular discipline. When applying for a job, it is important that young people are aware that in addition to knowledge, organisations look for observable behaviours such as leadership, innovation, adaptability and team work, which can be developed through all sorts of activities and experiences from either academic or professional life.

> Start to think about what makes you different from everyone else.
>
> Anonymous, 2017

My observations of the future are that the population and workforce will become even more diverse. Due to globalisation we are now seeing more migration, and more and more people are setting up their life in the UK. The position and power of women will continue to evolve; religion and race are becoming more transparent and sensitive; and more people are being open about their sexuality or even choosing gender re-assignment. There is also a paradox between the aging population versus millennials who are more likely to have boundaryless careers. This notion moves away from having a 'job for life' and towards a career spanning several organisations (Arthur & Rousseau, 1996). Individuals are also likely to have different expectations for a working life perspective (e.g., a work-home balance) and may be more likely to be reliant on technology.

This makes it even more important for all organisations to understand and value individual differences and be aware of what each employee can add to the organisation. In addition, the promotion of diversity and inclusion is more likely to lie in the heart of recruitment, development and retention strategies. For leadership roles, both technical and emotional competencies have become key differentiators for success. As people are promoted to more senior roles, their performance is measured not only on bottom-line results, but also on their emotional intelligence (how they deal and communicate with others).

It is essential for leaders to demonstrate self-awareness in their leadership style and encourage their teams to value each other by allocating tasks based on individuals' strengths. However, if someone lacks self–awareness and is unaware of what they can offer, this makes it difficult for others to understand. There are a number of psychometric tools on the market which can help an individual to understand themselves, their motives, strengths and preferences, as well as differences and how their differences can impact interactions. Leaders and managers may want to consider incorporating these tools into onboarding processes and whilst setting development plans for their team.

> On my own I'm a dot; with others I'm a masterpiece of dreamlike epic proportions and beauty.
>
> Anonymous, 2017

When building high performing teams, it is essential to acknowledge the similarities and differences between individuals and the most effective way for them to work together. Whereas one person may be great at generating exciting, out of the box ideas, another individual may have the necessary experience to investigate the detail and execute it; so it is essential to play on everyone's strengths and collaborate with others in the team.

Recently, I experienced a team development session and was posed a question of how I would react if I met my psychological opposite (highly people focused; inspiration driven; big picture oriented; and highly extroverted). A year ago I probably would that type of person, as I would have felt we had nothing in common; however, I now realise the value of working with people who are different than me and how together we can complement each other to create a bigger impact. Sometimes the most valuable perspective is the one you don't have.

Why is diversity important?

Organisations that understand the value of having a diverse workforce are more likely to benefit than those organisations that don't view diversity as a priority. In addition, ensuring the leadership team represents diversity sets the tone for the rest of the organisation. This isn't just a subjective fact; the research supports it (Stockdale & Crosby, 2004; Noe et al., 2003). Having a diverse workforce is linked to:

Improved employee engagement and performance—It is no surprise that employees are more likely to feel happy and supported in an environment where inclusivity is a priority. Equality in the workplace is essential if you want employees to feel confident in their ability and achieve their best. Increased morale is linked to increased productivity and performance (Downey et al., 2015).

A variety of talent, skills and experience—This is beneficial to the organisation and employees' work performance. Whilst it is important to hire individuals with the appropriate skills to fit role specifications, it is beneficial for employees to have crossover skills when managing, coaching and interacting with others. A variety of skills and experience means that employees can learn from each other and supports the notion of a learning organisation (Stewart, 2001). The 'Big 4' accountancy firms have started exploring the skills and behavioural characteristics a high performing accountant should possess (Edgley, Sharma & Anderson-Gough, 2016).

An innovation buzz—Creative concepts can be fuelled by working alongside people of different backgrounds, experiences and working styles. In particular, ideas can be bounced off each other, allowing for feedback, suggestions and improvements (Østergaard, Timmermans & Kristinsson, 2011). However, in practice, this is dependent on an organisation's culture. A great example is Google, which promotes diversity in thinking with their eight pillars of innovation (Wojcicki, 2011).

Language skills—Language barriers and cultural differences can often act as a bit of an obstacle for an organisation that seeks to operate globally.

However, it is often argued that multicultural organisations hold potential knowledge resources that can be used to increase performance (Lauring & Selmer, 2011). By acknowledging that employees speak a number of languages can make it easier to expand internationally and interact with a more varied client base. An organisation that represents a number of nationalities can also be considered as more reputable.

A culture of openness—By promoting diversity and inclusion practices, organisations are more likely to avoid change resistance. By fostering an attitude of openness, employees are more likely to feel part of decision making and buy into change initiatives (Pless & Maak, 2004). However, this is sometimes a challenge, as culture and openness in a team are often lead by the manager.

An increased talent pool—A company that embraces diversity will be viewed as a more progressive organisation, more appealing to work for and attract a wider range of candidates to vacancies. By attracting and retaining talent, this enables organisations to effectively plan their talent pipelining strategy and ensure there is a diverse spread of individuals in leadership positions. In practice, this can be challenging if there is not an in-house talent team; however, an excellent example of a progressive organisation is HSBC, which truly values diversity and has implemented a global talent management process to attract and retain individuals (Gakovic & Yardley, 2007).

I would like to thank everyone who put forward their thoughts and experiences for the purpose of this article. Your contributions enabled my analysis to represent diversity and inclusion practices across a number of organisations, industries and countries and made writing this piece truly enjoyable.

References

Arthur, M. B. & Rousseau, D. M. (1996). *The boundaryless career.* New York: Oxford University Press.

Barreto, M., Ryan, M. K., & Schmitt, M. T. (Eds.). (2008). *The glass ceiling in the 21ˢᵗ century: Understanding barriers to gender equality.* Washington, DC: American Psychological Association.

Biernat, M. (2012). Stereotypes and shifting standards: Forming, communicating, and translating person impressions. *Advances in Experimental Social Psychology, 45*, 1–59. Doi: https://doi.org/10.1016/B978-0-12-394286-9.00001-9

Burton, S., Cook, L., Howlett, E., & Newman, C. (2015). Broken halos and shattered horns: overcoming the biasing effects of prior expectations through objective information disclosure. *Journal of the Academy of Marketing Science, 43*(2), 240–256. Doi: https://doi.org/10.1007/s11747-014-0378-5

Downey, S. N., Werff, L., Thomas, K. M., & Plaut, V. C. (2015). The role of diversity practices and inclusion in promoting trust and employee engagement. *Applied Social Psychology*, 1–10. Doi: https://doi.org/10.1111/jasp.12273

Dweck, C. S. (2009). Mindsets: Developing talent through a growth mindset. *Olympic Coach, 21*(1), 4–7.

Edgley, C., Sharma, N., & Anderson-Gough, F. (2016). Diversity and professionalism in the Big Four Firms: Expectation, celebration and weapon in the battle for talent. *Critical Perspectives on Accounting, 35*, 13–34. Doi: https://doi.org/10.1016/j.cpa.2015.05.005

Gakovic, A. & Yardley, K. (2007). Global talent management at HSBC. *Organizational Development Journal, Summer*, 6–14.

Härtel, C. E. J. (2008). How to build a healthy emotional culture and avoid a toxic culture. In C. L. Cooper & N. M. Ashkanasy (Eds.), *Research Companion to Emotion in Organization* (pp. 1260–1291). Cheltenham, UK: Edwin Elgar Publishing.

Kanter, R. M. (2008). *Men and Women of the Corporation*. Basic Books, New York.

Lauring, J. & Selmer, J. (2011). Multicultural organizations: Common language, knowledge sharing and performance. *Personnel Review, 40*, 324–343. Doi: https://doi.org/10.1108/00483481111118649

Lee, D. (2000). An analysis of workplace bullying in the UK. *Personnel Review, 29*(5), 593–612. Doi: https://doi.org/10.1108/00483480010296410

Lipsitz, G. (2006). *The possessive investment in whiteness: How white people profit from identity politics*. Philadelphia: Temple University Press.

McIntosh, M. (2017). Making sense of idioms of distress and cultural expression in psychotherapeutic practice. In Y. Ade-Serrano, O. Nkansa-Dwamena. & M. McIntosh, M. (Eds.), *Race, Culture and diversity. A collection of articles*. Leicester: British Psychological Society, Division of Counselling Psychology.

Morisson, A. M., White, R. P., & Van Velsor, E. (1987). *Breaking the glass ceiling: Can women reach the top of America's largest corporations?* Addison-Wesley, Reading, MA.

Noe, R. A., Hollenbeck, J. R., Gerhart, B., & Wright, P. M., (1994). *Human Resource Management: Gaining a Competitive Advantage*. Burr Ridge, Illinois: Irwin.

Office for National Statistics. (2008). Modelling the gender pay gap in the UK: 1998 to 2006. *Economic and Labour Market Review, 2*(8), 18–24.

O'Neill, R. (2016). The importance of a diverse and culturally competent workforce. *Busidate, 24*(3), 9–13.

Østergaard, C. R., Timmermans, B. & Kristinsson, K. (2011). Does a different view create something new? The effect if employee diversity on innovation. *Research Policy, Elsevier, 40*(3), 500–509.

Pless, N. M. & Maak, T. (2004). Building an inclusive diversity culture: Principles, processes and practice. *Journal of Business Ethics, 54*, 129–147.

Roth, P. L., Bevier, C. A., Bobko, P., Switzer III, F. S. & Tyler, P. (2001). Ethnic group differences in cognitive ability in employment and educational settings: A meta-analysis. *Personnel psychology, 54*.

Stewart, D. (2001). Reinterpreting the learning organisation. *The Learning Organization, 8*(4), 141–142. Doi: https://doi.org/10.1108/EUM0000000005607

Stockdale, M. S. & Crosby, F. J., Eds. (2004). *The psychology and management of workplace diversity*. Malden, MA: Blackwell Publishers.

Toor, S. R. & Ofori, G. (2009). Ethical leadership: Examining the relationships with full range leadership model, employee outcomes, and organizational culture. *Journal of Business Ethics, 90*(4), 533–547.

Wojcicki, S. (2011). The Eight Pillars of Innovation – Think with Google. Retrieved from https://www.thinkwithgoogle.com/articles/8-pillars-of-innovation.html

Conclusion

Maureen McIntosh, Helen Nicholas and
Afreen Husain Huq

This book illustrates ways in which 'moving beyond the limits' concerning leadership and diversity is possible. The chapters come together to form a thought-provoking narrative that links with the overarching ideas in the book regarding leadership, diverse populations, styles of leadership and leadership in organizations. The authors have used their knowledge of what it is like to be part of a diverse community to present very personal accounts of discrimination, prejudice and sexuality and to promote a better understanding of the differences and similarities that make us human. Many people are part of overlapping intersections that are often misunderstood due to the negative stereotypes that are often portrayed within the media. Left unchallenged, these views permeate every part of society. More research is needed and training needs to be improved. We do not want to see 'cultural competency' become simply a popular phrase used in organizations to give the appearance of equality for diverse populations, with no true connection and understanding of what it means. The authors have been bold in their chapters as they talk about social justice, fairness, ethical positioning and using power to drive social, cultural and political change.

The book discusses developing leadership style at a personal and individual level. The authors reflect on their personal experience of leadership and diversity challenges. They encourage critical thinking about the leadership relationship and how this relates to diversity, equality and social justice. Moreover, they examine the negative construction of disability in psychology and beyond, with constructive ways of learning to be mindful, of noticing, naming and addressing exclusion, marginalisation and discrimination in the leadership role. Additionally, readers are exposed to living with dyslexia and surviving well in academia despite the challenges. This encourages us to have a keen knowledge of ourselves, our self-concept and identity, and to manage interactions with others using emotional intelligence as an essential feature of effective leadership.

Leadership within organisations demonstrates that over the years, great strides have been made to ensure larger organisations have a more diverse workforce.

The benefits for this are well known, as outlined in the book, where far more research has been published in this area. Missing in the research are the more personal reflective accounts of leaders in organisations and especially from psychologists' viewpoint, who have and continue to face unique challenges. Being a leader in an organisation can be difficult at times and in this part of the book, our authors have written very openly and reflectively about their experiences when faced with transitions, internal and external changes, building rapport with team members and working within their different contexts.

An area to be explored by future research is the inclusion of a reflective feedback loop into leadership models to highlight the importance of the voices of the leaders and in the context within which they work. The support and training needs of psychologists in leadership positions are not often acknowledged, with focus mainly on the outputs of the organisation rather than the workforce. This book highlights the importance of including clients within leadership models; women's contributions to the workplace; and some of the challenges faced by women in leadership positions. The importance of a strong awareness of diversity among psychology doctorate trainees, and the author evidences a positive movement towards a more diverse society is also highlighted. Trainee psychologists are the psychology leaders of the future and with this awareness they will hopefully have the confidence and competence to *move beyond the limits*.

We believe that future research should focus on the voices of psychologists in leadership positions to highlight the diverse perspectives of the leadership skills they have developed. We hope that this book has encouraged the reader to think critically about their own present or future leadership position and to understand some of the complexities they may face. If the readers of our book are inspired with constructive ideas on the challenges of leadership and diversity then it is vital that we address, traverse and map out some of the processes involved, and in so doing become more effective in leadership roles. This undertaking allows individuals to move from a change in insight to a change in action and to do this in a way which puts us in charge of the process of change.

Index

Printed in the United States
By Bookmasters